Maturin M. Ballou

Equatorial America

Maturin M. Ballou

Equatorial America

1st Edition | ISBN: 978-3-75238-349-2

Place of Publication: Frankfurt am Main, Germany

Year of Publication: 2020

Outlook Verlag GmbH, Germany.

EQUATORIAL AMERICA

BY

MATURIN M. BALLOU

PREFACE.

"I am a part of all that I have seen," says Tennyson, a sentiment which every one of large experience will heartily indorse. With the extraordinary facilities for travel available in modern times, it is a serious mistake in those who possess the means, not to become familiar with the various sections of the globe. Vivid descriptions and excellent photographs give us a certain knowledge of the great monuments of the world, both natural and artificial, but the traveler always finds the reality a new revelation, whether it be the marvels of a Yellowstone Park, a vast oriental temple, Alaskan glaciers, or the Pyramids of Ghiza. The latter, for instance, do not differ from the statistics which we have so often seen recorded, their great, dominating outlines are the same as pictorially delineated, but when we actually stand before them, they are touched by the wand of enchantment, and spring into visible life. Heretofore they have been shadows, henceforth they are tangible and real. The best descriptions fail to inspire us, experience alone can do that. What words can adequately depict the confused grandeur of the Falls of Schaffhausen; the magnificence of the Himalayan range,—roof-tree of the world; the thrilling beauty of the Yosemite Valley; the architectural loveliness of the Taj Mahal, of India; the starry splendor of equatorial nights; the maritime charms of the Bay of Naples; or the marvel of the Midnight Sun at the North Cape? It is personal observation alone which truly satisfies, educating the eye and enriching the understanding. If we can succeed in imparting, a portion of our enjoyment to others, we enhance our own pleasure, and therefore these notes of travel are given to the public.

M. M. B.

CHAPTER I.

In starting upon foreign travel, one drops into the familiar routine on
shipboard much after the same fashion wherever bound, whether crossing the
Atlantic eastward, or steaming to the south through the waters of the
Caribbean Sea; whether in a Peninsular and Oriental ship in the Indian Ocean,
or on a White Star liner in the Pacific bound for Japan. The steward brings a
cup of hot coffee and a slice of dry toast to one's cabin soon after the sun
rises, as a sort of eye-opener; and having swallowed that excellent stimulant,
one feels better fortified for the struggle to dress on the uneven floor of a
rolling and pitching ship. Then comes the brief promenade on deck before
breakfast, a liberal inhalation of fresh air insuring a good appetite. There is no
hurry at this meal. There is so little to do at sea, and so much time to do it in,
that passengers are apt to linger at table as a pastime, and even multiply their
meals in number. As a rule, we make up our mind to follow some instructive
course of reading while at sea, but, alas! we never fulfill the good resolution.
An entire change of habits and associations for the time being is not favorable
to such a purpose. The tonic of the sea braces one up to an unwonted degree,
evinced by great activity of body and mind. Favored by the unavoidable
companionship of individuals in the circumscribed space of a ship,
acquaintances are formed which often ripen into lasting friendship.
Inexperienced voyagers are apt to become effusive and over-confiding, abrupt
intimacies and unreasonable dislikes are of frequent occurrence, and before
the day of separation, the student of human nature has seen many phases
exhibited for his analysis.

Our vessel, the Vigilancia, is a large, commodious, and well-appointed ship, embracing all the modern appliances for comfort and safety at sea. She is lighted by electricity, having a donkey engine which sets in motion a dynamo machine, converting mechanical energy into electric energy. Perhaps the reader, though familiar with the effect of this mode of lighting, has never paused to analyze the very simple manner in which it is produced. The current is led from the dynamos to the various points where light is desired by means of insulated wires. The lamps consist of a fine thread of carbon inclosed in a glass bulb from which air has been entirely excluded. This offers such resistance to the current passing through it that the energy is expended in raising the carbon to a white heat, thus forming the light. The permanence of the carbon is insured by the absence of oxygen. If the glass bulb is broken and atmospheric air comes in contact with the carbon, it is at once destroyed by combustion, and all light from this source ceases. These lamps are so arranged that each one can be turned off or on at will without affecting others. The absence of offensive smell or smoke, the steadiness of the light, unaffected by the motion of the ship, and its superior brilliancy, all join to make this mode of lighting a vessel a positive luxury.

Some pleasant hours were passed on board the Vigilancia, between New York and the West Indies, in the study of the Gulf Stream, through which we were sailing,—that river in the ocean with its banks and bottom of cold water, while its current is always warm. Who can explain the mystery of its motive power? What keeps its tepid water, in a course of thousands of miles, from mingling with the rest of the sea? Whence does it really come? The accepted theories are familiar enough, but we place little reliance upon them, the statements of scientists are so easily formulated, but often so difficult to prove. As Professor Maury tells us, there is in the world no other flow of water so majestic as this; it has a course more rapid than either the Mississippi or the Amazon, and a volume more than a thousand times greater. The color of this remarkable stream, whose fountain is supposed to be the Gulf of Mexico and the Caribbean Sea, is so deep a blue off our southern shore that the line of demarcation from its surroundings is quite obvious, the Gulf water having apparently a decided reluctance to mingling with the rest of the ocean, a peculiarity which has been long and vainly discussed without a satisfactory solution having been reached. The same phenomenon has been observed in the Pacific, where the Japanese current comes up from the equator, along the shore of that country, crossing Behring's Sea to the continent of North America, and, turning southward along the coast of California, finally disappears. Throughout all this ocean passage, like the Gulf Stream in the Atlantic, it retains its individuality, and is quite separate from the rest of the ocean. The fact that the water is saltier than that of the Atlantic is by some supposed to account for the indigo blue of the Gulf Stream.

The temperature of this water is carefully taken on board all well regulated ships, and is recorded in the log. On this voyage it was found to vary from 75° to 80° Fahrenheit.

Our ship had touched at Newport News, Va., after leaving New York, to take the U. S. mail on board; thence the course was south-southeast, giving the American continent a wide berth, and heading for the Danish island of St. Thomas, which lies in the latitude of Hayti, but a long way to the eastward of that uninteresting island. We say uninteresting with due consideration, though its history is vivid enough to satisfy the most sensational taste. It has produced its share of native heroes, as well as native traitors, while the frequent upheavals of its mingled races have been no less erratic than destructive. The ignorance and confusion which reign among the masses on the island arc deplorable. Minister Douglass utterly failed to make anything out of Hayti. The lower classes of the people living inland come next to the inhabitants of Terra del Fuego in the scale of humanity, and are much inferior to the Maoris of New Zealand, or the savage tribes of Australia. It is satisfactorily proven that cannibalism still exists among them in its most repulsive form, so revolting, indeed, that we hesitate to detail the experience of a creditable eye-witness relating to this matter, as personally described to us.

Upon looking at the map it would seem, to one unaccustomed to the ocean, that a ship could not lay her course direct, in these island dotted waters, without running down one or more of them; but the distances which are so circumscribed upon the chart are extended for many a league at sea, and a good navigator may sail his ship from New York to Barbadoes, if he so desires, without sighting the land. Not a sailing vessel or steamship was seen, on the brief voyage from the American continent to the West Indies, these latitudes being far less frequented by passenger and freighting ships than the transatlantic route further north.

It is quite natural that the heart should throb with increased animation, the spirits become more elate, and the eyes more than usually appreciative, when the land of one's destination heaves in sight after long days and nights passed at sea. This is especially the case if the change from home scenes is so radical in all particulars as when coming from our bleak Northern States in the early days of spring, before the trees have donned their leaves, to the soft temperature and exuberant verdure of the low latitudes. Commencing the voyage herein described, the author left the Brooklyn shore of New York harbor about the first of May, during a sharp snow-squall, though, as Governor's Island was passed on the one hand, and the Statue of Liberty on the other, the sun burst forth from its cloudy environment, as if to smile a cheerful farewell. Thus we passed out upon the broad Atlantic, bound southward, soon feeling its half suppressed force in the regular sway and roll of the vessel. She was heavily laden, and measured considerably over four thousand tons, drawing twenty-two feet of water, yet she was like an eggshell upon the heaving breast of the ocean. As these mammoth ships lie in port beside the wharf, it seems as though their size and enormous weight would place them beyond the influence of the wind and waves: but the power of the latter is so great as to be beyond computation, and makes a mere toy of the largest hull that floats. No one can realize the great strength of the waves who has not watched the sea in all of its varying moods.

"Land O!" shouts the lookout on the forecastle.

A wave of the hand signifies that the occupant of the bridge has already made out the mote far away upon the glassy surface of the sea, which now rapidly grows into definite form.

When the mountain which rises near the centre of St. Thomas was fairly in view from the deck of the Vigilancia, it seemed as if beckoning us to its hospitable shore. The light breeze which fanned the sea came from off the land flavored with an odor of tropical vegetation, a suggestion of fragrant blossoms, and a promise of luscious fruits. On our starboard bow there soon came into view the well known Ship Rock, which appears, when seen from a short distance, almost precisely like a full-rigged ship under canvas. If the sky is clouded and the atmosphere hazy, the delusion is remarkable.

This story is told of a French corvette which was cruising in these latitudes at the time when the buccaneers were creating such havoc with legitimate commerce in the West Indies. It seems that the coast was partially hidden by a fog, when the corvette made out the rock through the haze, and, supposing it to be what it so much resembles, a ship under sail, fired a gun to leeward for her to heave to. Of course there was no response to the shot, so the Frenchman brought his ship closer, at the same time clearing for action. Being satisfied that he had to do with a powerful adversary, he resolved to obtain the advantage by promptly crippling the enemy, and so discharged the whole of his starboard broadside into the supposed ship, looming through the mist. The fog quietly dispersed as the corvette went about and prepared to deliver her port guns in a similar manner. As the deceptive rock stood in precisely the same place when the guns came once more to bear upon it, the true character of the object was discovered. It is doubtful whether the Frenchman's surprise or mortification predominated.

An hour of steady progress served to raise the veil of distance, and to reveal the spacious bay of Charlotte Amalie, with its strong background of abrupt hills and dense greenery of tropical foliage. How wonderfully blue was the water round about the island,—an emerald set in a sea of molten sapphire! It seemed as if the sky had been melted and poured all over the ebbing tide. About the Bahamas, especially off the shore at Nassau, the water is green,—a delicate bright green; here it exhibits only the true azure blue,—Mediterranean blue. It is seen at its best and in marvelous glow during the brief moments of twilight, when a glance of golden sunset tinges its mottled surface with iris hues, like the opaline flashes from a humming-bird's throat.

The steamer gradually lost headway, the vibrating hull ceased to throb with the action of its motive power, as though pausing to take breath after long days and nights of sustained effort, and presently the anchor was let go in the excellent harbor of St. Thomas, latitude 18° 20' north, longitude 64° 48' west. Our forecastle gun, fired to announce arrival, awakened the echoes in the hills, so that all seemed to join in clapping their hands to welcome us. Thus amid the Norwegian fiords the report of the steamer's single gun becomes a whole broadside, as it is reverberated from the grim and rocky elevations which line that iron-bound coast.

There was soon gathered about the ship a bevy of naked colored boys, a score or more, jabbering like a lot of monkeys, some in canoes of home construction, it would seem, consisting of a sugar box sawed in two parts, or a few small planks nailed together, forming more of a tub than a boat, and leaking at every joint. These frail floats were propelled with a couple of flat boards used as paddles. The young fellows came out from the shore to dive for sixpences and shillings, cast into the sea by passengers. The moment a piece of silver was thrown, every canoe was instantly emptied of its occupant, all diving pell-mell for the money. Presently one of the crowd was sure to come to the surface with the silver exhibited above his head between his fingers, after which, monkey-like, it was securely deposited inside of his cheek. Similar scenes often occur in tropical regions. The last which the author can recall, and at which he assisted, was at Aden, where the Indian Ocean and the Red Sea meet. Another experience of the sort is also well remembered as witnessed in the South Pacific off the Samoan islands. On this occasion the most expert of the natives, among the naked divers, was a young Samoan girl, whose agility in the water was such that she easily secured more than half the bright coins which were thrown overboard, though a dozen male competitors were her rivals in the pursuit. Nothing but an otter could have excelled this bronzed, unclad, exquisitely formed girl of Tutuila as a diver and swimmer.

But let us not stray to the far South Pacific, forgetting that we are all this time in the snug harbor of St. Thomas, in the West Indies.

A fidgety old lady passenger, half hidden in an avalanche of wraps, while the thermometer indicated 80° Fahr., one who had gone into partial hysterics several times during the past few days, upon the slightest provocation, declared that this was the worst region for hurricanes in the known world, adding that there were dark, ominous clouds forming to windward which she was sure portended a cyclone. One might have told her truthfully that May was not a hurricane month in these latitudes, but we were just then too earnestly engaged in preparing for a stroll on shore, too full of charming anticipations, to discuss possible hurricanes, and so, without giving the matter any special thought, admitted that it did look a little threatening in the northwest. This was quite enough to frighten the old lady half out of her senses, and to call the stewardess into prompt requisition, while the deck was soon permeated with the odor of camphor, sal volatile, and valerian. We did not wait to see how she survived the attack, but hastened into a shore boat and soon landed at what is known as King's wharf, when the temperature seemed instantly to rise about twenty degrees. Near the landing was a small plaza, shaded by tall ferns and cabbage palms, with here and there an umbrageous mango. Ladies and servant girls were seen promenading with merry children, whites and blacks mingling indiscriminately, while the Danish military band were producing most shocking strains with their brass instruments. One could hardly conceive of a more futile attempt at harmony.

There is always something exciting in first setting foot upon a foreign soil, in mingling with utter strangers, in listening to the voluble utterances and jargon of unfamiliar tongues, while noting the manners, dress, and faces of a new people. The current language of the mass of St. Thomas is a curious compound of negro grammar, Yankee accent, and English drawl. Though somewhat familiar with the West Indies, the author had never before landed upon this island. Everything strikes one as curious, each turn affords increased novelty, and every moment is full of interest. Black, yellow, and white men are seen in groups, the former with very little covering on their bodies, the latter in diaphanous costumes. Negresses sporting high colors in their scanty clothing, set off by rainbow kerchiefs bound round their heads, turban fashion; little naked blacks with impossible paunches; here and there a shuffling negro bearing baskets of fish balanced on either end of a long pole resting across his shoulders; peddlers of shells and corals; old women carrying trays upon their heads containing cakes sprinkled with granulated sugar, and displayed upon neat linen towels, seeking for customers among the newly arrived passengers,—all together form a unique picture of local life. The constantly shifting scene moves before the observer like a panorama unrolled for exhibition, seeming quite as theatrical and artificial.

St. Thomas is one of the Danish West Indian Islands, of which there are three belonging to Denmark, namely, St. Thomas, St. Croix, and St. John. For the possession of the first named Mr. Seward, when Secretary of State, in 1866, offered the King of Denmark five million dollars in gold, which proposition was finally accepted, and it would have been a cheap purchase for us at that price; but after all detail had been duly agreed upon, the United States Congress refused to vote the necessary funds wherewith to pay for the title deed. So when Mr. Seward consummated the purchase of Alaska, for a little over seven million dollars, there were nearly enough of the small-fry politicians in Congress to defeat the bargain with Russia in the same manner. The income from the lease of two islands alone belonging to Alaska—St. George and St. Paul—has paid four and one half per cent. per annum upon the purchase money ever since the territory came into our possession. There is one gold mine on Douglas Island, Alaska, not to mention its other rich and inexhaustible products, for which a French syndicate has offered fourteen million dollars. We doubt if St. Thomas could be purchased from the Danes to-day for ten million dollars, while the estimated value of Alaska would be at least a hundred million or more, with its vast mineral wealth, its invaluable salmon fisheries, its inexhaustible forests of giant timber, and its abundance of seal, otter, and other rich furs. A penny-wise and pound-foolish Congress made a huge mistake in opposing Mr. Seward's purpose as regarded the purchase of St. Thomas. The strategic position of the island is quite sufficient to justify our government in wishing to possess it, for it is geographically the keystone of the West Indies. The principal object which Mr. Seward had in view was to secure a coaling and refitting station for our national ships in time of war, for which St. Thomas would actually be worth more than the island of Cuba. Opposite to it is the continent of Africa; equidistant are the eastern shores of North and South America; on one side is western Europe, on the other the route to India and the Pacific Ocean; in the rear are Central America, the West Indies, and Mexico, together with those great inland bodies of salt water, the Caribbean Sea and the Gulf of Mexico. It requires no argument to show how important the possession of such an outpost might prove to this country.

Since these notes were written, it is currently reported that our government has once more awakened to the necessity of obtaining possession of this island, and fresh negotiations have been entered into. One thing is very certain, if we do not seize the opportunity to purchase St. Thomas at the present time, England, or some other important power, will promptly do so, to our serious detriment and just mortification.

St. Thomas has an area of nearly fifty square miles, and supports a population of about fourteen thousand. In many respects the capital is unique, and being our first landing-place after leaving home, was of more than ordinary interest to the writer. The highest point on the island, which comes first into view from the deck of a southern bound steamer, is West Mountain, rising sixteen hundred feet above the level of the surrounding waters. Geologists would describe St. Thomas as being the top of a small chain of submerged mountains, which would be quite correct, since the topography of the bottom of the sea is but a counterpart of that upon the more familiar surface of the earth we occupy. When ocean electric cables for connecting islands and continents are laid, engineers find that there are the same sort of plains, mountains, valleys, and gorges beneath as above the waters of the ocean. The skeletons of whales, and natural beds of deep-sea shells, found in valleys and hills many hundred feet above the present level of tide waters, tell us plainly enough that in the long ages which have passed, the diversified surface of the earth which we now behold has changed places with these submerged regions, which probably once formed the dry land. The history of the far past is full of instances showing the slow but continuous retreat of the water from the land in certain regions and its encroachment in others, the drying up of lakes and rivers, as well as the upheaval of single islands and groups from the bed of the ocean.

A range of dome-shaped hills runs through the entire length of this island of St. Thomas, fifteen miles from west to east, being considerably highest at the west end. As we passed between the two headlands which mark the entrance to the harbor, the town was seen spread over three hills of nearly uniform height, also occupying the gentle valleys between. Two stone structures, on separate hills, form a prominent feature; these are known respectively as Blue Beard and Black Beard tower, but their origin is a myth, though there are plenty of legends extant about them. Both are now utilized as residences, having mostly lost their original crudeness and picturesque appearance. The town, as a whole, forms a pleasing and effective background to the land-locked bay, which is large enough to afford safe anchorage for two hundred ships at the same time, except when a hurricane prevails; then the safest place for shipping is as far away from the land as possible. It is a busy port, considering the small number of inhabitants, steamers arriving and departing constantly, besides many small coasting vessels which ply between this and the neighboring islands. St. Thomas is certainly the most available commercially of the Virgin group of islands. Columbus named them "Las Vergines," in reference to the familiar Romish legend of the eleven thousand virgins, about as inappropriate a title as the fable it refers to is ridiculous.

Close in shore, at the time of our visit, there lay a schooner-rigged craft of more than ordinary interest, her jaunty set upon the water, her graceful lines, tall, raking masts, and long bowsprit suggesting the model of the famous old Baltimore clippers. There is a fascinating individuality about sailing vessels which does not attach to steamships. Seamen form romantic attachments for the former. The officers and crew of the Vigilancia were observed to cast admiring eyes upon this handsome schooner, anchored under our lee. A sort of mysterious quiet hung about her; every rope was hauled taut, made fast, and the slack neatly coiled. Her anchor was atrip, that is, the cable was hove short, showing that she was ready to sail at a moment's notice. The only person visible on board was a bareheaded, white-haired old seaman, who sat on the transom near the wheel, quietly smoking his pipe. On inquiry it was found that the schooner had a notable history and bore the name of the Vigilant, having been first launched a hundred and thirty years ago. It appeared that she was a successful slaver in former days, running between the coast of Africa and these islands. She was twice captured by English cruisers, but somehow found her way back again to the old and nefarious business. Of course, she had been overhauled, repaired, and re-rigged many times, but it is still the same old frame and hull that so often made the middle passage, as it was called. To-day she serves as a mail boat running between Santa Cruz and St. Thomas, and, it is said, can make forty leagues, with a fair wind, as quick as any steamer on the coast. The same evening the Vigilant spread her broad white wings and glided silently out of the harbor, gathering rapid way as she passed its entrance, until feeling the spur of the wind and the open sea, she quickly vanished from sight. It was easy to imagine her bound upon her old piratical business, screened by the shadows of the night.

Though it no longer produces a single article of export on its own soil, St. Thomas was, in the days of negro slavery, one of the most prolific sugar yielding islands of this region. It will be remembered that the emancipation of the blacks took place here in 1848. It was never before impressed upon us, if we were aware of the fact, that the sugar-cane is not indigenous to the West Indies. It seems that the plant came originally from Asia, and was introduced into these islands by Columbus and his followers. As is often the case with other representatives of the vegetable kingdom, it appears to have flourished better here than in the land of its nativity, new climatic combinations, together with the soil, developing in the saccharine plant better qualities and increased productiveness, for a long series of years enriching many enterprising planters.

When Columbus discovered St. Thomas, in 1493, it was inhabited by two tribes of Indians, the Caribs and the Arrowauks, both of which soon disappeared under the oppression and hardships imposed by the Spaniards. It is also stated that from this island, as well as from Cuba and Hayti, many natives were transported to Spain and there sold into slavery, in the days following close upon its discovery. Thus Spain, from the earliest date, characterized her operations in the New World by a heartlessness and injustice which ever attended upon her conquests, both among the islands and upon the continent of America. The Caribs were of the red Indian race, and appear to have been addicted to cannibalism. Indeed, the very word, by which the surrounding sea is also known, is supposed to be a corruption of the name of this tribe. "These Caribs did not eat their own babies," says an old writer apologetically, "like some sorts of wild beasts, but only roasted and ate their prisoners of war."

The island was originally covered with a dense forest growth, but is now comparatively denuded of trees, leaving the land open to the full force of the sun, and causing it to suffer at times from serious droughts. There is said to be but one natural spring of water on the island. This shows itself at the surface, and is of very limited capacity; the scanty rains which occur here are almost entirely depended upon to supply water for domestic use.

St. Thomas being so convenient a port of call for steamers from Europe and America, and having so excellent a harbor, is improved as a depot for merchandise by several of the neighboring islands, thus enjoying a considerable commerce, though it is only in *transitu*. It is also the regular coaling station of several steamship lines. Judging from appearances, however, it would seem that the town is not growing in population or business relations, but is rather retrograding. The value of the imports in 1880 was less than half the aggregate amount of 1870. We were told that green groceries nearly all come from the United States, and that even eggs and poultry are imported from the neighboring islands, showing an improvidence on the part of the people difficult to account for, since these sources of food supply can be profitably produced at almost any spot upon the earth where vegetation will grow. Cigars are brought hither from Havana in considerable quantities, and having no duty to pay, can be sold very cheap by the dealers at St. Thomas, and still afford a reasonable profit. Quite a trade is thus carried on with the passengers of the several steamers which call here regularly, and travelers avail themselves of the opportunity to lay in an ample supply. Cuban cigars of the quality which would cost nine or ten dollars a hundred in Boston are sold at St. Thomas for five or six dollars, and lower grades even cheaper in proportion. There is said to be considerable smuggling successfully carried on between this island and the Florida shore, in the article of cigars as well as in tobacco in the unmanufactured state. The high duty on these has always incited to smuggling, thus defeating the very object for which it is imposed. Probably a moderate duty would yield more to the government in the aggregate, by rendering it so much less of an object to smuggle.

Though the island is Danish in nationality, there are few surroundings calculated to recall the fact, save that the flag of that country floats over the old fort and the one or two official buildings, just as it has done for the last two centuries. The prominent officials are Danes, as well as the officers of the small body of soldiers maintained on the island. English is almost exclusively spoken, though there are French, Spanish, and Italian residents here. English is also the language taught in the public schools. People have come here to make what money they can, but with the fixed purpose of spending it and enjoying it elsewhere. As a rule, all Europeans who come to the West Indies and embark in business do so with exactly this purpose. In Cuba the Spaniards from the continent, among whom are many Jews, have a proverb the significance of which is: "Ten years of starvation, and a fortune," and most of them live up to this axiom. They leave all principles of honor, all sense of moral responsibility, all sacred domestic ties, behind them, forgetting, or at least ignoring, the significant query, namely, "What shall it profit a man, if he gain the whole world, and lose his own soul?"

About one third of the population is Roman Catholic. The Jews have a synagogue, and a membership of six hundred. They have a record on the island dating as far back as the year 1757, and add much to the activity and thrift of St. Thomas. No matter where we find the Jews, in Mexico, Warsaw, California, or the West Indies, they are all alike intent upon money making, and are nearly always successful. Their irrepressible energy wins for them the goal for which they so earnestly strive. That soldier of fortune, Santa Anna, formerly ruler of Mexico, when banished as a traitor from his native country, made his home on this island, and the house which he built and occupied is still pointed out to visitors as one of the local curiosities. The social life of St. Thomas is naturally very circumscribed, but is good so far as it goes. A few cultured people, who have made it their home for some years, have become sincerely attached to the place, and enjoy the climate. There are a small public library, a hospital, several charitable institutions, and a theatre, which is occupied semi-occasionally. The island is connected with the continent by cable, and has a large floating dock and marine railway, which causes vessels in distress to visit the port for needed repairs. The town is situated on the north side of the bay which indents the middle of the south side of the island. The harbor has a depth of water varying from eighteen to thirty-six feet, and has the advantage of being a free port, a fact, perhaps, of not much account to a place which has neither exports nor imports of its own. St. Thomas is the only town of any importance on the island, and is known locally as Charlotte Amalie, a fact which sometimes leads to a confusion of ideas.

The reader need not encounter the intense heat, which so nearly wilted us, in an effort to obtain a good lookout from some elevated spot; but the result will perhaps interest him, as it fully repaid the writer for all the consequent discomfort.

From the brow of a moderate elevation just behind the town, a delightful and far-reaching view is afforded, embracing St. Thomas in the foreground, the well-sheltered bay, dotted with vessels bearing the flags of various nations, an archipelago of islets scattered over the near waters, and numerous small bays indenting the coast. At a distance of some forty miles across the sea looms the island of Santa Cruz; and farther away, on the horizon's most distant limit, are seen the tall hills and mountains of Porto Rico; while the sky is fringed by a long trailing plume of smoke, indicating the course of some passing steamship. The three hills upon which the town stands are spurs of West Mountain, and the place is quite as well entitled to the name of Tremont —"tri-mountain"—as was the capital of Massachusetts, before its hills were laid low to accommodate business demands. On the seaward side of these elevations the red tiled roofs of the white houses rise in regular terraces from the street which borders the harbor, forming a very picturesque group as seen from the bay.

Though it has not often been visited by epidemics, Mr. Anthony Trollope pronounces the island, in his usual irresponsible way, to be "one of the hottest and one of the most unhealthy spots among all these hot and unhealthy regions," and adds that he would perhaps be justified in saying "that of all such spots it is the hottest and most unhealthy." This is calculated to give an incorrect idea of St. Thomas. True, it is liable to periods of unhealthiness, when a species of low fever prevails, proving more or less fatal. This is thought to originate from the surface drainage, and the miasma arising from the bay. All the drains of the town flow into the waters of the harbor, which has not sufficient flow of tide to carry seaward the foul matter thus accumulated. The hot sun pouring its heat down upon this tainted water causes a dangerous exhalation. Still, sharks do not seem to be sensitive as to this matter, for they much abound. It is yet to be discovered why these tigers of the sea do not attack the negroes, who fearlessly leap overboard; a white man could not do this with impunity. The Asiatics of the Malacca Straits do not enjoy any such immunity from danger, though they have skins as dark as the divers of St. Thomas. Sharks appear in the West Indies in small schools, or at least there are nearly always two or three together, but in Oriental waters they are only seen singly. Thus a Malay of Singapore, for a compensation, say an English sovereign, will place a long, sharp knife between his teeth and leap naked into the sea to attack a shark. He adroitly dives beneath the creature, and as it turns its body to bring its awkward mouth into use, with his knife the Malay slashes a deep, long opening in its exposed belly, at the same time forcing himself out of the creature's reach. The knife is sure and fatal. After a few moments the huge body of the fish is seen to rise and float lifeless upon the surface of the water.

A large majority of the people are colored, exhibiting some peculiarly interesting types, intermarriage with whites of various nationalities having produced among the descendants of Africans many changes of color and of features. One feels sure that there is also a trace of Carib or Indian blood mingled with the rest,—a trace of the aborigines whom Columbus found here. The outcome is not entirely a race with flat noses and protruding lips; straight Grecian profiles are not uncommon, accompanied by thin nostrils and Anglo-Saxon lips. Faultless teeth, soft blue eyes, and hair nearly straight are sometimes met with among the creoles. As to the style of walking and of carrying the head and body, the common class of women of St. Thomas have arrived at perfection. Some of them are notable examples of unconscious dignity and grace combined. This has been brought about by carrying burdens upon their heads from childhood, without the supporting aid of the hands. Modesty, or rather conventionality, does not require boys or girls under eight years of age to encumber themselves with clothing. The costume of the market women and the lower classes generally is picturesque, composed of a Madras kerchief carefully twisted into a turban of many colors, yellow predominating, a cotton chemise which leaves the neck and shoulders exposed, reaching just below the knees, the legs and feet being bare. The men wear cotton drawers reaching nearly to the knee, the rest of the body being uncovered, except the head, which is usually sheltered under a broad brimmed straw hat, the sides of which are perforated by many ventilating holes. The whites generally, and also the better class of natives, dress very much after the fashion which prevails in North America.

This is the negroes' paradise, but it is a climate in which the white race gradually wanes. The heat of the tropics is modified by the constant and grateful trade winds, a most merciful dispensation, without which the West Indies would be uninhabitable by man. On the hillsides of St. Thomas these winds insure cool nights at least, and a comparatively temperate state of the atmosphere during the day. Vegetation is abundant, the fruit trees are perennial, bearing leaf, blossom, and fruit in profusion, month after month, year after year. Little, if any, cultivation is required. The few sugar plantations which are still carried on yield from three to four successive years without replanting. It is a notable fact that where vegetation is at its best, where the soil is most rank and prolific, where fruits and flowers grow in wild exuberance, elevated humanity thrives the least. The lower the grade of man, the nearer he approximates to the animals, the less civilized he is in mind and body, the better he appears to be adapted to such localities. The birds and the butterflies are in exact harmony with the loveliness of tropical nature, however prolific she may be; the flowers are glorious and beautiful: it is man alone who seems out of place. A great variety of fruits are indigenous here,

15

such as the orange, lime, alligator pear, moss-apple, and mango, but none of them are cultivated to any extent; the people seem to lack the energy requisite to improve the grand possibilities of their fertile soil and prolific climate.

We were reminded by a resident of the town, before we left the harbor of St. Thomas, that the nervous old lady referred to was not entirely without reason for her anxiety. Some of our readers will remember, perhaps, that in October, 1867, a most disastrous hurricane swept over these Virgin Islands, leaving widespread desolation in its track. The shipping which happened to be in the bay of St. Thomas was nearly all destroyed, together with hundreds of lives, while on the land scores of houses and many lives were also sacrificed to the terrible cyclone of that date. Even the thoroughly built iron and stone lighthouse was completely obliterated. There is a theory that such visitations come in this region about once in every twelve or fifteen years, and upon looking up the matter we find them to have occurred, with more or less destructive force, in the years 1793, 1819, 1837, 1867, 1871, and so late as August, 1891. Other hurricanes have passed over these islands during the period covered by these dates, but of a mitigated character. August, September, and October are the months in which the hurricanes are most likely to occur, and all vessels navigating the West Indian seas during these months take extra precautions to secure themselves against accidents from this source. When such visitations happen, the event is sure to develop heroic deeds. In the hurricane of 1867, the captain of a Spanish man-of-war, who was a practical sailor, brought up from boyhood upon the ocean, seeing the oncoming cyclone, and knowing by experience what to expect, ordered the masts of his vessel to be cut away at once, and every portion of exposed top hamper to be cast into the sea. When thus stripped he exposed little but the bare hull of his steamer to the fury of the storm. After the cyclone had passed, it was found that he had not lost a man, and that the steamer's hull, though severely battered, was substantially unharmed. Keeping up all steam during the awful scene, this captain devoted himself and his ship to the saving of human life, promptly taking his vessel wherever he could be of the most service. Hundreds of seamen were saved from death by the coolness and intrepidity of this heroic sailor.

Since these notes were written among the islands, a terrible cyclone has visited them. This was on August 18, last past, and proved more destructive to human life, to marine and other property, than any occurrence of the kind during the last century. At Martinique a sharp shock of earthquake added to the horror of the occasion, the town of Fort de France being very nearly leveled with the ground. Many tall and noble palms, the growth of half a hundred years, were utterly demolished in the twinkling of an eye, and other trees were uprooted by the score.

The waters of this neighborhood teem with strange forms of animal and vegetable life. Here we saw specimens of red and blue snappers, the angel-fish, king-fish, gurnets, cow-fish, whip-ray, peacock-fish, zebra-fish, and so on, all, or nearly all, unfamiliar to us, each species individualized either in shape, color, or both. The whip-ray, with a body like a flounder, has a tail six or seven feet long, tapering from an inch and over to less than a quarter of an inch at the small end. When dried, it still retains a degree of elasticity, and is used by the natives as a whip with which to drive horses and donkeys. In some places, so singularly clear is the water that the bottom is distinctly visible five or six fathoms below the surface, where fishes of various sorts are seen in ceaseless motion. White shells, corals, star-fish, and sea-urchins mingle their various forms and colors, objects and hues seeming to be intensified by the strong reflected light from the surface, so that one could easily fancy them to be flowers blooming in the fairy gardens of the mermaids. The early morning, just after the sun begins to gild the surface of the sea, is the favorite time for the flying-fishes to display their aerial proclivities. They are always attracted by a strong light, and are thus lured to their destruction by the torches of the fishermen, who often go out for the purpose at night and take them in nets. In the early morning, as seen from the ship's deck, they scoot above the rippling waves in schools of a hundred and more, so compact as to cast fleeting shadows over the blue enameled surface of the waters. At St. Thomas, Martinique, and Barbadoes, as well as among the other islands bordering the Caribbean Sea, they form no inconsiderable source of food for the humble natives, who fry them in batter mixed with onions, making a savory and nutritious dish.

St. Thomas is, as we have said, a coaling station for steamships, and when the business is in progress a most unique picture is presented. The ship is moored alongside of the dock for this purpose, two side ports being thrown open, one for ingress, the other for egress. A hundred women and girls, wearing one scanty garment reaching to the knees, are in line, and commence at once to trot on board in single file, each one bearing a bushel basket of coal upon her head, weighing, say sixty pounds. Another gang fill empty baskets where the coal is stored, so that there is a continuous line of negresses trotting into the ship at one port and, after dumping their loads into the coal bunkers, out at the other, hastening back to the source of supply for more. Their step is quick, their pose straight as an arrow, while their feet keep time to a wild chant in which all join, the purport of which it is not possible to clearly understand. Now and again their voices rise in softly mingled harmony, floating very sweetly over the still waters of the bay. The scene we describe occurred at night, but the moon had not yet risen. Along the wharf, to the coal deposits, iron frames were erected containing burning bituminous coal, and the blaze, fanned by the open air, formed the light by which the women worked. It was a weird picture. Everything seemed quite in harmony: the hour, the darkness of night relieved by the flaming brackets of coal, the strange, dark figures hastening into the glare of light and quickly vanishing, the harmony of high-pitched voices occasionally broken in upon by the sharp, stern voice of their leader,—all was highly dramatic and effective.

Not unfrequently three or four steamers are coaling at the same time from different wharves. Hundreds of women and girls of St. Thomas make this labor their special occupation, and gain a respectable living by it, doubtless supporting any number of lazy, worthless husbands, fathers, and brothers.

After our ship was supplied with coal, these women, having put three hundred tons on board in a surprisingly short period of time, formed a group upon the wharf and held what they called a firefly dance, indescribably quaint and grotesque, performed by the flickering light of the flaming coal. Their voices were joined in a wild, quick chant, as they twisted and turned, clapping their hands at intervals to emphasize the chorus. Now and again a couple of the girls would separate from the rest for a moment, then dance toward and from each other, throwing their arms wildly about their heads, and finally, gathering their scanty drapery in one hand and extending the other, perform a movement similar to the French cancan. Once more springing back among their companions, all joined hands, and a roundabout romp closed the firefly dance. Could such a scene be produced in a city theatre *au naturel*, with proper accessories and by these actual performers, it would surely prove an attraction good for one hundred nights. Of course this would be impossible. Conventionality would object to such diaphanous costumes, and bare limbs, though they were of a bronzed hue, would shock Puritanic eyes.

Upon first entering the harbor, the Vigilancia anchored at a short distance from the shore; but when it became necessary to haul alongside the wharf, the attempt was made to get up the anchor, when it was found to require far more than the usual expenditure of power to do so. Finally, however, the anchor was secured, but attached to its flukes there came also, from the bottom of the bay, a second anchor, of antique shape, covered with rust and barnacles. It was such a one as was carried by the galleons of the fifteenth century, and had doubtless lain for over four hundred years just where the anchor of our ship had got entangled with it. What a remarkable link this corroded piece of iron formed, uniting the present with the far past, and how it stimulated the mind in forming romantic possibilities! It may have been the holding iron of Columbus's own caravel, or have been the anchor of one of Cortez's fleet, which touched here on its way into the Gulf of Mexico, or, indeed, it may have belonged to some Caribbean buccaneer, who was obliged to let slip his cable and hasten away to escape capture.

It was deemed a fortunate circumstance to have secured this ancient relic, and a sure sign of future good luck to the ship, so it was duly stored away in the lower hold of the Vigilancia.

That same night on which the coal bunkers were filled, our good ship was got under way, while the rising moon made the harbor and its surroundings as clearly visible as though it were midday. The light from the burning coal brackets had waned, only a few sparks bursting forth now and again, disturbed by a passing breeze which fanned them into life for a moment. When we passed through the narrow entrance by the lighthouse, and stood out once more upon the open sea, it was mottled, far and near, with argent ripples, that waltzed merrily in the soft, clear moonlight, rivaling the firefly dance on shore. Even to the very horizon the water presented a white, silvery, tremulous sheen of liquid light. One gazed in silent enjoyment until the eyes were weary with the lavish beauty of the scene, and the brain became giddy with its splendor. Is it idle and commonplace to be enthusiastic? Perhaps so; but we hope never to outlive such inspiration.

CHAPTER II.

Curious Seaweed.—Professor Agassiz.—Myth of a Lost Continent.—
Island of Martinique.—An Attractive Place.—Statue of the Empress
Josephine.—Birthplace of Madame de Maintenon.—City of St.
Pierre.—Mont Pelée.—High Flavored Specialty.—Grisettes of
Martinique.—A Botanical Garden.—Defective Drainage.—A Fatal
Enemy.—A Cannibal Snake.—The Climate.

Between St. Thomas and the island of Martinique, we fell in with some floating seaweed, so peculiar in appearance that an obliging quartermaster picked up a spray for closer examination. It is a strange, sponge-like plant, which propagates itself on the ocean, unharmed by the fiercest agitation of the waves, or the wildest raging of the winds, at the same time giving shelter to zoöphytes and mollusks of a species, like itself, found nowhere else. Sailors call it Gulf weed, but it has nothing to do with the Gulf Stream, though sometimes clusters get astray and are carried far away on the bosom of that grand ocean current. The author has seen small bodies of it, after a fierce storm in the Caribbean Sea, a thousand miles to the eastward of Barbadoes. Its special home is a broad space of ocean surface between the Gulf Stream and the equatorial current, known as the Sargasso Sea. Its limits, however, change somewhat with the seasons. It was first noticed by Columbus in 1492, and in this region it has remained for centuries, even to the present day.

Sometimes this peculiar weed is so abundant as to present the appearance of a submerged meadow, through which the ship ploughs its way as though sailing upon the land. We are told that Professor Agassiz, while at sea, having got possession of a small branch of this marine growth, kept himself busily absorbed with it and its products for twelve hours, forgetting all the intervening meals. Science was more than food and drink to this grand savant. His years from boyhood were devoted to the study of nature in her various forms. "Life is so short," said he, "one can hardly find space to become familiar with a single science, much less to acquire knowledge of many." When he was applied to by a lyceum committee to come to a certain town and lecture, he replied that he was too busy. "But we will pay you double price, Mr. Agassiz, if you will come," said the applicant. "I cannot waste time to make money," was the noble reply.

The myth of a lost continent is doubtless familiar to the reader,—a continent supposed to have existed in these waters thousands of years ago, but which, by some evolution of nature, became submerged, sinking from sight forever. It was the Atlantis which is mentioned by Plato; the land in which the Elysian Fields were placed, and the Garden of Hesperides, from which the early civilization of Greece, Egypt, and Asia Minor were derived, and whose kings and heroes were the Olympian deities of a later time. The poetical idea prevails that this plant, which once grew in those gardens, having lost its original home, has become a floating waif on the sapphire sea of the tropics. The color of the Sargasso weed is a faint orange shade; the leaves are pointed, delicate, and exquisitely formed, like those of the weeping willow in their youthful freshness, having a tiny, round, light green berry near the base of each leaf. Mother Cary's chickens are said to be fond of these berries, and that bird abounds in these waters.

Probably the main portion of the West Indian islands was once a part of the continent of America, many, many ages ago. There are trees of the locust family growing among the group to-day, similar to those found on our southern coast, which are declared to be four thousand years old. This statement is partially corroborated by known characteristics of the growth of the locust, and there are arborists who fully credit this great longevity. It is interesting to look upon an object which had a vital existence two thousand years and more before Christ was upon earth, and which is still animate.

* * * * *

Each new island which one visits in the West Indies seems more lovely than its predecessor, always leaving Hayti out of the question; but Martinique, at this moment of writing, appears to rival all those with which the author is familiar. It might be a choice bit out of Cuba, Singapore, or far-away Hawaii.

Its liability to destructive hurricanes is its only visible drawback. Having been discovered on St. Martin's day, Columbus gave it the name it now bears.

St. Pierre is the commercial capital of Martinique, one of the French West Indies, and the largest of the group belonging to that nation. Fort de France is the political capital, situated about thirty miles from St. Pierre. It was nearly ruined by the cyclone of last August, a few weeks after the author's visit. St. Pierre is the best built town in the Lesser Antilles, and has a population of about twenty-five thousand. The streets are well paved, and the principal avenues are beautified by ornamental trees uniformly planted. The grateful shade thus obtained, and the long lines of charming arboreal perspective which are formed, are desirable accessories to any locality, but doubly so in tropical regions. The houses are very attractive, while there is a prevailing aspect of order, cleanliness, and thrift everywhere apparent. It was not our experience to meet one beggar in the streets of St. Pierre. More or less of poverty must exist everywhere, but it does not stalk abroad here, as it does in many rich and pretentious capitals of the great world. The island is situated midway between Dominica and St. Lucia, and is admitted by all visitors to be one of the most picturesque of the West Indian groups. Irregular in shape, it is also high and rocky, thus forming one of the most prominent of the large volcanic family which sprang up so many ages ago in these seas. Its apex, Mont Pelée, an only partially extinct volcano, rises between four and five thousand feet above the level of the ocean, and is the first point visible on approaching the island from the north. It would be interesting to dilate upon the past history of Martinique, for it has known not a little of the checkered vicissitudes of these Antilles, having been twice captured by the English, and twice restored to France. But this would not be in accordance with the design of these pages.

St. Pierre is situated on the lee side of the island, something less than two thousand miles, by the course we have steered, from New York, and three hundred miles from St. Thomas. It comes down to the very water's edge, with its parti-colored houses and red-tiled roofs, which mingle here and there with tall, overhanging cocoa-palms. This is the most lavishly beautiful tree in the world, and one which never fails to impart special interest to its surroundings.

A marble statue in the Place de la Savane, at Fort de France, on the same side of the island as St. Pierre, recalls the fact that this was the birthplace of the Empress Josephine, born in 1763. Her memorable history is too familiar for us to repeat any portion of it here, but the brain becomes very active at the mere mention of her name, in recalling the romantic and tragic episodes of her life, so closely interwoven with the career of the first Napoleon. One instinctively recalls the small boudoir in the palace of Trianon, where her husband signed the divorce from Josephine. That he loved her with his whole power for loving is plain enough, as is also his well known reason for the separation, namely, the desire for offspring to transmit his name to posterity. There is one legend which is always rehearsed to strangers, relating to Josephine's youth upon the island. We refer to that of the old negress fortune-teller who prognosticated the grandeur of her future career, together with its melancholy termination, a story so tinctured with local color that, if it be not absolutely true, it surely ought to be. The statue, unless we are misinformed, was the gift of that colossal fraud, Napoleon III., though it purports to have been raised to the memory of Josephine by the people of Martinique, who certainly feel great pride in the fact of her having been born here, and who truly venerate her memory. The statue represents the empress dressed in the fashion of the First Empire, with bare arms and shoulders, one hand resting on a medallion bearing a profile of the emperor to whom she was devoted. The whole is partially shaded by a half dozen grand old palms. The group teems with historic suggestiveness, recalling one of the most tragic chapters of modern European history. It seemed to us that the artist had succeeded in imparting to the figure an expression indicating something of the sad story of the original.

This beautiful island, it will be remembered, also gave to France another remarkable historic character, Françoise d'Aubigné, afterwards Madame Scarron, but better known to the world at large as Madame de Maintenon. She, too, was the wife of a king, though the marriage was a left-handed one, but as the power behind the throne, she is well known to have shaped for years the political destinies of France.

St. Pierre has several schools, a very good hotel, a theatre, a public library, together with some other modern and progressive institutions; yet somehow everything looked quaint and olden, a sixteenth century atmosphere seeming to pervade the town. The windows of the ordinary dwellings have no glass, which is very naturally considered to be a superfluity in this climate; but these windows have iron bars and wooden shutters behind them, relics of the days of slavery, when every white man's house was his castle, and great precautions were taken to guard against the possible uprising of the blacks, who outnumbered their masters twenty to one.

Though so large a portion of the population are of negro descent, yet they are very French-like in character. The native women especially seem to be frivolous and coquettish, not to say rather lax in morals. They appear to be very fond of dress. The young negresses have learned from their white mistresses how to put on their diaphanous clothing in a jaunty and telling fashion, leaving one bronzed arm and shoulder bare, which strikes the eye in strong contrast with the snow white of their cotton chemises. They are Parisian grisettes in ebony, and with their large, roguish eyes, well-rounded figures, straight pose, and dainty ways, the half-breeds are certainly very attractive, and only too ready for a lark with a stranger. They strongly remind one of the pretty quadroons of Louisiana, in their manners, complexion, and general appearance; and like those handsome offspring of mingled blood, so often seen in our Southern States, we suspect that these of Martinique enjoy but a brief space of existence. The average life of a quadroon is less than thirty years.

Martinique is eight times as large as St. Thomas, containing a population of about one hundred and seventy-five thousand. Within its borders there are at least five extinct volcanoes, one of which has an enormous crater, exceeded by only three or four others in the known world. The island rises from the sea in three groups of rugged peaks, and contains some very fertile valleys. So late as 1851, Mont Pelée burst forth furiously with flames and smoke, which naturally threw the people into a serious panic, many persons taking refuge temporarily on board the shipping in the harbor. The eruption on this occasion did not amount to anything very serious, only covering some hundreds of acres with sulphurous débris, yet serving to show that the volcano was not dead, but sleeping. Once or twice since that date ominous mutterings have been heard from Mont Pelée, which it is confidently predicted will one day deluge St. Pierre with ashes and lava, repeating the story of Pompeii.

Sugar, rum, coffee, and cotton are the staple products here, supplemented by tobacco, manioc flour, bread-fruit, and bananas. Rum is very extensively manufactured, and has a good mercantile reputation for its excellence, commanding as high prices as the more famous article of the same nature produced at Jamaica. The purpose of the author is mainly to record personal impressions, but a certain sprinkling of statistics and detail is inevitable, if we would inform, as well as amuse, the average reader.

The flora of Martinique is the marvel and delight of all who have enjoyed its extraordinary beauty, while the great abundance and variety of its fruits are believed to be unsurpassed even in the prolific tropics. Of that favorite, the mango, the island produces some forty varieties, and probably in no other region has the muscatel grape reached to such perfection in size and flavor. The whole island looks like a maze of greenery, as it is approached from the sea, vividly recalling Tutuila of the Samoan group in the South Pacific. Like most of the West Indian islands, Martinique was once densely covered with trees, and a remnant of these ancient woods creeps down to the neighborhood of St. Pierre to-day.

The principal landing is crowded at all times with hogsheads of sugar and molasses, and other casks containing the highly scented island rum, the two sweets, together with the spirits, causing a nauseous odor under the powerful heat of a vertical sun. We must not forget to mention, however, that St. Pierre has a specific for bad odors in her somewhat peculiar specialty, namely, eau-de-cologne, which is manufactured on this island, and is equal to the European article of the same name, distilled at the famous city on the Rhine. No one visits the port, if it be for but a single day, without bringing away a sample bottle of this delicate perfumery, a small portion of which, added to the morning bath, is delightfully refreshing, especially when one uses salt water at sea, it so effectively removes the saline stickiness which is apt to remain upon the limbs and body after a cold bath.

The town is blessed with an inexhaustible supply of good, fresh, mountain water, which, besides furnishing the necessary quantity for several large drinking fountains, feeds some ornamental ones, and purifies the streets by a flow through the gutters, after the fashion of Salt Lake City, Utah. This is in fact the only system of drainage at St. Pierre. A bronze fountain in the Place Bertin is fed from this source, and is an object of great pleasure in a climate where cold water in abundance is an inestimable boon. This elaborate fountain was the gift of a colored man, named Alfred Agnew, who was at one time mayor of the city. Many of the gardens attached to the dwelling-houses are ornamented with ever-flowing fountains, which impart a refreshing coolness to the tropical atmosphere.

The Rue Victor Hugo is the main thoroughfare, traversing the whole length of the town parallel with the shore, up hill and down, crossing a small bridge, and finally losing itself in the environs. It is nicely kept, well paved, and, though it is rather narrow, it is the Broadway of St. Pierre. Some of the streets are so abrupt in grade as to recall similar avenues in the English portion of Hong Kong, too steep for the passage of vehicles, or even for donkeys, being ascended by means of much worn stone steps. Fine, broad roadways surround the town and form pleasant drives.

The cathedral has a sweet chime of bells, whose soft, liquid notes came to us across the water of the bay with touching cadence at the Angelus hour. It must be a sadly calloused heart which fails to respond to these twilight sounds in an isle of the Caribbean Sea. Millet's impressive picture was vividly recalled as we sat upon the deck and listened to those bells, whose notes floated softly upon the air as if bidding farewell to the lingering daylight. At the moment, all else being so still, it seemed as though one's heartbeat could be heard, while the senses were bathed in a tranquil gladness incited by the surrounding scenery and the suggestiveness of the hour.

Three fourths of the population are half-breeds, born of whites, blacks, or mulattoes, with a possible strain of Carib blood in their veins, the result of which is sometimes a very handsome type of bronzed hue, but of Circassian features. Some of the young women of the better class are very attractive, with complexions of a gypsy color, like the artists' models who frequent the "Spanish Stairs" leading to the Trinità di Monti, at Rome. These girls possess deep, dark eyes, pearly teeth, with good figures, upright and supple as the palms. In dress they affect all the colors of the rainbow, presenting oftentimes a charming audacity of contrasts, and somehow it seems to be quite the thing for them to do so; it accords perfectly with their complexions, with the climate, with everything tropical. The many-colored Madras kerchief is universally worn by the common class of women, twisted into a jaunty turban, with one well-starched end ingeniously arranged so as to stand upright like a soldier's plume. The love of ornament is displayed by the wearing of hoop earrings of enormous size, together with triple strings of gold beads, and bracelets of the same material. If any one imagines he has seen larger sized hoop earrings this side of Africa, he is mistaken. They are more like bangles than earrings, hanging down so as to rest upon the neck and shoulders. Those who cannot afford the genuine article satisfy their vanity with gaudy imitations. They form a very curious and interesting study, these black, brown, and yellow people, both men and women. In the market-place at the north end of the town, the women preside over their bananas, oranges, and other fruits, in groups, squatting like Asiatics on their heels. In the Havana fish market, one compares the variety of colors exhibited by the fishes exposed for sale to those of the kaleidoscope, but here the Cuban display is equaled if not surpassed.

St. Pierre has a botanical garden, situated about a mile from the centre of the town, so located as to admit of utilizing a portion of the native forest yet left standing, with here and there an impenetrable growth of the feathery bamboo, king of the grasses, interspersed with the royal palm and lighter green tree-ferns. The bamboo is a marvel, single stems of it often attaining a height in tropical regions of a hundred and seventy feet, and a diameter of a foot. So rapid is its growth that it is sometimes known to attain the height of a hundred feet in sixty days. Art has done something to improve the advantages afforded by nature in this botanical garden, arranging some pretty lakes, fountains, and cascades. Vistas have been cut through the dense undergrowth, and driveways have been made, thus improving the rather neglected grounds. One pretty lake of considerable size contains three or four small islands, covered with flowering plants, while on the shore are pretty summer houses and inviting arbors. The frangipanni, tall and almost leafless, but with thick, fleshy shoots and a broad-spread, single leaf, was recognized here among other interesting plants. This is the fragrant flower mentioned by the early discoverers. There was also the parti-colored passion-flower, and groups of odd-shaped cacti, whose thick, green leaves were daintily rimmed with an odorless yellow bloom. Here, also, is an interesting example of the ceba-tree, in whose shade a hundred persons might banquet together. The author has seen specimens of the ceba superbly developed in Cuba and the Bahamas, with its massive and curiously buttressed trunk, having the large roots half above ground. It is a solitary tree, growing to a large size and enjoying great longevity. Mangoes abound here, the finest known as the *mango d'or*. There is a certain air about the public garden of St. Pierre, indicating that nature is permitted in a large degree to have her own sweet will. Evidences enough remain to show the visitor that these grounds must once have been in a much more presentable condition. There is a musical cascade, which is well worth a long walk to see and enjoy. Just inside of the entrance, one spot was all ablaze with a tiny yellow flower, best known to us as English broom, *Cytisus genista*. Its profuse but delicate bloom was dazzling beneath the bright sun's rays. Could it possibly be indigenous? No one could tell us. Probably some resident brought it hither from his home across the ocean, and it has kindly adapted itself to the new soil and climate.

We were cautioned to look out for and to avoid a certain poisonous snake, a malignant reptile, with fatal fangs, which is the dread of the inhabitants, some of whom are said to die every year from the venom of the creature. It will be remembered that one of these snakes, known here as the *fer-de-lance*, bit Josephine, the future empress, when she was very young, and that her faithful negro nurse saved the child's life by instantly drawing the poison from the wound with her own lips. It is singular that this island, and that of St. Lucia, directly south of it, should be cursed by the presence of these poisonous creatures, which do not exist in any other of the West Indian islands, and, indeed, so far as we know, are not to be found anywhere else. The fer-de-lance has one fatal enemy. This is a large snake, harmless so far as poisonous fangs are concerned, called the *cribo*. This reptile fearlessly attacks the fer-de-lance, and kills and eats him in spite of his venom, a perfectly justifiable if not gratifying instance of cannibalism, where a creature eats and relishes the body of one of its own species. The domestic cat is said also to be more than a match for the dreaded snake, and instinctively adopts a style of attack which, while protecting itself, finally closes the contest by the death of the fer-de-lance, which it seizes just back of the head at the spine, and does not let go until it has severed the head from the body; and even then instinct teaches the cat to avoid the head, for though it be severed from the body, like the mouth of a turtle under similar circumstances, it can still inflict a serious wound.

The fer-de-lance is a great destroyer of rats, this rodent forming its principal source of food. Now as rats are almost as much of a pest upon the island, and especially on the sugar plantations, as rabbits are in New Zealand, it will be seen that even the existence of this poisonous snake is not an unmitigated evil.

Crosses and wayside shrines of a very humble character are to be seen in all directions on the roadsides leading from St. Pierre, recalling similar structures which line the inland roads of Japan, where the local religion finds like public expression, only varying in the character of the emblems. At Martinique it is a Christ or a Madonna; in Japan it is a crude idol of some sort, the more hideous, the more appropriate. The same idea is to be seen carried out in the streets of Canton and Shanghai, only Chinese idols are a degree more unlike anything upon or below the earth than they are elsewhere.

It was observed that while there were plenty of masculine loafers and careless idlers of various colors, whose whole occupation seemed to be sucking at some form of burning tobacco in the shape of cigarette, cigar, or pipe, the women, of whatever complexion, seen in public, were all usefully employed. They are industrious by instinct; one almost never sees them in repose. In the transportation of all articles of domestic use, women bear them upon their heads, whether the article weighs one pound or fifty, balancing their load without making use of the hands except to place the article in position. The women not infrequently have also a baby upon their backs at the same time. Negresses and donkeys perform nine tenths of the transportation of merchandise. Wheeled vehicles are very little used in the West Indian islands. As we have seen, even in coaling ship, it is the women who do the work.

The Hotel des Bains, at St. Pierre, is an excellent hostelry, as such places go in this part of the world. The stranger will find here most of the requisites for domestic comfort, and at reasonable prices. As a health resort the place has its advantages, and a northern invalid, wishing to escape the rigor of a New England winter, would doubtless find much to occupy and recuperate him here. St. Pierre, however, has times of serious epidemic sickness, though this does not often happen in the winter season. Three or four years ago the island was visited by a sweeping epidemic of small-pox, but it raged almost entirely among the lowest classes, principally among the negroes, who seem to have a great prejudice and superstitious fear relating to vaccination, and its employment as a preventive against contracting the disease. In the yellow fever season the city suffers more or less, but the health of St. Pierre will average as good as that of our extreme Southern States; and yet, after all, with the earthquakes, hurricanes, tarantulas, scorpions, and deadly fer-de-lance, as Artemus Ward would say, Martinique presents many characteristics to recommend protracted absence. A brief visit is like a poem to be remembered, but one soon gets a surfeit of the circumscribed island.

Our next objective point was Barbadoes, to reach which we sailed one hundred and fifty miles to the eastward, this most important of the Lesser Antilles being situated further to windward, that is, nearer the continent of Europe. Our ponderous anchor came up at early morning, just as the sun rose out of the long, level reach of waters. It looked like a mammoth ball of fire, which had been immersed during the hours of the night countless fathoms below the sea. Presently everything was aglow with light and warmth, while the atmosphere seemed full of infinitesimal particles of glittering gold. At first one could watch the face of the rising sun, as it came peering above the sea, a sort of fascination impelling the observer to do so, but after a few moments, no human eye could bear its dazzling splendor.

Said an honest old Marshfield farmer, in 1776, who met the clergyman of the village very early in the opening day: "Ah, good mornin', Parson, another fine day," nodding significantly towards the sun just appearing above the cloudless horizon of Massachusetts Bay. "They do say the airth moves, and the sun stands still; but you and I, Parson, we git up airly and we *see* it rise!"

CHAPTER III.

English Island of Barbadoes.—Bridgetown the Capital.—The
Manufacture of Rum.—A Geographical Expert.—Very English.—A
Pest of Ants.—Exports.—The Ice House.—A Dense Population.—
Educational.—Marine Hotel.—Habits of Gambling.—Hurricanes.—
Curious Antiquities.—The Barbadoes Leg.—Wakeful Dreams.—
Absence of Twilight.—Departure from the Island.

Bridgetown is the capital of Barbadoes, an English island which, unlike St. Thomas, is a highly cultivated sugar plantation from shore to shore. In natural beauty, however, it will not compare with Martinique. It is by no means picturesquely beautiful, like most of the West Indian islands, being quite devoid of their thick tropical verdure. Nature is here absolutely beaten out of the field by excessive cultivation. Thirty thousand acres of sugar-cane are cut annually, yielding, according to late statistics, about seventy thousand hogsheads of sugar. We are sorry to add that there are twenty-three rum distilleries on the island, which do pecuniarily a thriving business. "The poorest molasses makes the best rum," said an experienced manager to us. He might well have added that it is also the poorest use to which it could be put. This spirit, like all produced in the West Indies, is called Jamaica rum, and though a certain amount of it is still shipped to the coast of Africa, the return cargoes no longer consist of kidnapped negroes. The article known as New

England rum, still manufactured in the neighborhood of Boston, has always disputed the African market, so to speak, with the product of these islands. Rum is the bane of Africa, just as opium is of China, the former thrust upon the native races by Americans, the latter upon the Chinese by English merchants, backed by the British government. Events follow each other so swiftly in modern times as to become half forgotten by contemporary people, but there are those among us who remember when China as a nation tried to stop the importation of the deadly drug yielded by the poppy fields of India, whereupon England forced the article upon her at the point of the bayonet.

Bridgetown is situated at the west end of the island on the open roadstead of Carlisle Bay, and has a population of over twenty-five thousand. Barbadoes lies about eighty miles to the windward of St. Vincent, its nearest neighbor, and is separated from Europe by four thousand miles of the Atlantic Ocean. It is comparatively removed from the chain formed by the Windward Isles, its situation being so isolated that it remained almost unnoticed until a century had passed after Columbus's first discovery in these waters. The area of the British possessions in the West Indies is about one seventh of the islands. It is often stated that Barbadoes is nearly as large as the Isle of Wight, but the fact is, it exceeds that island in superficial area, being a little over fifty-five miles in circumference. The reader will perhaps remember that it was here Addison laid the scene of his touching story of "Inkle and Yarico," published so many years ago in the "Spectator."

Though it is not particularly well laid out, Bridgetown makes a very pleasing picture, as a whole, when seen from the harbor. Here and there a busy windmill is mixed with tall and verdant tropical trees, backed by far-reaching fields of yellow sugar-cane, together with low, sloping hills. The buildings are mostly of stone, or coral rock, and the town follows the graceful curve of the bay. The streets are macadamized and lighted with gas, but are far too narrow for business purposes. The island is about twenty-one miles long and between fourteen and fifteen broad, the shores being nearly inclosed in a cordon of coral reefs, some of which extend for two or three miles seaward, demanding of navigators the greatest care on seeking a landing, though the course into the roads to a suitable anchorage is carefully buoyed.

Barbadoes was originally settled by the Portuguese, who here found the branches of a certain forest tree covered with hair-like hanging moss, from whence its somewhat peculiar name, Barbadoes, or the "bearded place," is supposed to have been derived. Probably this was the Indian fig-tree, still found here, and which lives for many centuries, growing to enormous proportions. In India, Ceylon, and elsewhere in Asia, it is held sacred. The author has seen one of these trees at Kandy, in the island of Ceylon, under which sacred rites have taken place constantly for a thousand years or more, and whose widespread branches could shelter five hundred people from the heat of the sun. It stands close by the famous old Buddhist temple wherein is preserved the tooth of the prophet, and before which devout Indians prostrate themselves daily, coming from long distances to do so. Indeed, Kandy is the Mecca of Ceylon.

A good share of even the reading public of England would be puzzled to tell an inquirer exactly where Barbadoes is situated, while most of those who have any idea about it have gained such knowledge as they possess from Captain Marryat's clever novel of "Peter Simple," where the account is, to be sure, meagre enough. Still later, those who have read Anthony Trollope's "West Indies and the Spanish Main" have got from the flippant pages of that book some idea of the island, though it is a very disagreeable example of Trollope's pedantic style.

"Barbadoes? Barbadoes?" said a society man to the writer of these pages, in all seriousness, just as he was about to sail from New York, "that's on the coast of Africa, is it not?" "Oh, no," was the reply, "it is one of the islands of the Lesser Antilles."

"Where are the Antilles, pray?" "You must surely know."

"But I do not, nevertheless; haven't the remotest idea. Fact is, geography never was one of my strong points."

With which remark we silently agreed, and yet our friend is reckoned to be a fairly educated, cultured person, as these expressions are commonly used. Probably he represents the average geographical knowledge of one half the people to be met with in miscellaneous society.

This is the first English possession where the sugarcane was planted, and is one of the most ancient colonies of Great Britain. It bears no resemblance to the other islands in these waters, that is, topographically, nor, indeed, in the character of its population, being entirely English. The place might be a bit taken out of any shire town of the British home island, were it only a little more cleanly and less unsavory; still it is more English than West Indian. The manners and customs are all similar to those of the people of that nationality; the negroes, and their descendants of mixed blood, speak the same tongue as the denizens of St. Giles, London. The island has often been called "Little England." There is no reliable history of Barbadoes before the period when Great Britain took possession of it, some two hundred and sixty years ago. Government House is a rather plain but pretentious dwelling, where the governor has his official and domestic residence. In its rear there is a garden, often spoken of by visitors, which is beautified by some of the choicest trees and shrubs of this latitude. It is really surprising how much a refined taste and skillful gardening can accomplish in so circumscribed a space.

Barbadoes is somewhat remarkable as producing a variety of minerals; among which are coal, manganese, iron, kaolin, and yellow ochre. There are also one or two localities on the island where a flow of petroleum is found, of which some use is made. It is called Barbadoes tar, and were the supply sufficient to warrant the use of refining machinery, it would undoubtedly produce a good burning fluid. There is a "burning well," situated in what is known as the Scotland District, where the water emerging from the earth forms a pool, which is kept in a state of ebullition from the inflammable air or gas which passes through it. This gas, when lighted by a match, burns freely until extinguished by artificial means, not rising in large enough quantities to make a great flame, but still sufficient to create the effect of burning water, and forming quite a curiosity.

There are no mountains on the island, but the land is undulating, and broken into hills and dales; one elevation, known as Mount Hillaby, reaches a thousand feet and more above the level of tide waters.

One of the most serious pests ever known at Barbadoes was the introduction of ants, by slave-ships from Africa. No expedient of human ingenuity served to rid the place of their destructive presence, and it was at one time seriously proposed to abandon the island on this account. After a certain period nature came to the rescue. She does all things royally, and the hurricane of 1780 completely annihilated the vermin. Verily, it was appropriate to call Barbadoes in those days the Antilles! It appears that there is no affliction quite unmixed with good, and that we must put a certain degree of faith in the law of compensation, however great the seeming evil under which we suffer. To our limited power of comprehension, a destructive hurricane does seem an extreme resort by which to crush out an insect pest. The query might even arise, with some minds, whether the cure was not worse than the disorder.

The exports from the island consist almost wholly of molasses, sugar, and rum, products of the cane, which grows all over the place, in every nook and corner, from hilltop to water's edge. The annual export, as already intimated, is considerably over sixty thousand hogsheads. Sugar cannot, however, be called king of any one section, since half of the amount manufactured in the whole world is the product of the beet root, the growth of which is liberally subsidized by more than one European government, in order to foster local industry. Like St. Thomas, this island has been almost denuded of its forest growth, and is occasionally liable, as we have seen, to destructive hurricanes.

Bridgetown is a place of considerable progress, having several benevolent and educational institutions; it also possesses railway, telephone, and telegraphic service. Its export trade aggregates over seven million dollars per annum, to accommodate which amount of commerce causes a busy scene nearly all the time in the harbor. The steam railway referred to connects the capital with the Parish of St. Andrews, twenty-one miles away on the other side of the island, its terminus being at the thrifty little town of Bathsheba, a popular resort, which is noted for its fine beach and excellent sea bathing.

The cathedral is consecrated to the established religion of the Church of England, and is a picturesque, time-worn building, surrounded, after the style of rural England, by a quaint old graveyard, the monuments and slabs of which are gray and moss-grown, some of them bearing dates of the earlier portion of the sixteenth century. This spot forms a very lovely, peaceful picture, where the graves are shaded by tree-ferns and stately palms. Somehow one cannot but miss the tall, slim cypress, which to the European and American eye seems so especially appropriate to such a spot. There were clusters of low-growing mignonette, which gave out a faint perfume exactly suited to the solemn shades which prevailed, and here and there bits of ground enameled with blue-eyed violets. The walls of the inside of the church are covered with memorial tablets, and there is an organ of great power and sweetness of tone.

The "Ice House," so called, at Bridgetown is a popular resort, which everybody visits who comes to Barbadoes. Here one can find files of all the latest American and European papers, an excellent café, with drinks and refreshments of every conceivable character, and can purchase almost any desired article from a toothpick to a set of parlor furniture. It is a public library, an exchange, a "Bon Marché," and an artificial ice manufactory, all combined. Strangers naturally make it a place of rendezvous. It seemed to command rather more of the average citizen's attention than did legitimate business, and one is forced to admit that although the drinks which were so generously dispensed were cool and appetizing, they were also very potent. It was observed that some individuals, who came into the hospitable doors rather sober and dejected in expression of features, were apt to go out just a little jolly.

The Ice House is an institution of these islands, to be found at St. Thomas, Demerara, and Trinidad, as well as at Barbadoes. Havana has a similar retreat, but calls it a café, situated on the Paseo, near the Tacon Theatre.

The population of the island amounts to about one hundred and seventy-two thousand,—the census of 1881 showed it to be a trifle less than this,—giving the remarkable density of one thousand and more persons to the square mile, thus forming an immense human beehive. It is the only one of the West Indian islands from which a certain amount of emigration is necessary annually. The large negro population makes labor almost incredibly cheap, field-hands on the plantations being paid only one shilling per day; and yet, so ardent is their love of home—and the island is home to them—that only a few can be induced to leave it in search of better wages. When it is remembered that the State of Massachusetts, which is considered to be one of the most thickly populated sections of the United States, contains but two hundred and twenty persons to the square mile, the fact that this West Indian island supports over one thousand inhabitants in the same average space will be more fully appreciated. Notwithstanding this crowded state of the population, we were intelligently informed that while petty offenses are common, there is a marked absence of serious crimes.

One sees few if any signs of poverty here. It is a land of sugar-cane, yams, and sweet potatoes, very prolific, and very easily tilled. Some of the most prosperous men on the island are colored planters, who own their large establishments, though born slaves, perhaps on the very ground they now own. They have by strict economy and industry saved money enough to make a fair beginning, and in the course of years have gradually acquired wealth. One plantation, owned by a colored man, born of slave parents, was pointed out to us, with the information that it was worth twenty thousand pounds sterling, and that its last year's crop yielded over three hundred hogsheads of sugar, besides a considerable quantity of molasses.

England maintains at heavy expense a military depot here, from which to draw under certain circumstances. There is no local necessity for supporting such a force. Georgetown is a busy place. Being the most seaward of the West Indies, it has become the chief port of call for ships navigating these seas. The Caribbees are divided by geographers into the Windward and Leeward islands, in accordance with the direction in which they lie with regard to the prevailing winds. They are in very deep water, the neighboring sea having a mean depth of fifteen hundred fathoms. Being so far eastward, Barbadoes enjoys an exceptionally equable climate, and it is claimed for it that it has a lower thermometer than any other West Indian island. Its latitude is 13° 4' north, longitude 59° 37' west, within eight hundred miles of the equator. The prevailing wind blows from the northeast, over the broad, unobstructed Atlantic, rendering the evenings almost always delightfully cool, tempered by this grateful tonic breath of the ocean.

Trafalgar Square, Bridgetown, contains a handsome fountain, and a bronze statue of Nelson which, as a work of art, is simply atrocious. From this broad, open square the tramway cars start, and it also forms a general business centre.

The home government supports, besides its other troops, a regiment of negroes uniformed as Zouaves and officered by white men. The police of Bridgetown are also colored men. Slavery was abolished here in 1833. Everything is so thoroughly English, that only the temperature, together with the vegetation, tells the story of latitude and longitude. The soil has been so closely cultivated as to have become partially exhausted, and this is the only West Indian island, if we are correctly informed, where artificial enrichment is considered necessary to stimulate the native soil, or where it has ever been freely used. "I question," said an intelligent planter to us, "whether we should not be better off to-day, if we had not so overstimulated, in fact, burned out, our land with guano and phosphates." These are to the ground like intoxicants to human beings,—if over-indulged in they are fatal, and even the partial use is of questionable advantage. The Chinese and Japanese apply only domestic refuse in their fields as a manure, and no people obtain such grand results as they do in agriculture. They know nothing of patent preparations employed for such purposes, and yet will render a spot of ground profitable which a European would look upon as absolutely not worth cultivating.

In any direction from Bridgetown going inland, miles upon miles of plantations are seen bearing the bright green sugar-cane, turning to yellow as it ripens, and giving splendid promise for the harvest. Here and there are grouped a low cluster of cabins, which form the quarters of the negroes attached to the plantation, while close at hand the tall chimney of the sugar mill looms over the surrounding foliage. A little one side, shaded by some palms, is the planter's neat and attractive residence, painted snow white, in contrast to the deep greenery surrounding it, and having a few flower beds in its front.

The Marine Hotel, which is admirably situated on a rocky point at Hastings, three hundred feet above the beach, is about a league from the city, and forms a favorite resort for the townspeople. The house is capable of accommodating three hundred guests at a time. Its spacious piazzas fronting the ocean are constantly fanned by the northeast trades from October to March. Some New York families regard the place as a choice winter resort, the thermometer rarely indicating over 80° Fahr., or falling below 70°. This suburb of Hastings is the location of the army barracks, where a broad plain affords admirable space for drill and military manœuvres. There is a monument at Hastings, raised to the memory of the victims of the hurricane of 1831, which seems to be rather unpleasantly suggestive of future possibilities. Near at hand is a well-arranged mile racecourse, a spot very dear to the army officers, where during the racing season any amount of money is lost and won. There seems to be something in this tropical climate which incites to all sorts of gambling, and the habit among the people is so common as to be looked upon with great leniency. Just so, at some of the summer resorts of the south of France, Italy, and Germany, ladies or gentlemen will frankly say, "I am going to the Casino for a little gambling, but will be back again by and by."

The roads in the vicinity of Bridgetown are admirably kept, all being macadamized, but the dust which rises from the pulverized coral rock is nearly blinding, and together with the reflection caused by the sun on the snow white roads proves very trying to the eyesight. The dust and glare are serious drawbacks to the enjoyment of these environs.

As we have said, hurricanes have proved very fatal at Barbadoes. In 1780, four thousand persons were swept out of existence in a few hours by the irresistible fury of a tornado. So late as 1831, the loss of life by a similar visitation was over two thousand, while the loss of property aggregated some two million pounds sterling. The experience has not, however, been so severe here as at several of the other islands. At the time of the hurricane just referred to, Barbadoes was covered with a coat of sulphurous ashes nearly an inch thick, which was afterwards found to have come from the island of St. Vincent, where what is called Brimstone Mountain burst forth in flames and laid that island also in ashes. It is interesting to note that there should have been such intimate relationship shown between a great atmospheric disturbance like a hurricane and an underground agitation as evinced by the eruption of a volcano.

It should be mentioned that these hurricanes have never been known to pass a certain limit north or south, their ravages having always been confined between the eleventh and twenty-first degrees of north latitude.

It appears that some curious Carib implements were found not long since just below the surface of the earth on the south shore of the bay, which are to be forwarded to the British Museum, London. These were of hard stone, and were thought by the finders to have been used by the aborigines to fell trees. Some were thick shells, doubtless employed by the Indians in the rude cultivation of maize, grown here four or five hundred years ago. It was said that these stone implements resembled those which have been found from time to time in Norway and Sweden. If this is correct, it is an important fact for antiquarians to base a theory upon. Some scientists believe that there was, in prehistoric times, an intimate relationship between Scandinavia and the continent of America.

Though there are several public schools in Bridgetown, both primary and advanced, we were somehow impressed with the idea that education for the common people was not fostered in a manner worthy of a British colony of so long standing; but this is the impression of a casual observer only. There is a college situated ten or twelve miles from the city, founded by Sir Christopher Codrington, which has achieved a high reputation as an educational institution in its chosen field of operation. It is a large structure of white stone, well-arranged, and is, as we were told, consistent with the spirit of the times. It has the dignity of ripened experience, having been opened in 1744. The professors are from Europe. A delicious fresh water spring rises to the surface of the land just below the cliff, at Codrington College, a blessing which people who live in the tropics know how to appreciate. There is also at Bridgetown what is known as Harrison's College, which, however, is simply a high school devoted exclusively to girls.

The island is not exempt from occasional prevalence of tropical fevers, but may be considered a healthy resort upon the whole. Leprosy is not unknown among the lower classes, and elephantiasis is frequently to be met with. This disease is known in the West Indies as the "Barbadoes Leg." Sometimes a native may be seen on the streets with one of his legs swollen to the size of his body. There is no known cure for this disease except the surgeon's knife, and the removal of the victim from the region where it first developed itself. The author has seen terrible cases of elephantiasis among the natives of the Samoan group of islands, where this strange and unaccountable disease is thought to have reached its most extreme and repulsive development. Foreigners are seldom if ever afflicted with it, either in the West Indies or the South Pacific.

We are to sail to-night. A few passengers and a quantity of freight have been landed, while some heavy merchandise has been received on board, designed for continental ports to the southward. The afternoon shadows lengthen upon the shore, and the sunset hour, so brief in this latitude, approaches. The traveler who has learned to love the lingering twilight of the north misses these most charming hours when in equatorial regions, but as the goddess of night wraps her sombre mantle about her, it is so superbly decked with diamond stars that the departed daylight is hardly regretted. It is like the prompter's ringing up of the curtain upon a complete theatrical scene; the glory of the tropical sky bursts at once upon the vision in all its completeness, its burning constellations, its solitaire brilliants, its depth of azure, and its mysterious Milky Way.

While sitting under the awning upon deck, watching the gentle swaying palms and tall fern-trees, listening to the low drone of busy life in the town, and breathing the sweet exhalations of tropical fruits and flowers, a trance-like sensation suffuses the brain. Is this the *dolce far niente* of the Italians, the sweet do-nothing of the tropics? To us, however defined, it was a waking dream of sensuous delight, of entire content. How far away sounds the noise of the steam-winch, the sharp chafing of the iron pulleys, the prompt orders of the officer of the deck, the swinging of the ponderous yards, the rattling of the anchor chain as it comes in through the hawse hole, while the ship gradually loses her hold upon the land. With half closed eyes we scarcely heard these many significant sounds, but floated peacefully on in an Eden of fancy, quietly leaving Carlisle Bay far behind.

Our course was to the southward, while everything, high and low, was bathed in a flood of shimmering moonlight, the magic alchemy of the sky, whose influence etherealizes all upon which it rests.

CHAPTER IV.

Curious Ocean Experiences.—The Delicate Nautilus.—Flying-Fish.—
The Southern Cross.—Speaking a Ship at Sea.—Scientific
Navigation.—South America as a Whole.—Fauna and Flora.—
Natural Resources of a Wonderful Land.—Rivers, Plains, and
Mountain Ranges.—Aboriginal Tribes.—Population.—Political
Divisions.—Civil Wars.—Weakness of South American States.

The sudden appearance of a school of flying-fish gliding swiftly through the air for six or eight rods just above the rippling waves, and then sinking from sight; the sportive escort of half a hundred slate-colored porpoises, leaping high out of the water on either bow of the ship only to plunge back again, describing graceful curves; the constant presence of that sullen tiger of the ocean, the voracious, man-eating shark, betrayed by its dorsal fin showing above the surface of the sea; the sporting of mammoth whales, sending columns of water high in air from their blowholes, and lashing the waves playfully with their broad-spread tails, are events at sea too commonplace to comment upon in detail, though they tend to while away the inevitable monotony of a long voyage.

Speaking of flying-fish, there is more in the flying capacity of this little creature than is generally admitted, else why has it wings on the forward part of its body, each measuring seven inches in length? If designed only for fins, they are altogether out of proportion to the rest of its body. They are manifestly intended for just the use to which the creature puts them. One was brought to us by a seaman; how it got on board we know not, but it measured eleven inches from the nose to the tip of the tail fin, and was in shape and size very much like a small mackerel. After leaving Barbadoes, we got into what sailors call the flying-fish latitudes, where they appear constantly in their low, rapid flight, sometimes singly, but oftener in small schools of a score or more, creating flashes of silvery-blue lustre. The most careful observation could detect no vibration of the long, extended fins; the tiny fish sailed, as it were, upon the wind, the flight of the giant albatross in miniature.

One afternoon, when the sea was scarcely dimpled by the soft trade wind, we came suddenly upon myriads of that little fairy of the ocean, the gossamer nautilus, with its Greek galleon shape, and as frail, apparently, as a spider's web. What a gondola it would make for Queen Mab! How delicate and transparent it is, while radiating prismatic colors! A touch might dismember it, yet what a daring navigator, floating confidently upon the sea where the depth is a thousand fathoms, liable at any moment to be changed into raging billows by an angry storm! How minute the vitality of this graceful atom, a creature whose existence is perhaps for only a single day; yet how grand and limitless the system of life and creation of which it is so humble a representative! Sailors call these frail marine creatures Portuguese men-of-war. Possessing some singular facility for doing so, if they are disturbed, they quickly furl their sails and sink below the surface of the buoyant waves into deep water, the home of the octopus, the squid, and the voracious shark. Did they, one is led to query, navigate these seas after this fashion before the Northmen came across the ocean, and before Columbus landed at San Salvador? At night the glory of the southern hemisphere, as revealed in new constellations and brighter stars brought into view, was observed with keenest interest,—"Everlasting Night, with her star diadems, with her silence, and her verities." The phosphorescence of the sea, with its scintillations of brilliant light, its ripples of liquid fire, the crest of each wave a flaming cascade, was a charming phenomenon one never tired of watching. If it be the combination of millions and billions of animalculæ which thus illumines the waters, then these infinitesimal creatures are the fireflies of the ocean, as the cucuios, that fairy torch-bearer, is of the land. Gliding on the magic mirror of the South Atlantic, in which the combined glory of the sky was reflected with singular clearness, it seemed as though we were sailing over a starry world below.

While observing the moon in its beautiful series of changes, lighting our way by its chaste effulgence night after night, it was difficult to realize that it shines entirely by the light which it borrows from the sun; but it was easy to believe the simpler fact, that of all the countless hosts of the celestial bodies, she is our nearest neighbor. "An eighteen-foot telescope reveals to the human eye over forty million stars," said Captain Baker, as we stood together gazing at the luminous heavens. "And if we entertain the generally accepted idea," he continued, "we must believe that each one of that enormous aggregate of stars is the centre of a solar system similar to our own." The known facts relating to the stars, like stellar distances, are almost incomprehensible.

One cannot but realize that there is always a certain amount of sentiment wasted on the constellation known as the Southern Cross by passengers bound to the lands and seas over which it hangs. Orion or the Pleiades, either of them, is infinitely superior in point of brilliancy, symmetry, and individuality.

A lively imagination is necessary to endow this irregular cluster of stars with any real resemblance to the Christian emblem for which it is named. It serves the navigator in the southern hemisphere, in part, the same purpose which the north star does in our portion of the globe, and there our own respect for it as a constellation ends. Much poetic talent has been expended for ages to idealize the Southern Cross, which is, alas! no cross at all. We have seen a person unfamiliar with the locality of this constellation strive long and patiently, but in vain, to find it. It should be remembered that two prominent stars in Centaurus point directly to it. The one furthest from the so called cross is held to be the fixed star nearest to the earth, but its distance from us is twenty thousand times farther than that of the sun.

We have never yet met a person, looking upon this cluster of the heavens for the first time, who did not frankly express his disappointment. Anticipation and fruition are oftenest at antipodes.

The graceful marine birds which follow the ship, day after day, darting hither and thither with arrowy swiftness, lured by the occasional refuse thrown from on board, would be seriously missed were they to leave us. Watching their aerial movements and untiring power of wing, while listening to their sharp complaining cries, is a source of constant amusement. Even rough weather and a raging sea, if not accompanied by too serious a storm, is sometimes welcome, serving to awaken the ship from its dull propriety, and to put officers, crew, and passengers upon their mettle. To speak a strange vessel at sea is always interesting. If it is a steamer, a long, black wake of smoke hanging among the clouds at the horizon betrays her proximity long before the hull is sighted. All eyes are on the watch until she comes clearly within the line of vision, gradually increasing in size and distinctness of outline, until presently the spars and rigging are minutely delineated. Then speculation is rife as to whence she comes and where she is going. By and by the two ships approach so near that signal flags can be read, and the captains talk with each other, exchanging names, whither bound, and so on. Then each commander dips his flag in compliment to the other, and the ships rapidly separate. All of this is commonplace enough, but serves to while away an hour, and insures a report of our progress and safety at the date of meeting, when the stranger reaches his port of destination.

We have spoken of the pleasure experienced at sea in watching intelligently the various phases of the moon. The subject is a prolific one; a whole chapter might be written upon it.

It is perhaps hardly realized by the average landsman, and indeed by few who constantly cross the ocean, with their thoughts and interests absorbed by the many attractive novelties of the ocean, how important a part this great luminary plays in the navigation of a ship. It is to the intelligent and observant mariner the never-failing watch of the sky, the stars performing the part of hands to designate the proper figure upon the dial. If there is occasion to doubt the correctness of his chronometer, the captain of the ship can verify its figures or correct them by this planet. Every minute that the chronometer is wrong, assuming that it be so, may put him fifteen miles out of his reckoning, which, under some circumstances, might prove to be a fatal error, even leading to the loss of his ship and all on board. To find his precise location upon the ocean, the navigator requires both Greenwich time and local meridian time, the latter obtained by the sun on shipboard, exactly at midday. To get Greenwich time by lunar observation, the captain, for example, finds that the moon is three degrees from the star Regulus. By referring to his nautical almanac he sees recorded there the Greenwich time at which the moon was three degrees from that particular star. He then compares his chronometer with these figures, and either confirms or corrects its indication. It is interesting to the traveler to observe and understand these important resources, which science has brought to bear in perfecting his safety on the ocean, promoting the interests of commerce, and in aid of correct navigation. The experienced captain of a ship now lays his course as surely by compass, after satisfying himself by these various means of his exact position, as though the point of his destination was straight before him all the while, and visible from the pilot house.

How indescribable is the grandeur of these serene nights on the ocean, fanned by the somnolent trade winds; a little lonely, perhaps, but so blessed with the hallowed benediction of the moonlight, so gorgeously decorated by the glittering images of the studded heavens, so sweet and pure and fragrant is the breath of the sleeping wind! If one listens intently, there seems to come to the senses a whispering of the waves, as though the sea in confidence would tell its secrets to a willing ear.

The ship heads almost due south after leaving Barbadoes, when her destination is, as in our case, Pará, twelve hundred miles away. On this course we encounter the equatorial current, which runs northward at a rate of two miles in an hour, and at some points reaches a much higher rate of speed.

As eternal vigilance is the price of liberty, so eternal scrubbing is the price of cleanliness on shipboard. The deck hands are at it from five o'clock in the morning until sunset. Our good ship looks as if she had just come out of dock. Last night's gale, which in its angry turmoil tossed us about so recklessly, covered her with a saline, sticky deposit; but with the rising of the sun all this disappears as if by magic. The many brass mountings shine with dazzling lustre, and the white paint contrasts with the well-tarred cordage which forms the standing rigging.

While the ship pursues her course through the far-reaching ocean, let us sketch in outline the general characteristics of South America, whither we are bound.

It is a country containing twice the area, though not quite one half the amount of population, of the United States, a land which, though now presenting nearly all phases of civilization, was four centuries ago mostly inhabited by nomadic tribes of savages, who knew nothing of the horse, the ox, or the sheep, which to-day form so great and important a source of its wealth, and where wheat, its prevailing staple, was also unknown. It is a land overflowing with native riches, which possesses an unlimited capacity of production, and whose large and increasing population requires just such domestic supplies as we of the north can profitably furnish. The important treaty of reciprocity, so lately arranged between the giant province of Brazil—or rather we should say the Republic of Brazil—and our own country, is already developing new and increasing channels of trade for our shippers and producers of the great staples, as well as throwing open to us a new nation of consumers for our special articles of manufacture. Facts speak louder than words. On the voyage in which the author sailed in the Vigilancia, she took over twenty thousand barrels of flour to Brazil from the United States, and would have taken more had her capacity admitted. Every foot of space on board was engaged for the return voyage, twelve thousand bags of coffee being shipped from Rio Janeiro alone, besides nearly as large a consignment of coffee from Santos, in the same republic. The great mutual benefit which must accrue from this friendly compact with an enterprising foreign country can hardly be overestimated. These considerations lead to a community of interests, which will grow by every reasonable means of familiarizing the people of the two countries with each other. Hence the possible and practical value of such a work as the one in hand.

By briefly consulting one of the many cheap and excellent maps of the western hemisphere, the patient reader will be enabled to follow the route taken by the author with increased interest and a clearer understanding.

It is surprising, in conversing with otherwise intelligent and well-informed people, to find how few there are, comparatively speaking, who have any fixed and clear idea relative to so large a portion of the habitable globe as South America. The average individual seems to know less of the gigantic river Amazon than he does of the mysterious Nile, and is less familiar with that grand, far-reaching water-way, the Plate, than he is with the sacred Ganges; yet one can ride from Buenos Ayres in the Argentine Republic, across the wild pampas, to the base of the Andes in a Pullman palace car.

There is no part of the globe concerning which so little is written, and no other portion which is not more sought by travelers; in short, it is less known to the average North American than New Zealand or Australia.

The vast peninsula which we call South America is connected with our own part of the continent by the Isthmus of Panama and the territory designated as Central America. Its configuration is triangular, and exhibits in many respects a strong similarity to the continents of Africa and Australia, if the latter gigantic island may be called a continent. It extends north and south nearly five thousand miles, or from latitude 12° 30' north to Cape Horn in latitude 55° 59' south. Its greatest width from east to west is a little over three thousand miles, and its area, according to the best authorities, is nearly seven million square miles. Three fourths of this country lie in the torrid zone, though as a whole it has every variety of climate, from equatorial heat to the biting frosts of alpine peaks. Its widespread surface consists principally of three immense plains, watered respectively by the Amazon, Plate, and Orinoco rivers. This spacious country has a coast line of over sixteen thousand miles on the two great oceans, with comparatively few indentures, headlands, or bays, though at the extreme south it consists of a maze of countless small islands, capes, and promontories, of which Cape Horn forms the outermost point.

The Cordillera of the Andes extends through the whole length of this giant peninsula, from the Strait of Magellan to the Isthmus of Panama, a distance of forty-five hundred miles, forming one of the most remarkable physical features of the globe, and presenting the highest mountains on its surface, except those of the snowy Himalayas which separate India from Thibet. The principal range of the Andes runs nearly parallel with the Pacific coast, at an average distance of about one hundred miles from it, and contains several active volcanoes. If we were to believe a late school geography, published in London, Cotopaxi, one famous peak of this Andean range, throws up flames three thousand feet above the brink of its crater, which is eighteen thousand feet above tide water; but to be on the safe side, let us reduce these extraordinary figures at least one half, as regards the eruptive power of Cotopaxi. This mountain chain, near the border between Chili and Peru, divides into two branches, the principal one still called the Cordillera of the Andes, and the other, nearer to the ocean, the Cordillera de la Costa. Between these ranges, about three thousand feet above the sea, is a vast table-land with an area larger than that of France.

It will be observed that we are dealing with a country which, like our own, is one of magnificent distances. It is difficult for the nations of the old world, where the population is hived together in such circumscribed space, to realize the geographical extent of the American continent. When informed that it required six days and nights, at express speed upon well-equipped railroads, to cross the United States from ocean to ocean, a certain editor in London doubted the statement. Outside of Her Majesty's dominions, the average Englishman has only superficial ideas of geography. The frequent blunders of some British newspapers in these matters are simply ridiculous.

It should be understood that South America is a land of plains as well as of lofty mountains, having the *llanos* of the Orinoco region, the *selvas* of the Amazon, and the *pampas* of the Argentine Republic. The llanos are composed of a region about as large as the New England States, so level that the motion of the rivers can hardly be discerned. The selvas are for the most part vast unbroken forests, in which giant trees, thick undergrowth, and entwining creepers combine to form a nearly impenetrable region. The pampas lie between the Andes and the Atlantic Ocean, stretching southward from northern Brazil to southern Patagonia, affording grass sufficient to feed innumerable herds of wild cattle, but at the extreme south the country sinks into half overflowed marshes and lagoons, resembling the glades and savannahs of Florida.

The largest river in the world, namely, the Amazon, rises in the Peruvian Andes, within sixty miles of the Pacific Ocean, and flows thousands of miles in a general east-northeast direction, finally emptying into the Atlantic Ocean. This unequaled river course is navigable for over two thousand miles from its mouth, which is situated on the equatorial line, where its outflow is partially impeded by the island of Marajo, a nearly round formation, one hundred and fifty miles or thereabouts in diameter. This remarkable island divides the river's outlet into two passages, the largest of which is a hundred and fifty miles in width, forming an estuary of extraordinary dimensions. The Amazon has twelve tributaries, each one of which is a thousand miles in length, not to count its hundreds of smaller ones, while the main stream affords water communication from the Atlantic Ocean to near the foothills of the Andes.

We are simply stating a series of condensed geographical facts, from which the intelligent reader can form his own deductions as regards the undeveloped possibilities of this great southland.

Our own mammoth river, the Mississippi, is a comparatively shallow stream, with a shifting channel and dangerous sandbanks, which impede navigation throughout the most of its course; while the Amazon shows an average depth of over one hundred feet for the first thousand miles of its flow from the Atlantic, forming inland seas in many places, so spacious that the opposite banks are not within sight of each other. It is computed by good authority that this river, with its numerous affluents, forms a system of navigable water twenty-four thousand miles in length! There are comparatively few towns or settlements of any importance on the banks of the Amazon, which flows mostly through a dense, unpeopled evergreen forest, not absolutely without human beings, but for very long distances nearly so. Wild animals, anacondas and other reptiles, together with many varieties of birds and numerous tribes of monkeys, make up the animal life. Now and again a settlement of European colonists is found, or a rude Indian village is seen near the banks, but they are few and far between. There are occasional regions of low, marshy ground, which are malarious at certain seasons, but the average country is salubrious, and capable of supporting a population of millions.

This is only one of the large rivers of South America; there are many others of grand proportions. The Plate comes next to it in magnitude, having a length of two thousand miles, and being navigable for one half the distance from its mouth at all seasons. It is over sixty miles wide at Montevideo, and is therefore the widest known river. Like the great stream already described, it traverses a country remarkable for the fertility of its soil, but very thinly settled. The Plate carries to the ocean four fifths as much, in volume of water, as does the mighty Amazon, the watershed drained by it exceeding a million and a half square miles. One can only conceive of the true magnitude of such figures when applied to the land by comparing the number of square miles contained in any one European nation, or any dozen of our own States.

Juan Diaz de Solis discovered the estuary of the Plate in 1508, and believed it at that time to be a gulf, but on a second voyage from Europe, in 1516, he ascended the river a considerable distance, and called it Mar Dulce, on account of the character of the waters. Unfortunately, this intelligent discoverer was killed by Indian arrows on attempting to land at a certain point. For a considerable period the river was called after him, and we think should have continued to be so, but its name was changed to the Plate on account of the conspicuous silver ornaments worn in great profusion by the natives, which they freely exchanged for European gewgaws.

Though nearly four hundred years have passed since its discovery, a large portion of the country still remains comparatively unexplored, much of it being a wilderness sparsely inhabited by Indians, many of whom are without a vestige of civilization. We know as little of portions of the continent as we do of Central Africa, yet there is no section of the globe which suggests a greater degree of physical interest, or which would respond more readily and profitably to intelligent effort at development. When the Spaniards first came to South America, it was only in Peru, the land of the Incas, that they found natives who had made any substantial progress in civilization. The earliest history extant relating to this region of the globe is that of the Incas, a warlike race of sun-worshipers, who possessed enormous treasures of gold and silver, and who erected magnificent temples enriched with the precious metals. It was the almost fabulous wealth of the Incas that led to their destruction, tempting the cupidity of the avaricious Spaniards, and causing them to institute a system of cruelty, oppression, robbery, and bloodshed which finally obliterated an entire people from the face of the globe. The empire of the Incas extended from Quito, in Ecuador (on the equator), to the river Monté in Chili, and eastward to the Andes. The romantic career of Pizarro and Cortez is familiar to us all. There are few palliating circumstances connected with the advent of the Spaniards, either here, in the West Indies, or in Mexico. The actual motive which prompted their invasion of this foreign soil was to search for mineral treasures, though policy led them to cover their bloodthirsty deeds with a pretense of religious zeal. Their first acts were reckless, cruel, and sanguinary, followed by a systematic oppression of the native races which was an outrage upon humanity. The world at large profited little by the extortion and golden harvest reaped by Spain, to realize which she adopted a policy of extermination, both in Peru and in Mexico; but let it be remembered that her own national ruin was brought about with poetical justice by the very excess of her ill-gotten, blood-stained treasures. The Spanish historians tell us, as an evidence of the persistent bravery of their ancestors, that it took them eight hundred years of constant warfare to wrest Spain from her Moorish conquerors. It is for us to remind them how brief has been the continuance of their glory, how rapid their decline from splendid continental and colonial possessions to their present condition, that of the weakest and most insignificant power in Europe.

There are localities which have been visited by adventurous explorers, especially in Chili and Peru, where ruins have been found, and various monuments of antiquity examined, of vast interest to archæologists, but of which scarcely more than their mere existence is recorded. Some of these ruins are believed to antedate by centuries the period of the Incas, and are supposed to be the remains of tribes which, judging from their pottery and other domestic utensils, were possibly of Asiatic origin. Comparatively few travelers have visited Lake Titicaca, in the Peruvian Andes, with its sacred islands and mysterious ruins, from whence the Incas dated their mythical origin. The substantial remains of some grand temples are still to be seen on the islands near the borders of the lake, the decaying masonry decked here and there with a wild growth of hardy cactus. This remarkable body of water, Lake Titicaca, in the mountain range of Peru, lies more than twelve thousand feet above the level of the Pacific; yet it never freezes, and its average depth is given as six hundred feet, representing an immense body of water. It covers an area of four thousand square miles, which is about four fifths as large as our own Lake Ontario, the average depth being about the same. Titicaca is the largest lake in the world occupying so elevated a site.

The population of South America is mostly to be found on the coast, and is thought to be about thirty-five millions, though, all things considered, we are disposed to believe this an overestimate. There are tribes far inland who are not brought in contact with civilization at all, and whose numbers are not known. The magnitude and density of the forests are remarkable; they cover, it is intelligently stated, nearly two thirds of the country. The vegetation, in its various forms, is rich beyond comparison. Professor Agassiz, who explored the valley of the Amazon under the most favorable auspices, tells us that he found within an area of half a mile square over one hundred species of trees, among which were nearly all of the choicest cabinet and dye woods known to the tropics, besides others suitable for shipbuilding. Some of these trees are remarkable for their gigantic size, others for their beauty of form, and still others are valuable for their gums and resins. Of the latter, the india-rubber tree is the most prolific and important known to commerce. From Brazil comes four fifths of the world's supply of the raw material of rubber.

The great fertility of the soil generally would seem to militate against the true progress of the people of South America, absolutely discouraging, rather than stimulating national industry. One cannot but contrast the state of affairs in this respect with that of North America, where the soil is so much less productive, and where the climate is so universally rigorous. The deduction is inevitable that, to find man at his best, we must observe him where his skill, energy, and perseverance are all required to achieve a livelihood, and not where exuberant nature is over-indulgent, over-productive. The coast, the valleys, and indeed the main portion of South America are tropical, but a considerable section of the country is so elevated that its climate is that of perpetual spring, resembling the great Mexican plateau, both physically and as regards temperature. The population is largely of Spanish descent, and that language is almost universally spoken, though Portuguese is the current tongue in Brazil. These languages are so similar, in fact, that the people of the two nations can easily understand each other. It is said to be true that, in the wild regions of the country, there are tribes of Indians found to-day living close to each other, separated by no physical barriers, who differ materially in language, physiognomy, manners, and customs, having absolutely nothing in common but their brown or copper colored skins. Furthermore, these tribes live most frequently in deadly feuds with each other. That cannibalism is still practiced among these interior tribes is positively believed, especially among some of the tribes of the extreme south, that is, among the Patagonians and the wild, nomadic race of Terra del Fuego. These two tribes, on opposite sides of the Strait of Magellan, are quite different from each other in nearly every respect, especially in size, nor will they attempt to hold friendly intercourse of any sort with each other.

There are certain domestic animals which are believed to be improved by crossing them with others of a different type, but this does not seem to apply, very often, advantageously to different races of human beings. It is plain enough in South America that the amalgamation of foreigners and natives rapidly effaces the original better qualities of each, the result being a mongrel, nondescript type, hard to analyze and hard to improve. That keen observer, Professor Agassiz, especially noticed this during his year of scientific research in Brazil. This has also been the author's experience, as illustrated in many lands, where strictly different races, the one highly civilized, the other barbarian, have unitedly produced children. It is a sort of amalgamation which nature does not favor, recording her objections in an unmistakable manner. It is the flow of European emigration towards these southern republics which will infuse new life and progress among them. The aboriginal race is slowly receding, and fading out, as was the case in Australia, in New Zealand, and in the instance of our western Indians. A new people will eventually possess the land, composed of the several European nationalities, who are already the virtual masters of South America so far as regards numbers, intelligence, and possession.

Since these notes were written, the Argentine government has sold to Baron Hirsch three thousand square leagues of land in the province of Chaco, for the formation of a Jewish colony. Agents are already at work, aided by competent engineers and practical individuals, in preparing for the early reception of the new occupants of the country. The first contingent, of about one thousand Jews, have already arrived and are becoming domesticated. Argentina wants men perhaps more than money; indeed, one will make the other. A part of Baron Hirsch's scheme is to lend these people money, to be repaid in small installments extending over a considerable period. For this extensive territory the Baron paid one million three hundred thousand dollars in gold, thus making himself the owner of the largest connected area of land in the world possessed by a single individual. It exceeds that of the kingdom of Montenegro.

As to the zoölogy of this part of the continent, it is different from that of Europe, Africa, Asia, and North America. The number of dangerous beasts of prey is quite limited. There is nothing here to answer to the African lion, the Asiatic tiger, the elephant of Ceylon, or the grisly bear of Alaska. The jaguar is perhaps the most formidable animal, and resembles the leopard. There are also the cougar, tiger-cat, black bear, hyena, wolf, and ocelot. The llama, alpaca, and vicuña are peculiar to this country. The monkey tribe exceeds all others in variety and number. There are said to be nearly two hundred species of them in South America, each distinctly marked, and varying from each other, in size, from twelve pounds to less than two. The smallest of the little marmosets weigh less than a pound and a half each, and are the most intelligent animal of their size known to man. There are also the deer, tapir, armadillo, anteater, and a few other minor animals. The pampas swarm with wild cattle and horses, descended from animals originally brought from Europe. In the low, marshy grounds the boa-constrictor and other reptiles abound. Eagles, vultures, and parrots are found in a wild state all over the country, while the rivers and the waters near the coast are well filled with fish, crocodiles, and turtles. Scientists have found over two thousand species of fish in the Amazon River alone.

The pure aboriginal race are copper colored, resembling the Mexicans in character and appearance. Like most natives of equatorial regions, they are indolent, ignorant, superstitious, sensuous, and by no means warlike. Forced into the ranks and drilled by Europeans, they make fairly good soldiers, and when well led will obey orders and fight. There can be no *esprit de corps* in soldiers thus organized; the men neither know nor care what they fight for, their incentive in action being first a natural instinct for brutality, and second the promise of booty. In some parts of the country the half-breeds show themselves skillful workmen in certain simple lines of manufacture, but the native pure and simple will not work except to keep from starving.

The Spaniards conquered nearly all parts of South America except Brazil, which was subject to Portugal until 1823, when it achieved its independence. The Spanish colonies also revolted, one by one, until they all became independent of the mother country. The history of these republics, as in the instance of Mexico, has been both stormy and sanguinary. Foreign and civil wars have reigned among them incessantly for half a century and more.

The present political divisions are: Brazil, British Guiana, Dutch Guiana, French Guiana, Ecuador, United States of Colombia, Venezuela, Bolivia, Chili, Peru, Argentine Republic, Uruguay, and Paraguay. Brazil is the most extensive of these states, and is thought to enjoy the largest share of natural advantages, including in its area nearly one half as many square miles as all the rest combined. Its seaboard at Parahiba, and for hundreds of miles north and south of it, projects into the Atlantic a thousand miles to the east of the direct line between its northern and southern extremities. Besides her diamond and gold mines, she possesses what is much more desirable, namely, valuable deposits of iron, copper, silver, and other metals. We have before us statistics which give the result of diamond mining in Brazil from 1740 to 1823, when national independence was won, which show the aggregate for that entire period to have been less than ten million dollars in value; while that of the coffee alone, exported from Rio Janeiro in one year, exceeded twenty million dollars, showing that, however dazzling the precious stones may appear in the abstract, they are not even of secondary consideration when compared with the agricultural products of the country. The export of coffee has increased very much since the year 1851, which happens to be that from which we have quoted. It must also be admitted that probably twice the amount of diamonds recorded were actually found and enriched somebody, all which were duly reported, having to pay a government royalty according to the pecuniary exigency of those in authority.

The population of Brazil is between fourteen and fifteen million, and it is thought to be more advanced in civilization than other parts of South America, though in the light of our own experience we should place the Argentine Republic first in this respect. Indeed, so far as a transient observer may speak, we are inclined to place Argentina far and away in advance of Brazil as regards everything calculated to invite the would-be emigrant who is in search of a new home in a foreign land. Were it not that intestine wars are of such frequent occurrence among these states, and national bankruptcy so common, voluntary emigration would tend towards South America in far larger numbers than it does now. The revolutions are solely to promote personal aggrandizement; it is individual interest, not principle, for which these people fight so often. Unfortunately, every fresh outbreak throws the country back a full decade as regards national progress. The late civil wars in Chili and the Argentine Republic are illustrations in point. The first-named section of South America has suddenly sunk from a condition of remarkable pecuniary prosperity to one of actual poverty. Thousands of valuable lives have been sacrificed, an immense amount of property has been destroyed, her commerce crippled, and for the time being paralyzed. Ten years of peace and reasonable prosperity could hardly restore Chili to the position she was in twelve months ago. The country is to-day in a terrible condition, while many of the best families mourn the death of a father, a son, or both, whose lives have been sacrificed to the mad ambition of a usurper. Numerous families, once rich, have now become impoverished by the confiscation of their entire property. The Chilians do not carry on warfare in European style, by organized armies; there is a semblance only of such bodies. The fighting is mostly after the fashion of free lances, guerrilla bands, and highwaymen. There seems to be no sense of honor or chivalry among the common people, while the only idea of the soldiery is to plunder and destroy.

The Peruvians whose cities were despoiled by Chili must have regarded the recent cutting of each other's throats by the Chilian soldiery with something like grim satisfaction.

The obvious weakness of the South American states lies in their bitter rivalry towards each other, a condition which might be at once obviated by their joining together to form one united nation. The instability which characterizes their several governments in their present isolated interests has passed into a byword. Divided into nine unimportant states,—leaving out the three Guianas, which are dependent upon European powers,—any one of them could be erased from the map and absorbed by its stronger neighbor, or by a covetous foreign power. On the contrary, by forming one grand republic, it would stand eighth in the rank of nations as regards wealth, importance, and power, amply able to take care of itself, and to maintain the integrity of its territory. A community of interest would also be established between our government and that of these South American provinces, which would be of immense commercial and political importance to both nations.

To those who have visited the country, and who have carefully observed the conditions, it is clear that this division of the continent will never thrive and fully reap the benefit of its great natural advantages until the independent republics assume the position of sovereign states, subservient to a central power, a purpose which has already been so successfully accomplished in Mexico.

While we have been considering the great southern continent as a whole, our good ship, having crossed the equator, has been rapidly approaching its northern shore. After entering the broad mouth of the Amazon and ascending its course for many miles, we are now in sight of the thriving metropolis of Pará.

CHAPTER V.

City of Pará.—The Equatorial Line.—Spanish History.—The King of
Waters.—Private Gardens.—Domestic Life in Northern Brazil.—
Delicious Pineapples.—Family Pets.—Opera House.—Mendicants.—
A Grand Avenue.—Botanical Garden.—India-Rubber Tree.—
Gathering the Raw Material.—Monkeys.—The Royal Palm.—
Splendor of Equatorial Nights.

Pará is the most northerly city of Brazil. It also bears the name of Belem on some maps, and is the capital of a province of the first designation. The full official title of the place is, in the usual style of Portuguese and Spanish hyperbole, Santa Maria do Belem do Grão Pará, which has fortunately and naturally simplified itself to Pará. It was founded in 1615, and the province of which it is the capital was the last in Brazil to declare its independence of the mother country, and to acknowledge the authority of the first emperor, Dom Pedro. It is the largest political division of the republic, and in some respects the most thriving. The city is situated about ninety miles south of the equator, and eighty miles from the Atlantic Ocean on the Pará River, so called, but which is really one of the mouths of the Amazon. It is thus the principal city at the mouth of the largest river in the world, a fact quite sufficient to indicate its present, and to insure its continued commercial importance.

As we entered the muddy estuary of the river, whose wide expanse was lashed into short, angry waves by a strong wind, large tree trunks were seen floating seaward, rising and sinking on the undulating surface of the water. Some were quite entire, with all of their branches still attached to the main trunk. They came, perhaps, from two thousand miles inland, borne upon the swift current from where it had undermined the roots in their forest home. Among the rest was a cocoa-palm with its full tufted head, some large brown nuts still hanging tenaciously to the parent stem. It had fallen bodily, while in its prime and full bearing, suddenly unearthed by some swift deviation of the river, which brooks no trifling impediment to its triumphal march seaward. How long, one would be glad to know, has this vast stream, fed by the melted snow of the Andes, poured its accumulated waters into the bosom of the ocean? A thousand years is but as a day, in reckoning the age of a mountain range or of a mammoth river.

As we approached the city, the channel became gradually narrowed by several prominent islands, crowded with rich green vegetation, forest trees of various sorts, mangoes, bananas, and regal palms. Though it is thus broken by islands, the river is here over twenty miles in width.

Pará is yielded precedence over the other cities on the east coast of South America in many respects, and is appreciatively called "Queen of the Amazon," her water communication reaching into the very heart of some of the most fertile valleys on the continent. One incorporated company has established a score of well-appointed steamers, averaging five hundred tons each, which navigate the river for a distance of two thousand miles from its mouth. Pará has an excellent harbor, of large capacity, accommodating an extensive commerce, a considerable portion of which is with the United States of North America. It has a mixed population of about fifty thousand, composed of an amalgamation of Portuguese, Italians, Indians, and negroes, and is the only town of any importance, except Quito, situated so near to the equatorial line, where the interested observer has the privilege of beholding the starry constellations of both hemispheres. Ships of five thousand tons measurement can lie within a hundred yards of the wharves of Pará, where the accumulation of coffee, dyewoods, drugs, tobacco, cotton, cocoa, rice, sugar, and raw india-rubber, indicates the character of the principal exports. Of all these staples, the last named is the most important, in a commercial point of view, occupying the third place on the list of national exports. As we have shown, the import and export trade of the Amazon valley naturally centres here, and Pará need fear no commercial rival.

For a considerable period this unequaled water-way, forming the spacious port, and conveying the drainage of nearly half of South America into the Atlantic, bore the name of its discoverer, Orellana, one of Pizarro's captains; but the fabulous story of a priest called Friar Gaspar, self-constituted chronicler of the expedition, gave to it the designation which it now bears. All the Spanish records of the history and conquests in the New World, relating to the doings of Columbus, Cortez, Pizarro, and others, without an exception, were written in the same spirit of exaggeration and untruthfulness, leading that pious witness and contemporary writer, Las Casas, to pronounce them, with honest indignation, to be a tissue of falsehoods. Even our own popular historian, Prescott, who drew so largely upon these sources for his poetical productions, was forced to admit their manifest incongruities, contradictions, and general irresponsibility. This Munchausen of a priest, Friar Gaspar, recorded that a tribe of Amazons, or fighting women, was encountered far inland, on the banks of the mighty river, who were tall in stature, symmetrical in form, and had a profusion of long hair, which hung in braids down their backs. They were represented to be as warlike as they were beautiful, and as carrying shields and spears, the latter of which they could use with great skill and effect. It was this foolish story of the Amazons, hatched in the prolific brain of Friar Gaspar, which gave the river its lasting name.

The Indian designation of the mammoth watercourse was significant and appropriate, as their names always are. They called it *Parana-tinga*, meaning "King of Waters," and it seems to us a great pity that the name could not have been retained.

Pará has the advantage of being much nearer to the United States and to Europe than Rio Janeiro, the capital of Brazil. Though the commerce of Rio is constantly increasing, in spite of its miserable sanitary condition, it is confidently believed by intelligent persons engaged in the South American trade, that Pará will equal it erelong in the aggregate of its shipments. All freight is now landed by means of lighters, a process which is an awkward drawback upon commerce, and what makes it still more aggravating is that it seems to be an entirely needless one. Certainly a good, substantial, capacious pier might be easily built, which would obviate this objection, accommodating a dozen large vessels at the same time. The Brazilians are slow to adopt any modern improvement. Portuguese and Spaniards are very much alike in this respect. Wharves will be built at Pará by and by, after a few more millions have been wasted upon the inconvenient process now in vogue, which involves not only needless expense, but causes most awkward and unreasonable delay, both in landing merchandise and in shipping freight for export. This serious objection applies to all the ports along the east coast of South America. There is always some private interest which exerts itself to prevent any progressive movement, and it is this which retards improved facilities for unloading and shipping of cargoes at Pará. In this instance the owners of the steam tugs which tow the flat-bottomed lighters from ship to shore, and vice versa, oppose the building of piers, because, if they were in existence, these individuals would find their profitable occupation gone. If proper wharf facilities were to be furnished, commerce generally would be much benefited, though a few persons would suffer some pecuniary loss. As we have said, the wharves will come by and by, when the people realize that private interest must be subservient to the public good.

The city of Pará is situated upon slightly elevated ground, and makes a fine appearance from the river, with its lofty cathedral, numerous churches, convents, custom house, and arsenal standing forth in bold relief against an intensely blue sky, while fronting the harbor, like a line of sentinels, is a row of tall, majestic palms, harmonizing admirably with the local surroundings, though in the very midst of a busy commercial centre. The buildings are painted yellow, blue, or pink, the façades contrasting strongly with the dark red of the heavily tiled roofs, which, having no chimneys, present an odd appearance to a northern eye. Here and there a mass of greenery indicates some domestic garden, or a plaza presided over by tall groups of trees, among which the thick, umbrageous mangoes prevail. The Rua da Imperatriz is the principal wholesale street of the city, where the large warehouses are to be found, but the Rua dos Mercadores is the fashionable shopping street, through which the tramway also passes. The shops are rather small, but have a fair stock of goods offered at reasonable rates, though strangers are apt to be victimized by considerably higher prices than a native would pay.

This, however, is not unusual in all foreign countries, so far as our experience goes. North Americans are looked upon as possessing unlimited pecuniary means, and as lavish in their expenditures, prices being gauged accordingly. This is a universal practice in Europe, and especially so in Germany.

The climate is very moist, and it has been facetiously remarked that it rains here eight days in the week. One cannot speak approvingly of the sanitary condition of a place where turkey buzzards are depended upon to remove the garbage which accumulates in the thoroughfares. It is unaccountable that the citizens should submit to such filthy surroundings, especially in a locality where malarial fever is acknowledged to prevail in the summer season. Though at this writing it is the latter part of May, yellow fever is still rife here, and we hear of many particularly sad cases, ending fatally, all about us. This destroyer is especially apt to carry off people who have newly arrived in the country. The present year has been unusually fatal among the residents of Pará, as regards yellow fever, which seems to linger longer and longer each year of its visitation. Our own conviction is that the people have themselves to thank for this lingering of the pest into the winter months, since the sanitary conditions of the place are inexcusably defective.

Gardens in and about the city quickly catch and delight the eye,—gardens where flowers and fruits grow in great luxuriance. Among the latter are oranges, mangoes, guavas, figs, and bananas. The glossy green fronds of the bananas throw other verdure altogether into the shade, while in dignity and beauty the cocoanut palms excel all other trees. The tall, straight stem of the palm rises from the roots without leaf or branch until the plumed head is reached, which bends slightly under its wealth of pinnated leaves and fruit combined. If you happen to pass these gardens after nightfall, especially those in the immediate environs of the city, mark the phosphorescent clouds of dancing lights which fill the still atmosphere round about the vegetation. This peculiar effect is produced by the busy cucuios, or tropical fireflies, each vigorously flashing its individual torch. Do they shine thus in the daytime, we are led to wonder, like the constellations in the heavens, though hidden by the greater light of the sun? They are always demonstrative in the night, be it never so cloudy, foggy, or damp in the low latitudes. They keep their sparkling revels, their torchlight dances, all heedless of the grim and deadly fever which lurks in the surrounding atmosphere, claiming human victims right and left, among high and low, from the ranks of age and of youth. Insect life is redundant here. It is the very paradise of butterflies, whose size, wide spread of wing, variety, and striking beauty of colors, we have only seen equaled at Penang and Singapore, in the Malacca Straits. Some of the avenues leading to the environs are lined with handsome trees, which add greatly to their attractiveness and comfort. The silk cotton tree and the almond are favorites here as ornamental shade trees. The cape jessamine is universally cultivated at Pará, and grows to a large size, filling the air with its agreeable fragrance. Here the oleander, covered with clusters of bloom, grows to the height of twenty feet and more. The lime, with its fine acid fruit, which is in great request in making cooling drinks, also abounds.

The glimpses of domestic life which one gets in passing the better class of dwellings reveal rooms with tiled or polished wooden floors, cane-finished chairs, sofas, and rockers to match, a small foot rug here and there, a group of flowering plants in one corner, while hammocks seem to take the place of bedsteads. The temperature is high at Pará in summer, and woolen carpets, or even mattresses, are too warm for use in this climate. Bignonias, oleanders, and other blooming plants abound in the flower-plots about the city, besides many flowering vines which are strangers to us, half orchids, half creepers. One is apt to jump at conclusions. These people dearly love flowers, so we conclude they cannot be very wicked.

The families live, as it were, in the open patios, which form the centres of their dwellings, are shaded by broad verandas, and upon which the domestic apartments all open. The accessories are few, and not entirely convenient, according to a northerner's ideas of comfort; but this is compensated for by the fragrance of flowers, the picturesqueness of the surroundings, and the free and easy out-of-door atmosphere which ignores conventionalities. These attractive interiors suggest a sort of picnic mode of life which has conformed itself to climatic influences. Everything is very quiet, there is no hurry, and the stillness is occasionally interrupted by the musical laughter of children, which rings out clear and pleasantly, entirely in harmony with the surroundings. And such children! Artists' models, every one of them. It all seems to a stranger to be the very poetry of living, yet we venture to say that each household has its skeleton in the closet, and some a whole anatomical museum!

At Bahia, further south, a revelation awaits the traveler in the delicious richness, size, and delicacy of the oranges which grow there in lavish abundance, and which are famous, all along the coast. Here at Pará, the same may be said of the pineapple, the raising of which is a local specialty. These are not picked until fully ripe, and often weigh ten pounds each. When cut open, the inside can be eaten with a spoon, if one fancies that mode. They require no sugar; nature has supplied the saccharine principle in abundance. They are absolutely perfect in themselves alone. People sailing northward lay in a great store of this admirable fruit, which is as cheap as it is delicious and appetizing. In New England, the pines of which we partake have been picked in a green condition in Bermuda, the Bahamas, or Florida, to enable them to bear transportation. They ripen only partially off the stem, and after a very poor style, decay setting in at the same time; consequently the pulp is not suitable to swallow, and is always more or less indigestible. The Pará pines are seedless, and are propagated by replanting the suckers. The crown, we were told, would also thrive and reproduce the fruit if properly planted, but the first named process is that generally employed, and is probably the best.

In the neighborhood of Pará are many large and profitable cocoa plantations, the industry connected with which is a growing one, representing a considerable amount of capital. But above all others, the gathering and preparing of raw india-rubber for exportation is the prevailing industry of this Brazilian capital.

The common people seem to be an uncertain mixture of races, confounding all attempts properly to analyze their antecedents. They have touches of refinement and underlying tenderness of instinct, as exhibited in their home associations, but also evince a coarseness which is not inviting, to say the least. They are universal lovers of pet birds and small animals. No household seems to be complete without some representatives of the sort. Among these are cranes, ibises, herons, turtle-doves, parrots, macaws, and paroquets. Monkeys of various tribes, the little marmoset being the favorite, are seen domesticated in almost every private garden, full of fun and mischief, and affording infinite amusement to the youthful members of the household. Young anacondas, sometimes ten feet long, are kept in and about the dwellings, to catch and drive away the rats! The reader smiles half incredulously at this, and we do not wonder. If one of these rodents be caught in a trap and killed, it is useless to offer it to an anaconda as food. That fastidious reptile will eat only such creatures as it kills itself. This is also characteristic of the African lion and the tiger of India, when in the wild state; neither will molest a dead body, of man or beast, which they have not themselves deprived of life, though hyenas, wolves, and some other animals will even rob the graves of human bodies for food. We had never heard of anacondas employed as ratters before we came to Pará, but we were assured by those who should know that they are especially effective in warfare against this domestic pest.

Broad verandas give a grateful shade to most of the dwelling-houses, which are seldom over one story in height, each one, however, extending over considerable ground space. In the business part of the town, fronting the harbor, the houses are generally two or even three stories in height, it being necessary in such localities to economize the square feet of ground occupied. The same sort of external ornamentation is seen here as upon the house fronts in Mexico, namely, the profuse decoration of the walls with glazed earthen tiles, often of fancy colors, which gives a checkerboard appearance to a dwelling-house not calculated to please a critical eye.

The Opera House of Pará is a large and imposing structure, one of the finest edifices in the town, and the largest theatre, we believe, in South America, quite uncalled for, it would seem, by any local demand. It is built of brick, finished in stucco, the front being decorated with marble columns having handsome and elaborate Corinthian capitals. The house lights up brilliantly at night, being finished in red, white, and gold. It has four narrow galleries supported upon brackets, thus obviating the necessity for the objectionable upright posts which so provokingly interfere with the line of sight. The cathedral is a substantial and handsome structure, with a couple of tall towers, after the usual Spanish style, each containing a dozen bells. The interior has all the florid and tawdry ornamentation always to be found in Roman Catholic churches, together with the usual complement of bleeding figures, arrow-pierced saints, high-colored paper rosettes, utterly meaningless, together with any amount of glittering tinsel, calculated to catch the eye and captivate the imagination of the grossly ignorant native population.

There are many minor churches in the city, and judging by the number seen in the streets, there must be at least a thousand priests, whose sole occupation, when they are not gambling or cock-fighting, is to cajole and impoverish the common people. It was a church festival when we visited the cathedral. There are over two hundred such days, out of every three hundred and sixty-five, in Roman Catholic countries,—not days of humiliation and prayer, but days of gross latitude, of bull-fights, occasions when the decent amenities of life are ignored, days when the broadest license prevails, and all excesses are condoned. There were a large number of women present in the cathedral on this day, but scarcely half a dozen men. The better class were dressed gayly, and wore some rich jewelry. The love of finery prevails, and pervades all classes. Some of the ladies were clad in costly silks and laces, set off by brilliants and pearls. Diamonds and precious stones are very common in this country, and a certain class seem to carry a large share of their worldly possessions showily displayed upon their persons. What the humbler class lacked in richness of material, they made up in gaudy colors, blazing scarfs, and imitation gold and silver jewelry. Nature sets the example of bright colors in these latitudes, in gaudy plumed birds and high-tinted flowers and fruits. The natives only follow her. The few men who were present came to ogle the women, and having satisfied their low-bred curiosity, soon retired to the neighboring bar-rooms and gambling saloons. On special festal days temporary booths are erected in the squares, in which intoxicants are sold, together with toys, cakes, cigars, and charms, the latter said to have been blessed by the priests, and therefore sure to prevent any injury from the evil eye!

As in most of the South American cities, there are several elaborate buildings here, formerly used as convents, which are now devoted to more creditable purposes. The present custom house occupies one of these edifices, which is crowned with two lofty towers.

There are plenty of mendicants in the streets of Pará, who are very ready with their importunities, especially in appealing to strangers. The average citizens seemed to be liberal in dealing with these beggars. Saturday is called "poor day" in Pará, as it is also in Havana, Matanzas, Cienfuegos, etc., when every housekeeper who is able to give something does so, if it be only a small roll of bread, to each visiting beggar. At most houses these small rolls are baked regularly for this purpose, and the applicant is nearly sure to get one upon calling, and if he represents a large family he may receive two. Money is rarely, if ever, given by residents, nor is it expected; but strangers are surrounded as by an army with banners, and vigorously importuned for centavos. The Spaniards and Portuguese are natural beggars.

Here let us digress for a moment. The system of beggary prevailing in Spanish countries is very trying to all sensitive travelers. In Italy, Spain, and the south of France, especially at the watering-places, it is a terrible pest. Naples has become almost unendurable on this account. At every rod one is constantly importuned and followed by beggars of all sizes, ages, and of both sexes,—individuals who should be placed in asylums and cared for by the state. No reasonable person would object to paying a certain sum on entering these resorts, to be honestly devoted to charitable purposes, provided it would insure him against the disgusting importunities of which strangers are now the victims. Visitors hasten away from the localities where these things are not only permitted but are encouraged. It is thought to be quite the thing to fleece foreigners of every possible penny, and by every possible means. The contrast in this respect between the cities of the United States and those of Europe and South America is eminently creditable to the former. In the beautiful little watering-place known as Luchon, in the south of France, at the foot of the Pyrenees, with scarcely four thousand inhabitants, there are over one hundred professional beggars, who constantly beset and drive away visitors. Some of these, as usual in such cases, are known to be well off pecuniarily, but are marked by some physical deformity upon which they trade. If the stranger gives, he is oftenest encouraging a swindle, rarely performing a true charity. This is one of the increasing disgraces of Paris. Beggars know too much to importune citizens, but strangers are beset at every corner of the boulevards and public gardens, particularly by children, girls and boys, trained for the purpose.

Of all the races seen in Brazil, the half-breed Indian girls are the most attractive, and until they are past the age of twenty-five or thirty years they are almost universally handsome, no matter to what class they belong. Those who have the advantage of domestic comforts, good food, and delicate associations develop accordingly, and are especially beautiful. They would make charming artists' models. The remarkably straight figure of the native women is noticeable, caused by the practice referred to of carrying burdens on the head. As already mentioned, if a negro or Indian woman has an article to transport, even if it be but a quart bottle, or an umbrella, it is placed at once upon the head. The article may weigh five pounds or fifty, it is all the same; everything but the babies is thus transported. These little naked creatures, always suggestive of monkeys, are supported on the mother's back, held there by a shawl or rebozo tied securely across the chest. When the children are six or eight years old, they are promoted to the dignity of wearing one small garment, an abbreviated shirt or chemise.

The principal food of the common people of northern Brazil is farina and dried fish, with fried plantains and ripe bananas. Crabs and oysters of a poor description abound along the coast, and are eaten by the people, both in a raw and cooked condition. But the white people avoid the coast oysters, which sometimes poison those not accustomed to them.

The finest avenue in Pará is the Estrada de São José, bordered by grand old palms, which form a beautiful perspective and a welcome shade, the feathery tops nearly embracing each other overhead. The tramway takes one through the environs by the Rua de Nazareth, for five miles to Marco da Legua, where the public wells of the city are situated. The way thither is lined with neat and handsome dwellings, shaded by noble trees. The botanical garden is well worth a visit by all lovers of horticulture. The forest creeps up towards the environs of the town, wherein many of the trees are rendered beautiful by clinging orchids of gorgeous blue; others are of blood red, and some of orange yellow, presenting also a great diversity of form. One has not far to go to see specimens of the india-rubber tree, growing from ninety to a hundred feet in height, while measuring from four to five feet in diameter. This tree begins to produce gum at the age of fifteen years. The trunk is smooth and perfectly round, the bark of a buff color. It bears a curious fruit, of which some animals are said to be fond. The author has seen the india-rubber tree growing in the island of Ceylon, where it seemed to reach a greater height and dimensions than it does in the district of Pará. A considerable portion of the roots lie above ground, stretching away from the base of the tree like huge anacondas, and finally disappearing in the earth half a rod or more from the parent trunk. The reader can hardly fail to be familiar with the simple wild plant, which grows so abundantly by our New England roadsides, known as the milk-weed, which, when the stem is cut or broken, emits a creamy, pungent smelling liquid. In the latitude of Pará, this little weed, of the same family, assumes the form of a colossal tree, and is known as the india-rubber tree. The United States takes of Brazilian rubber, in the crude state, over twenty-five thousand tons annually. As to coffee, Brazil supplies one half of all which is consumed in the civilized world; but we should frankly tell the reader, if he does not already realize the fact, that it is most frequently marked and sold for "Old Government Java."

The india-rubber tree is tapped annually very much after the same style in which we treat the sugar-maple in Vermont, and elsewhere, to procure its sap. A yellow, creamy liquid flows forth from the rubber tree into small cups placed beneath an incision made in the trunk. When the cup becomes full, its contents is emptied into a large common receptacle, where it is allowed to partially harden, and in which form it is called caoutchouc. The tapping of the trees and attending to the gathering of the sap furnish employment to hundreds of the natives, who, however, make but small wages, being employed by contractors, who either lease the trees of certain districts, or own large tracts of forest land. These Brazilian forests are very grand, abounding in valuable aromatic plants, precious woods, gaudy birds, and various wild animals. The number of monkeys is absolutely marvelous, including many curious varieties. A native will not kill a monkey; indeed, it must be difficult for a European to make up his mind to shoot a creature so nearly human in its actions, and whose pleading cries when wounded are said to be so pitiable.

One of the peculiar street sights in Pará is that of native women with a dozen young monkeys of different species for sale. Marmosets can be bought for a quarter of a dollar each. So tame are the little creatures that they cling about the woman's person, fastening upon her hair, arms, and neck, not in the least inclined to escape from her. It is remarkable and interesting to see how very fond they become of their owner, if he is kind to them. Like the dog and the cat, they seem to have a strong desire for human companionship. When seen running wild in the woods, leaping from tree to tree, and from branch to branch, they do not try to get far away from the presence of man, but only to keep, in their untamed state, just out of reach of his hands. Ships sailing hence generally take away a few of these animals, but as they are delicate, and very sensitive to climatic changes, many of them die before reaching Europe or North America.

The great beauty of Pará is its abundance of palm trees. The palm is always an interesting object, as well as a most valuable one; interesting because of its historical and legendary associations, and valuable, since it would be almost impossible to enumerate the number of important uses to which it and its products are put. To the people of the tropics it is the prolific source of food, shelter, clothing, fuel, fibre for several uses, sugar, oil, wax, and wine. It has been aptly termed the "princess of the vegetable world." One indigenous species, the Piassaba, is a palm which yields a most valuable fibre, extensively manufactured into cordage and ships' cables, for which purpose it is much in use on the coast of South America. It is found to be stronger and more elastic than hemp when thus employed, besides which it is far more durable. The product of this species of palm is also exported in large quantities to North America and to England, for the purpose of making brushes, brooms, and various sorts of domestic matting.

The nights are especially beautiful in this region. We were interested in observing the remarkable brilliancy of the sky; the stars do not seem to sparkle, as with us at the north, but shed a soft, steady light, making all things luminous. This is the natural result of the clearness of the atmosphere. One is surprised at first to find the moon apparently so much increased in size and effulgency. The Southern Cross is ever present, though it is dominated by the Centaur. Orion is seen in his glory, and the Scorpion is clearly defined. In the author's estimation, there is no exhibition of the heavens in these regions which surpasses the magnificence of the far-reaching Milky Way.

CHAPTER VI.

Island of Marajo.—Rare and Beautiful Birds.—Original Mode of
Securing Humming-Birds.—Maranhão.—Educational.—Value of

The island of Marajo, situated at the mouth of the Amazon, opposite Pará, and belonging to the province or state of that name, is a hundred and eighty miles in length and about one hundred and sixty in width, nearly identical in size with the island of Sicily, and almost oval in form. One of the principal shore settlements is Breves, on the southeastern corner of the island, which lies somewhat low, and consists of remarkably fertile soil, so abounding in wild and beautiful vegetation and exquisite floral varieties, that it is called in this region "the Island of Flowers." We can easily believe the name to be appropriately chosen, since, as we skirt its verdant shores hour after hour, they seem to emit the drowsy, caressing sweetness of fragrant flowers so sensibly as to almost produce a narcotic effect. The easterly or most seaward part of Marajo is open, marshy, sandy land, but back from the shore the soil is of a rich, black alluvium, supporting in very large tracts a dense forest growth, similar to all the low-lying tropical lands of South America. The population is recorded as numbering about twenty thousand, divided into several settlements, mostly on the coast, and consists largely of the aboriginal race found by the first comers upon this island, who, on account of their somewhat isolated condition, have amalgamated less with Europeans and the imported colored race than any other tribe on the east coast of the continent.

The extensive meadows of Marajo are the grazing fields of numerous herds of wild horses and horned cattle, the former of a superior breed, highly prized on the mainland; and yet so rapidly do they increase in this climate, in the wild state, that every few years they are killed in large numbers for their hides alone. The exports from the island consist of rice, cattle, horses, and hides. There are some large plantations devoted to the cultivation of rice, the soil and water supply of certain districts being especially favorable to this crop. As intimated, a considerable portion of Marajo is covered with a forest growth so dense as to be compared to the jungles of Africa and India, and which, so far as is known, has never been penetrated by the foot of man. Travelers who have visited the borders of this leafy wilderness expatiate upon the strange, inexplicable sounds which are heard at times, amid the prevailing stillness and sombre aspect of these primeval woods. Sometimes there comes, it is said, from out the forest depth a wild cry, like that of a human being in distress, but which, however long one may listen, is not repeated. Again, there is heard an awful crash, like the falling of some ponderous forest giant, then stillness once more settles over the mysterious, tangled woods. Every time the silence is broken it seems to be by some new and inexplicable sound, not to be satisfactorily accounted for.

The lagoons near the centre of Marajo are said to abound in alligators, which are sometimes sought for by the natives for their hides, for which a fair price is realized, since fashion has rendered this article popular in a hundred different forms. The number and variety of birds and lesser animals to be found upon the island are marvelous. Certain species of birds seem to have retreated to this spot from the mainland, before the tide of European immigration; indeed, it has for a long time been considered the paradise of the naturalist. Over thirty species of that peculiar bird, the toucan, have been secured here.

When Professor Agassiz was engaged in his scientific exploration of the Amazon, he dispatched a small but competent party especially to obtain specimens from this island, the result being both a surprise and a source of great gratification to the king of naturalists. Many of the objects secured by these explorers were rare and beautiful birds, not a few of which are unique, and of which no previous record existed. There were also many curious insects and other specimens particularly valuable to naturalists, most of which are preserved to-day in the Agassiz Museum at Cambridge, Massachusetts. The toucan, just spoken of, is most remarkable for its beauty and variety of colors, as well as for the very peculiar form and size of its elephantine bill, which makes it look singularly ill-balanced. This ludicrous appendage is nine inches long and three in circumference; the color is vermilion and yellow delicately mingled. The toucan is much coveted for special collections by all naturalists, and is becoming very scarce, except in this one equatorial locality. Scarlet ibises and roseate spoonbills are also found at Marajo, both remarkably fine examples of semi-aquatic fowl, and when these are secured in good condition for preservation, the natives realize good prices for them. In order to procure desirable specimens of the humming-bird species, which are also abundant on this island, the native hunters resort to an ingenious device, so as not to injure the skin or the extremely delicate plumage of this butterfly-bird. For this purpose they use a peculiar syringe made from reeds, and charged with a solution of adhesive gum, which, when directed by an experienced hand, clogs the bird's wings at once, stopping its flight and causing it to fall to the ground. Some are caught by means of nets set on the end of long bamboo poles, such as are used to secure butterflies, but this method is poorly adapted to catch so quick moving a creature as a humming-bird. The author has seen, in southern India, butterflies of gaudiest texture with bodies as large as small humming-birds, which were quite as brilliant as they in lovely colors. The variety and beauty of this insect, as found anywhere from Tuticorin to Darjeeling, is notable. Wherever British troops are permanently settled, the wives of the common soldiers become very expert in catching and arranging these attractive objects, preserving them in frames under glass. These find ready purchasers for museums and private collections all over Europe, and are sold at moderate prices, but serve to add a welcome trifle to the extremely poor pay of a common soldier having perhaps a wife and one or two children to support.

The island of Marajo was not formed at the Amazon's mouth of soil brought down from the interior by the river's current, as is often the case with islands thus situated, but is a natural, rocky formation which serves to divide the channel and give the river a double outlet into the Atlantic. Agassiz studied its character, and gives us an interesting statement as the result. He declared, after careful geological examination, that it is an island which was once situated far inland, away from the river's mouth, but which is now brought near to it by the gradual encroachment of the Atlantic Ocean, whose waves and restless currents have slowly worn away the northeastern part of the continent. This abrasion must have been going on for many thousand years, to have produced such a decided topographical change. For the word years, upon second thought, read ages, which will undoubtedly express the true idea much more correctly.

There are over twenty species of palms indigenous to Marajo, which, as one skirts the water front, are seen growing along the far-reaching shore, fostered by the humidity of the atmosphere arising from the ever-flowing waters of the great river. Among these the peach-palm is quite conspicuous, with its spiny stems and mealy, nutritious fruit. There are also the cocoa-palm and the assai-palm, the latter gayly decorated with its delicate green plumes and long spear pointing heavenward, an emblem borne by no other tree in existence. The great variety of forms of plant life and giant grasses is extremely curious and beautiful on this interesting island. We heard, while at Pará, of a proposal made by some European party to thoroughly explore Marajo, which has never yet been done, so far as is known to our time, and it is believed that some very interesting and valuable discoveries may be the result of such an expedition, composed of engineers, scientists, and naturalists.

A day's sail to the eastward, bearing a little to the south along the coast, brings us to the port of Maranhão, which is the capital of a province of Brazil known by the same name, situated a little over three hundred miles from Pará. The place is picturesquely nestled, as it were, in the very lap of the mountains, which come boldly down to the coast at this point. It was founded nearly three hundred years ago, is regularly built, and contains between thirty and forty thousand inhabitants. Nearly all of the houses, which are generally of two stories, are ornamented with attractive balconies, and have handsome gardens attached to them, where the luxurious verdure is with difficulty kept within proper bounds. Vegetation runs riot in equatorial regions. It is the one pleasing outlet of nature, whose overcharged vitality, spurred on by the climate, must find vent either in teeming vegetation or in raging volcanoes, tidal waves, and unwelcome earthquakes, though sometimes, to be sure, we find them all combined in the tropics.

The harbor of Maranhão is excellent and sheltered, the depth of water permitting the entrance of ships drawing full twenty feet, an advantage which some of the ports to the southward would give millions of dollars to possess. According to published statistics, the exports during 1890 were as follows: thirty-six hundred tons of cotton, six hundred tons of sugar, seven hundred tons of hides, a large amount of rice, and some other minor articles. The imports for the same period were estimated at something less than three million dollars in value. This is the entrepôt of several populous districts, besides that of which it is the capital. The province itself contains a number of navigable rivers, with some thrifty towns on their banks. The bay gives ample evidence of commercial activity, containing at all times a number of foreign steamships, with a goodly show of coasting vessels. The place is slowly but steadily growing in its business relations, and in the number of its permanent population.

It cannot make any pretension to architectural excellence, though the Bishop's palace and the cathedral are handsome structures. There are two or three other prominent edifices, quaint and Moorish, which were once nunneries or monasteries; also a foundling institution, a special necessity in all Roman Catholic countries. We found here a public library, and a botanical garden. Not far inland there are some extensive rice plantations, the province in some portions being specially adapted to producing this valuable staple. We were informed by those whose opinion was worthy of respect, that educational advantages are rather remarkable here, the Lyceum having in the past few years graduated some of the most prominent statesmen and professionals in Brazil. One thing is very certain, the authorities cannot multiply educational facilities any too rapidly in this country, nor give the subject any too much attention, especially as regards the rising generation of both sexes. So far as we could learn by inquiry, or judge by careful observation, the ignorance of the mass of the people is simply deplorable.

Maranhão is situated about fourteen hundred miles north of Rio Janeiro, with which port it carries on an extensive coasting trade. The exports, besides the staples already spoken of, are various, including annotto, sarsaparilla, balsam copaiba, and other medicinal extracts, together with rum and crude india-rubber. The climate is torrid, the city being one hundred and fifty miles south of the equator; and though, like most of the towns on the eastern coast of the continent, it is rather an unhealthy locality, it is much less so than Pará, and is a far more cleanly place than that city, its situation giving it the advantage of a system of natural drainage. The country near Maranhão abounds in native forests of exuberant richness, producing a valuable quality of timber, and affording some of the finest cabinet woods known to commerce, as well as a practically inexhaustible supply of various dyewoods, a considerable business being done in the export of the latter article. It was observed that the assai-palm, from which the palm wine is made, was also a prominent feature here. The trunk is quite smooth, the fruit growing in heavy bunches like grapes, dark brown in color, and about the size of cranberries, hanging in heavy clusters just below the bunch of long leaves which forms the top of the tree. The native drink which is made from these palm grapes is a favorite beverage in northern Brazil, and when properly fermented it contains about the same percentage of alcohol as English pale ale.

To the author, the town of Maranhão was quite unknown; even its place upon the maps had never attracted his attention until after it was seen lying peacefully in an amphitheatre of tall hills, which come down close to the rock-ribbed shore of the Atlantic Ocean. This acknowledgment is between ourselves, for such a confession would sound very ridiculous to the good people of Maranhão.

After leaving its harbor, our next objective point was Pernambuco, which is situated about four days' sail from Pará by steamship, and about three from Maranhão.

This well known port, with its one hundred and fifty thousand inhabitants, is reckoned as the third city of Brazil in point of size and commercial importance. It lacks elevation to produce a good effect, and recalls the low-lying city of Havana in general appearance, as one approaches it from the sea. The harbor is not what could be desired for a commercial city, having hardly sufficient depth of water for vessels of heavy tonnage, and being also too narrow for a modern long steamship to safely turn in. The American line of steamships come to a mooring inside the harbor, but the European lines, or at least the Pacific Mail, in which we made the home passage, anchor in the open roadstead, three quarters of a mile from the shore. The harbor is formed by a long natural reef, which makes a breakwater between it and the open sea, a portion of the reef having been built up with solid masonry to render it more effective. This remarkable coral formation, which is more or less clearly defined, extends along the coast for a considerable distance,—it is said for four hundred miles. Opposite Pernambuco it rises six feet above the water, that is, above high-water mark, and runs parallel to the front street of the city at the distance from it of about a third of a mile or less. A wide opening in the reef at the northern end of the town makes the entrance to the harbor. Off the northeast coast of Australia, there is a very similar reef-formation, fully as long as this on the South American coast, but situated much further from the shore.

It is a serious drawback that passengers by large ocean steamers cannot enter the harbor of Pernambuco except by lighters or open boats; all freight brought by these steamers must also be transhipped. Landing here is often accomplished at considerable personal risk, and a thorough ducking with salt water is not at all uncommon in the attempt to reach the shore. To pull a boat from the open roadstead into the harbor, or vice versa, requires six stout oarsmen and an experienced man at the helm, so that landing from the Pacific Mail steamers is both a serious and an expensive affair. If a very heavy sea is running, the thing cannot be done, and no one will attempt it. The powerful wind which so often prevails on the coast occasionally creates quite a commotion even inside the harbor, among the shipping moored there, causing the largest cables to part and vessels to drag their anchors. Of course a vessel lying in the open roadstead, outside of the reef, has no protection whatever, and is in a critical situation if the wind blows towards the land. If it comes on to blow suddenly, she buoys and slips her anchor at once; she dares not waste the time to hoist it, but gets away as quickly as possible to where there is plenty of sea room and no lee shore to fear. Fortunately, though so fierce for the time being, and of a cyclonic character, the storms upon the coast are generally of brief duration, and like the furious pamperos, which are so dreaded by mariners further south, they blow themselves out in a few hours.

The geographical situation of Pernambuco is such, in the track of commerce, that vessels bound north or south, from Europe or from North America, naturally make it a port of call to obtain late advices and provisions. The name has been singularly chosen, no one can say how or by whom, but it signifies "the mouth of hell," a cognomen which we do not think the place at all deserves. It is a narrow, crowded, picturesque old seaport.

The town is situated at the mouth of the Biberibe River, just five hundred miles south of the equator, and is divided in rather a peculiar manner into three distinct parts: Recife, on a narrow peninsula; Boa Vista, on the river shore; and San Antonio, on an island in the river; all being connected, however, by six or eight substantial iron bridges. The first named division is the business portion of the capital, about whose water front the commercial life of Pernambuco centres, but the streets of Recife are very narrow and often confusingly crooked. Boa Vista is beautified by pleasant domestic residences, delightful gardens, and attractive promenades, far beyond anything which a stranger anticipates meeting in this part of the world. Though the business portion of the city is so low, the other sections are of better and more recent construction.

The view of the town and harbor to be had from some portions of Olinda is very fine and comprehensive, taking in a wide reach of land and ocean. When a brief storm is raging, spending its force against the reef, the view from this point is indeed grand. The sea, angered at meeting a substantial impediment, seethes and foams in wild excitement, dashing fifty feet into the air, and, falling over the reef, lashes the inner waters of the harbor into waves which mount the landing piers, and set everything afloat in the broad plaza which lines the shore. The big ships rock and sway incessantly, straining at their anchors, or chafing dangerously at their moorings. Precautions are taken to avert damage, but man's strength and skill count for little when opposed by the enraged elements.

This plaza, or quay, is shaded by aged magnolias of great height, and is the resort of unemployed seamen, fruit dealers, and idlers of all degrees. The house fronts in the various sections of the town are brilliantly colored, yellow, blue, white, and pink, also sometimes being covered halfway up the first story with glittering tiles of various hues. At nearly every turn one comes upon the moss-grown, crumbling façade of some old church, about the corners of which there is often a grossly filthy receptacle, the vile odor from which permeates the surrounding atmosphere. This was found to be almost insupportable with the thermometer standing at 90° Fahr. in the shade, forming so obvious a means for propagating malarial fever and sickness generally as to be absolutely exasperating. Notwithstanding all appearances, the American consul assured us that Pernambuco is one of the healthiest cities on the east coast of South America. The yellow fever, however, does not by any means forget to visit the place annually. Experience showed us that the residents along the coast were accustomed to give their own city precedence in the matter of hygienic conditions, and to admit, with serious faces, that the other capitals, north and south, were sadly afflicted by epidemics at nearly all seasons.

Pernambuco has several quite small but well-arranged public squares, decorated with fountains, trees, and flowers of many species. Two of these plazas have handsome pagodas, from which outdoor concerts are often given by military bands. The city is a thriving and progressive place, has extensive gas works, an admirable system of water supply, tramways, good public schools, and one college or high school. We must not forget to add to this list a very *flourishing* foundling asylum, where any number of poor little waifs are constantly being received, and no questions asked. A revolving box or cradle is placed in a wall of the hospital, next to the street, in which any person can deposit an infant, ring the bell, and the cradle will revolve, leaving the child on the inside of the establishment, where the little deserted object will be duly cared for. Connected with the hospital are several outlying buildings, where children are placed at various stages of growth. We were told that about forty per cent. of such children live to grow up to maturity, and leave the care of the government fairly well fitted to take their place in the world, and to fight the battle of life so very inauspiciously begun. It has been strongly argued that such an establishment offers a premium upon illegitimacy and immorality; but one thing is to be considered, it prevents the terrible crime of infanticide, which is said to have prevailed here to an alarming extent before this hospital was founded.

There is a passably good system of drainage, which was certainly very much needed, and since its completion the general health of the place is said to have considerably improved. This is not all that is required, however. There should be a decided reform in the habits of the people as regards cleanliness. At present they are positively revolting. The inhabitants are the very reverse of neat in their domestic associations, and home arrangements for natural conveniences are inexcusably objectionable; such, indeed, as would in a North American city, or even small town, call for the prompt interference of the local board of health. These remarks do not apply to isolated cases; the trouble is universal. Families living otherwise in comparative affluence utterly disregard neatness and decency in the matter to which we allude.

The districts neighboring to Pernambuco form extensive plains, well adapted to the raising of sugar, coffee, and cotton, as well as all sorts of tropical fruits and vegetables. There are many flourishing plantations representing these several interests, more especially that of sugar. The storehouses on the wharves and in the business sections of the city, the oxcarts passing through the streets, drawn each by a single animal, and even the very atmosphere, seem to be full of sugar. It is, in fact, the great sugar mart of South America. The annual amount of the article which is exported averages some twelve hundred thousand tons. Sugar is certainly king at Pernambuco. People not only drink, but they talk sugar. It is the one great interest about which all other business revolves. The article is mostly of the lower grade, and requires to be refined before it is suitable for the market. The refining process is being generally adopted at the plantations. American machinery is introduced for the purpose with entire success. The export of the crude article will, it is believed, be much less every year for the future, until it ceases altogether. It was a singular sight to observe the naked negroes carrying canvas bags of crude sugar upon their heads through the streets, each bag weighing a hundred pounds or more. The intense heat caused the canvas to exude quantities of syrup or molasses, which covered their dark, glossy bodies with small streams of fluid. They trotted along in single file, and at a quick pace, towards their destination, unheeding the sticky condition of their woolly heads and naked bodies.

Not far inland there are extensive meadows, where large herds of horned cattle are raised, together with a breed of half-wild horses, the breaking and domesticating of which, as here practiced, is a most cruel process. A certain set of men devote themselves to this business; rough riders, we should call them, very rough. Good horses are to be had at extraordinarily low prices. In the back country there are some grand and extensive forests, which produce fine cabinet woods and superior dye woods.

By consulting a map of the western hemisphere, it will be seen that Pernambuco is situated on the great eastern shoulder of South America, where it pushes farthest into the Atlantic Ocean, fifteen hundred miles south of Pará, and about five hundred north of Bahia. On the long coral reef which separates the harbor from the open sea is a picturesque lighthouse, also a quaint old watch tower which dates from the time of the Dutch dominion here. It is proposed to build additional layers of heavy granite blocks upon the reef, so as to raise it about six or eight feet higher and make it of a uniform elevation along the entire city front, and thus afford almost complete protection for the inner anchorage. It will be only possible to make any real improvement of the harbor by adopting a thorough system of dredging and deepening. There was evidence of such a purpose being already in progress on our second visit, two large steam dredging machines being anchored at the southerly end of the harbor.

The people of this hot region know the great value of shade trees, consequently they abound, half hiding from view the numerous handsome villas which form the attractive suburbs of the city. Everywhere one sees tall cocoanut palms, clusters of feathery bamboos, widespread mangoes, prolific bananas, guavas, and plantains growing among other graceful tropical trees, rich in the green texture of their foliage, and thrice rich in their luscious and abundant fruits. Among the vine products we must not forget to mention a rich, high flavored grape, which is native here, and which all people praise after once tasting. The water, which is brought into the city by a system of double iron pipes, comes from a neighboring lake, and is a pure and wholesome drink, a most incomparable blessing in equatorial regions, which no person who has not suffered for the want of it can duly appreciate.

The International Hotel is the favorite resort of strangers, and is situated a couple of miles from the harbor. It is surrounded by beautiful trees and flowers, the golden oranges weighing down the branches nearly to the ground by their size and abundance, while the young blossoms fill the air with their delicate perfume,—fruit and blossoms on the tree at the same time. The garden is thronged by household pets, and contains a spacious aviary. The monkey tribe is fully represented; gaudy winged parrots dazzle the eye with impossible colors. One partakes here, in the open air, of the refreshing viands amid the songs of birds, the occasional scream of the cockatoo, the cooing of turtle-doves, and the fragrance of a profusion of tropical flowers. The native servants are well-trained, and there is a French chef. We were told that this attractive place had once belonged to a very wealthy Brazilian, a planter, who had come to grief financially, and as the house was offered for sale, it had been purchased for one fifth of its original cost and adapted to hotel purposes. While enjoying our fruit at dessert, a somewhat similar experience was recalled as having taken place at Christiania, in Norway, where visitors enjoy the meals in a sort of outdoor museum and garden, surrounded by curious preserved birds mingled with living ones, the latter so tame as to alight fearlessly upon the table and await any choice bit guests may offer them.

We shall not soon forget the very appetizing dinner of which we partook, amid such attractive surroundings, in the gardens of the International Hotel at Pernambuco. One fruit which was served to us is known by the name of the loquat. It is round, dark yellow, and about the size of a Tangerine orange,—a great favorite with the natives, though it is mostly stone and skin, and tastes like turpentine.

This city is often called the Venice of Brazil, but why, it is difficult for one to understand. It is only poetical license, for there is not the first actual resemblance between the two cities. True, there are several watercourses, and half a dozen bridges, intersecting this Brazilian capital. One would be equally justified in calling the frail catamarans which are used by the fishermen in these waters, gondolas. This singular craft, by the way, consists of four or five logs of the cork-palm tree, confined together by a series of strong lashings, no nails being used, thus securing a necessary degree of elasticity. One end of the logs is hewn down to a smaller size or width than the other, thus forming stem and stern, while a single thick plank serves as a keel. There are no bulwarks to this crazy craft,—for it can hardly be called anything else,—the whole being freely washed by the sea; but yet, with a rude mast carrying a triangular sail, and with a couple of oars, two or three fishermen venture far away from the shore; indeed, we encountered them out of sight of land. A couple of upright stakes are driven into the logs, to hold on by when occasion requires. It is really wonderful to see how weatherly such a frail affair can be, and how literally safe in a rough seaway. The boatmen who navigate these catamarans (they are called here *janguardas*) manage to keep the market of Pernambuco abundantly supplied with the strange, fantastic fish which so prevail along the Atlantic coast in equatorial regions.

We have seen a craft very similar to these catamarans in use off the Coromandel coast, between Madras and the mouth of the Hoogly River, which leads up to Calcutta. Here the natives manage them in a sea so rough that an ordinary ship's boat, if exposed, would surely be swamped. The Madras catamaran consists of three pieces of timber, mere logs twelve or fourteen feet long, securely bound together with ropes made from the fibre of the cocoanut palm. Nails are no more available here than in the former crafts we have named. No nails could withstand the wrenching which this raft is subjected to. The middle log is a little longer than the two outside ones, and is given a slight upward turn at the end which forms the prow. No sail is used, but two fishermen generally go out with each of these rafts, propelling them with broad-bladed paddles, used alternately on either side. Of course the natives who navigate these crafts are naked, with the exception of a breech-cloth at the loins. They are very frequently thrown off by the sea, but regain their places with remarkable agility. They manage also, somehow, to secure their fishing gear, and generally to bring in a remunerative fare from their excursions. Strange as the catamaran is, it must yet be described as breezy, watery, and safe—for amphibious creatures. There is one enemy these fishermen have to look out for, namely the shark, both on the coast of Madras and South America. It is more common to say when one is lost that the sharks got him, than it is to say he was drowned.

The reef so often referred to, forming the breakwater opposite Pernambuco, is about forty feet in width at the surface, and is the marvelous architecture of that tiny coral builder which works beneath these southern seas. When it has reared a pyramid reaching from the far bottom of the ocean to the surface, its mission is performed and it dies. It lives and works only beneath the surface of the sea; atmospheric air is fatal to it. The pyramids of Egypt cannot compare with these submerged structures for height, solidity, or magnitude. One is the product of a creature of such seeming unimportance as to require microscopic aid to detect its existence; the other are monuments erected by ancient kings commanding infinite resources; the former being the process of nature in carrying out her great and mysterious plan; the latter, the ambitious work of men whose very identity is now questionable. If we were to enter into a calculation based upon known scientific facts, as to how many thousands of years were required for this minute animal to rear this massive structure, the result would astonish the average reader.

On approaching Pernambuco from the sea, the first object to attract the eye is the long line of snow white breakers, caused by the incessant swell of the sea striking against the firmly planted reef with a deafening surge, breaking into foam and spray which are thrown forty feet and more into the air. As we drew near for the first time, the extended line of breakers was illumined by the early morning sun, making fancy rainbows and misty pictures in the mingled air and water. We were escorted by myriads of sea-birds, whose sharp cries came close upon the ear, as they flew in and about the rigging. Behind the reef lay the comparatively smooth waters of the harbor, dotted here and there by tiny white sails, curious-shaped coasting craft, rowboats, and steam tugs, while the background was formed by a leafless forest of tall ships' masts which lined the wharves, and partially screened the low-lying capital from view.

We have remained quite long enough at this city of the reef, and now turn southward towards the more attractive port of Bahia.

In running down the coast, the Brazilian shore is so near as to be distinctly visible, with its surf-fringed beach of golden sands extending mile after mile, beyond which, far inland, rise ranges of forest-clad hills, and beyond these, sky-reaching alps. It is often necessary to give the land a wide berth, as at certain points dangerous sandbars make out from it far to seaward; but whenever near enough to the coast to make out the character of the vegetation, it was of deepest green and exuberantly tropical. With the exception of one or two small towns, and an occasional fisherman's hamlet, the shore presented no signs of habitation, being mostly a sandy waste adjoining the sea, where heavy rollers spent their force upon the smooth, water-worn, yellow beach.

CHAPTER VII.

Port of Bahia.—A Quaint Old City.—Former Capital of Brazil.—
Whaling Interests.—Beautiful Panorama.—Tramways.—No Color
Line Here.—The Sedan Chair.—Feather Flowers.—Great Orange
Mart.—Passion Flower Fruit.—Coffee, Sugar, and Tobacco.—A
Coffee Plantation.—Something about Diamonds.—Health of the City.
—Curious Tropical Street Scenes.

Bahia,—pronounced Bah-ee´ah,—situated three hundred and fifty miles south of Pernambuco, is the capital of a province of the same name in Brazil, and contains nearly two hundred thousand inhabitants. It is admirably situated on elevated ground at the entrance of All Saints Bay,—*Todos os Santos*,—just within Cape San Antonio, eight hundred miles or thereabouts north of Rio Janeiro. The entrance of the bay is seven miles broad. For its size, there are few harbors in the world which present a more attractive picture as one first beholds it on entering from the open Atlantic. The elevated site of the city, with its close array of neat, white three and four story houses, breaks the sky-line in front of the anchorage, while the town forms a half moon in shape, extending for a couple of miles each way, right and left. Near the water's edge, on the lower line of the city, are many substantial warehouses, official establishments, the custom house, and the like. Between the lower and the upper town is a long reach of green terraced embankment, intense in its bright verdure. Probably no other city on the globe, certainly not so far as our experience extends, is so peculiarly divided.

A sad episode marked our first experience here. We came to anchor in the harbor, according to custom, at what is known as the Quarantine. About a cable's length from us lay a large European steamship, flying the yellow flag at the fore. She came into port from Rio Janeiro on the previous evening; five of her passengers who had died of yellow fever on the passage were buried at sea, while two more were down with it, and were being taken to the lazaretto on shore, as we dropped our anchor. Probably they went there to die. This was naturally depressing, more so, perhaps, as we were bound direct for Rio Janeiro; but as we now came from a northern port with a clean bill of health, we were finally released from quarantine and permitted to land. It is late in the season—last of May—for this pest of the coast to prevail, but the year 1891 has been one of unusual fatality in the South American ports, and none of them have been entirely exempt from the scourge, some showing a fearful list of mortality among both citizens and strangers. We were conversant with many instances of a particularly trying and sad nature, if any distinction can be made where death intervenes with such a rude hand. Victims who were in apparent good health in the morning were not infrequently buried on the evening of the same day! But we will spare the reader harrowing details.

Americus Vespucius discovered Bahia in 1503, while sailing under the patronage of Portugal, and as it was settled in 1511, it is the oldest city in the country, being also the second in size, though not in commercial importance. The excellent harbor is so spacious as to form a small inland sea, the far-reaching shores of which are beautified by mingled green foliage and pretty villas stretching along the bay, while the business portion gives evidence of a growing and important foreign trade. This deduction is also corroborated by the presence of numerous European steamships, and full-rigged sailing vessels devoted to the transportation of merchandise. The buildings are generally of a substantial appearance, whether designed as residences or for business purposes, but are mostly of an antique pattern, old and dingy. Though the city is divided into the lower and the upper town, the latter two or three hundred feet above the former, it is made easily accessible by mechanical means. A large elevator, run by hydraulic power, is employed for the purpose, which was built by an energetic Yankee, and has been in successful operation several years, taking the citizens from the lower to the upper town, as we pass from basement to attic in our tall North American buildings. Between the two portions of Bahia there are streets for the transportation of merchandise, which wind zigzag fashion along the ravine to avoid the abruptness of the ascent. Besides these means, there are narrow stone steps leading upwards to the first level, among the tropical verdure, the deep green branches and leaves nodding to one from out of narrow lanes and quiet nooks. There is still another way of reaching the upper town, namely, a cable road, of very steep grade, one car ascending while another descends, thus forming a sort of counterbalance. By all these facilities united, the population manage very comfortably to overcome the topographical difficulties of the situation.

Though there are few buildings of any special note in Bahia, the general architecture being quaint and nondescript, still the combined view of the city, as we have endeavored to show, is of no inconsiderable beauty. We approached it from the north, doubling Light House Point in the early morning, just as the rising sun lighted up the bay. Seen from the harbor, the large dome of the cathedral overlooks the whole town very much like the gilded dome which forms so conspicuous an object on approaching the city of Boston. The dark, low-lying, grim-looking fort, which presides over the quarantine anchorage, is built upon a natural ledge of rock, half a mile from the shore of the town, and looks like a huge cheese-box.

In the upper portion of Bahia the streets are narrow, and the houses so tall as to nearly exclude the sun when it is not in the zenith. They are built of a native stone, and differ from the majority of South American dwellings, which are rarely over two stories in height, and generally of one only. We have heard it argued that it is advantageous to build tropical cities with narrow streets, so as to exclude the heat of the sun's rays and thus keep the houses cooler. This is not logical. Wide avenues and broad streets give ventilation which cannot be obtained in any other way in populous centres. Narrow lanes invite epidemics, fevers, and malarial diseases; broad thoroughfares give less opportunity for their lodgment. A beehive of human beings, crowded together in a narrow space, exhausts the life-giving principle of the surrounding atmosphere, but this is impossible where plenty of room is given for the circulation of fresh air.

These tall houses of Bahia have overhanging ornamental balconies, which towards evening are filled with the female portion of the families, laughing, chatting, singing, and smoking, for the ladies of these latitudes smoke in their domestic circles. Narrow as the streets of Bahia are, room is found for a well patronized tramway to run through them. No one thinks of walking, if it be for only a couple of hundred rods, on the line of the street cars. All of the civilized world seems to have grown lazy since the introduction of this modern facility for cheap transportation.

Bahia was the capital of Brazil until 1763, during which year the headquarters of the government were removed to Rio Janeiro.

This is a sort of New Bedford, so to speak, having been for more than a century extensively engaged in the whaling business, an occupation which is still pursued to a limited extent. Whales frequent the bay of Bahia, where they are sometimes captured by small boats from the shore. It is supposed that the favorite food of this big game is found in these waters. There was a time when the close pursuit by fishing fleets fitted out in nearly all parts of the world rendered the whales wary and scarce. The catching and killing of so many seemed to have thinned out their number in most of the seas of the globe. Then came the great discovery of rock oil, which rapidly superseded the whale oil of commerce in general use. Thereupon the pursuit of the gigantic animal ceased to be of any great moment, while there was oil enough spontaneously pouring out of the wells of Pennsylvania, and elsewhere, to fully satisfy the demand of the world at large. Being no longer hunted, the whales gradually became tame and increased in numbers, so that to-day there are probably as many in the usual haunts of these leviathans in either hemisphere as there ever were. The briefest sea voyage can hardly be made without sighting one or more of them, and sometimes in large schools.

There is a portion of the elevated section of Bahia which is called Victoria, a really beautiful locality, having delightful gardens, attractive walks, and myriads of noble shade trees. From here the visitor overlooks the bay, with its islands and curving shore decked with graceful palms, bamboos, and mango groves; upon the water are numerous tiny boats, while white winged sailing ships and dark, begrimed steamers unite in forming a picture of active life and maritime beauty. In the distance lies the ever green island of Itaparica, named after the first governor's Indian bride, while still farther away is seen range after range of tall, purple hills, multiplied until lost in the distance.

A few grim looking convents and monasteries, which have gradually come into the possession of the government, are now used as free schools, libraries, and hospitals. There is a medical college here which has a national reputation for general excellence, and many students come from Rio Janeiro, eight hundred miles away, to avail themselves of its advantages, receiving a diploma after attending upon its three years' course of studies. From subsequent inquiry, however, not only here but in Rio and elsewhere, we are satisfied that the science of medicine and surgery stands at a very low ebb throughout this great southland. Foreign doctors are looked upon with great distrust and jealousy; indeed, it is very difficult for them to obtain a suitable license to practice in Brazil. This does not apply to dentistry, of which profession there are many American experts in the country, who have realized decided pecuniary and professional success. There were six or eight on board the Vigilancia, who had been on a visit to their North American homes during the summer season, at which time the fever is most to be dreaded here.

The city contains over sixty churches, some of which are fine edifices, built of stone brought from Europe. This could easily be done without much extra expense, as the vessels visiting the port in those early days required ballast with which to cross the ocean. They brought no other cargo of any account, but were sure at certain seasons of the year to obtain a suitable return freight, which paid a good profit on the round voyage. Several of these churches are in a very dilapidated condition, and probably will not be repaired. The cathedral is one of the largest structures of the sort in Brazil, and is thought by many to be one of the finest. The cathedral at Rio, however, is a much more elaborate structure, and far more costly. It takes enormous sums, wrung from the poorest class of people, to maintain these gorgeous temples and support the horde of fat, licentious, useless priests attached to them, while the mass of humanity find life a daily struggle with abject want and poverty. Does any thoughtful person believe for one moment that such hollow service can be grateful to a just and merciful Supreme Being?

Bahia was a flourishing port before Rio Janeiro was known commercially, and was the first place of settlement by English traders on this coast. The present population is of a very mixed character, composed of nearly all nationalities, white and black, European and natives. There is no prejudice evinced as regards color. Mulatto or negro may once have been a slave, but he is a freeman now, both socially and in the eyes of the law. He is eligible for any position of trust, public or private, if he develops the requisite degree of intelligence. Men who have been slaves in their youth are now filling political offices here, with credit to themselves and satisfaction to the public. The actual reform from being a degraded land of slavery to one of human freedom is much more radical and thorough in Brazil than it is in our own Southern States, where the pretended equality of the colored race is simply a burlesque upon constitutional liberty.

The occasional use of that quaint mode of conveyance, the sedan chair, was observable, taking one back to the days of Queen Anne. Only a few years ago it was the one mode of transportation from the lower to the upper part of the town; but modern facilities, already referred to, have thrown the sedan chair nearly out of use. A few antique representatives of this style of vehicle, some quite expensive and elaborately ornamented, are still seen obstructing the entrances to the houses. The local name they bear is *cadeira*. When these chairs are used, they are borne upon the shoulders of two or four stalwart blacks, and are hung upon long poles, like a palanquin, after the fashion so often seen in old pictures and ancient tapestry.

We have spoken of the narrowness of the streets through which the tramways pass. In many places, pedestrians are compelled to step into the doorways of dwellings to permit the cars to pass them. This is not only the case at Bahia, but also in half the busy portion of South American cities. These mule propelled cars are now adopted all over this country and Mexico; even fourth class cities have tramways, and many towns which have not yet risen to the dignity of having a city organization are thus supplied with transportation. The Bahia tramway, on its route to the suburbs, passes through fertile districts of great rural beauty, among groves of tropical fruits, orange orchards, tall overshadowing mangoes, and cultivated flowers. There is an attempt at a public garden, though it is an idea only half carried out; but there is a terrace in connection here called "The Bluff," from whence one gets a magnificent view, more especially of the near and the distant sea. These delightful and comprehensive natural pictures are photographed upon the memory, forming a charming cabinet of scenic views appertaining to each special locality, choice, original, and never to be effaced.

We must not omit to mention a specialty of this city, an article produced in one or two of the charitable institutions, as well as in many humble family circles, namely, artificial flowers made from the choicest feathers of the most brilliant colored birds. None of these articles are poor, while some of them are exquisite in design and execution, produced entirely from the plumage of native birds. A considerable aggregate sum of money is realized by a certain portion of the community, in the regular manufacture of these delicate ornaments. Girls begin to learn the art at a very early age, and in a few years arrive at a marvelous degree of perfection, producing realistic pictures which rival the brush and pencil of a more pretentious department of art. Nearly all visitors carry away with them dainty examples of this exquisite and artistic work, which has a reputation beyond the seas. Thousands of beautiful birds are annually sacrificed to furnish the necessary material. Thus the delicate family of the humming-bird, whose variety is infinite in Brazil, has been almost exterminated in some parts of the country. There is one other specialty here, namely, the manufacture of lace, which gives constant employment to many women of Bahia, their product being much esteemed all over South America for the beauty of the designs and the perfection of the manufacture.

The special fruit of this province, as already intimated, is oranges, and it is safe to say that none produced elsewhere can excel them. They are not picked until they are thoroughly ripe, and are therefore too delicate, in their prime condition, to sustain transportation to any considerable distance. Those sold in our northern cities are picked in a green condition and ripened off the trees, a process which does not injure some fruits, but which detracts very materially from the orange and the pineapple. The oranges of Bahia average from five to six inches in diameter, have a rather thin skin, are full of juice, and contain no pips; in short, they are perfectly delicious, being delicately sweet, with a slight subacid flavor. The first enjoyment of this special fruit in Bahia is a gastronomic revelation. The maracajus is also a favorite fruit here, but hardly to be named beside the orange. It is the product of the vine which bears the passion flower, but this we could not relish. It is a common fruit in Australia and New Zealand, where the author found it equally unpalatable, yet people who have once acquired the taste become very fond of it. The vine with its flower is common enough in the United States, but we have never seen it in a fruit-bearing condition in our country.

The province of Bahia has an area of two hundred thousand square miles, and is represented as containing some of the most fertile land in Brazil, capable of producing immense crops of several important staples. It is especially fertile near the coast, where there are some large and thriving tobacco, sugar, and coffee plantations. The first mentioned article, owing to some favorable peculiarity of the soil in this vicinity, is held to be nearly equal to the average Cuban product, and it is being more and more extensively cultivated each year. Bahia cigars are not only very cheap, but they are remarkably fine in flavor. It was observed that old travelers on this coast made haste to lay in a goodly supply of them for personal use.

A coffee plantation situated not far from this city was visited, affording a small party of strangers to the place much pleasure and information. The coffee plant is an evergreen, and thus the foliage is always fresh in appearance, yielding two harvests annually. Boa Vista, the plantation referred to, covers about one hundred acres, much of which is also devoted to the raising of fodder, fruit, corn, and beans, with some special vegetables, forming the principal sustenance of the people and animals employed upon the estate. At first, in laying out such a plantation, the coffee sprouts are started in a nursery, and when they have had a year's growth are transplanted to the open field, where they are placed with strict uniformity in long rows at equal distances apart. After the second year these young plants begin to bear, and continue to do so for twenty-five or thirty years, at which period both the trees and the soil become in a measure exhausted, and a new tract of land is again selected for a plantation. By proper management the new plantation can be made to begin bearing at the same time that the old one ceases to be sufficiently productive and remunerative to cultivate for the same purpose. The coffee-tree is thought to be in its prime at from five to ten years of age. Fruit trees, such as bananas, oranges, mandioca, guavas, and so on, are planted among the coffee-trees to afford them a partial shelter, which, to a certain degree, is requisite to their best success, especially when they are young and throwing out thin roots. The coffee bushes are kept trimmed down to about the height of one's head, which facilitates the harvesting of the crop, and also throws the sap into the formation and growth of berries. The coffee-tree, when permitted to grow to its natural height, reaches between twenty and thirty feet, and, with its deep green foliage, is a handsome ornamental garden tree, much used for this purpose in Brazil. The coffee pods, when ripe, are scarlet in color, and resemble cherries, though they are much smaller. Each berry contains two seeds, which, when detached from the pod and properly dried, form the familiar article of such universal domestic use. A coffee plantation well managed, in Brazil, is an almost certain source of ample fortune. The crop is sure; that is to say, it has scarcely any drawbacks, and is always in demand. Of course there are inconveniences of climate, and other things needless to enumerate, as regards entering into the business, but the growth and ripening of a coffee crop very seldom fail.

As has been intimated, this port is famous for the production of oranges and tobacco; so Rio is famous for coffee, Pernambuco for sugar, and Pará for crude india-rubber.

We must not forget to mention one other, and by no means insignificant product of Brazil which is exported from Bahia, namely, diamonds of the very first quality, which for purity of color far exceed those of Africa and elsewhere. It appears that a syndicate in London control the world's supply of this peculiar gem from all the mines on the globe, permitting only a certain quantity of diamonds to go on to the market annually, and thus keeping up the selling price and the market value. No one is permitted to know the real product of the mines but the managers of this syndicate. The quantity of the sparkling gems which are held back by the dealers in London, Paris, and Vienna is really enormous; were they to be placed in the retail dealers' hands as fast as they are produced from the various sources of supply, they would be erelong as cheap and plenty as moonstones. This sounds like an extravagant assertion, but still there is far more truth in it than is generally realized. One of the public journals of London lately spoke of a proposed corporation, to be known as the "Diamond Trust," which is certainly a significant evidence that the market requires to be carefully controlled as to the quantity which is annually put upon it. In old times a diamond was simply valued as a diamond; its cutting and polishing were of the simplest character. A series of irregular plane surfaces were thought to sufficiently bring out its reflective qualities, but the stone is now treated with far more care and intelligence. A large portion of the value of a diamond has come to consist in the artistic, and we may say scientific, manner in which it is cut. By this means its latent qualities of reflection of light are brought to perfection, developing its real brilliancy. Accomplished workmen realize fabulous wages in this employment. A stone of comparatively little value, by being cut in the best manner, can be made to outshine a much finer stone which is cut after the old style. Amsterdam used to control the business of diamond cutting, but it is now as well done in

Boston and New York as in any part of the world.

The largest diamond yet discovered came from Brazil, and is known as the Braganza. The first European expert in precious stones has valued this extraordinary gem, which is still in the rough, at three hundred million sterling! Its actual weight is something over one pound troy. In the light of such a statement, we pause to ask ourselves, What is a diamond? Simply carbon crystallized, that is, in its greatest purity, and carbon is the combustible principle of charcoal. The author was told, both here and in Rio Janeiro, that there is a considerable and profitable mining industry carried on in this country, of which the general public hear nothing. The results are only known to prominent and interested Brazilians, the whole matter being kept as secret as possible for commercial reasons. No one reads anything about the products of the diamond mines in the local papers.

We cannot say that the city of Bahia is a very healthy locality, though it certainly seems that it ought to be, it is so admirably situated. Yellow fever and other epidemics prevail more or less every year. The lower part of the town, on the water front, is so shamefully filthy as to induce fever. Upon first landing, the stranger finds himself almost nauseated by the vile smells which greet him. This section of the town is also very hot, the cliff, or upper town, shutting off almost entirely the circulation of air. It is here that sailors, particularly, indulge in all sorts of excesses, especially in drinking the vile, raw liquor sold by negresses, besides eating unripe and overripe fruit, thus inviting disease. One favorite drink produced here, very cheap and very potent, is a poisonous but seductive white rum.

The trade and people in this part of the town form a strange conglomerate,—monkeys, parrots, caged birds, tame jaguars, mongrel puppies, pineapples, oranges, mangoes, and bananas, these being flanked by vegetables and flowers. The throng is made up of half-naked boatmen, indolent natives from the country, with negresses, both as venders and purchasers. As we look at the scene, in addition to what we have depicted there is a jovial group of sailors from a man-of-war in the harbor enjoying their shore leave, while not far away a small party of yachtsmen from an English craft are amusing themselves with petty bargains, close followed by half a dozen Americans, who came hither in the last mail steamer. A polyglot scene of mixed tongues and gay colors.

In passing into and out of the harbor of Bahia, one can count a dozen forts and batteries, all constructed after the old style, and armed in the most ineffective manner. These would count as nothing in a contest with modern ships of war having plated hulls and arms of precision. Land fortifications, designed to protect commercial ports from foreign enemies, have not kept pace with the progress in naval armament.

Bahia is connected by submarine telegraph with Pernambuco, Pará, and Rio Janeiro, and through them with all parts of the civilized world.

CHAPTER VIII.

Cape Frio.—Rio Janeiro.—A Splendid Harbor.—Various Mountains.—
Botafogo Bay.—The Hunchback.—Farewell to the Vigilancia.—
Tijuca.—Italian Emigrants.—City Institutions.—Public Amusements.
—Street Musicians.—Churches.—Narrow Thoroughfares.—
Merchants' Clerks.—Railroads in Brazil.—Natural Advantages of the
City.—The Public Plazas.—Exports.

After a three days' voyage down the coast, between Bahia and Rio Janeiro, the tall lighthouse of Cape Frio—"Cool Cape"—was sighted. This promontory is a large oval mass of granite, sixteen hundred feet in height, quite isolated from other highlands, protruding boldly into the Atlantic Ocean. It forms the southeastern extremity of the coast of Brazil, and in clear weather can be seen, it is said, forty miles or more away. Here the long swell of the open sea is unobstructed and finds full sway, asserting its giant power at all seasons of the year. Experienced travelers who rarely suffer from seasickness are apt to succumb to this trying illness off Cape Frio. It is situated in latitude 22° 59' south, longitude 41° 57' west, which is particularly specified because the line of no magnetic variation touches on this cape,—that line which Columbus was so amazed at discovering one hundred leagues west of Flores, in the Azores, nearly four hundred years ago. We had been running almost due south for the last eight hundred miles, but in doubling Cape Frio, and making for Rio harbor, the ship was headed to the westward, while the mountains on the coast assumed the most grotesque and singular shapes, the range extending from west to east until it ends at Cape Frio. The continent of South America here forms a sharp angle, but we were too full of expectancy as to the king of harbors towards which we were heading, to speculate much about Cape Frio and its ocean-swept surroundings.

Rio Janeiro, the capital of Brazil, is also the largest, if not the most important city in South America, situated about twelve hundred miles north of Montevideo and Buenos Ayres, just within the borders of the southern torrid zone. The distance of Rio from New York direct is five thousand miles, but most voyagers, on the way through the West Indies, stop at three or four of these islands, and also at some of the northern ports of the continent of South America, the same as in our own case, so that about five hundred miles may be fairly added to the distance we have just named. Though the vessel was a month in making the voyage to this port, had we sailed direct it might have been done in two thirds of the time.

After doubling the cape and sailing some sixty or eighty miles, we steered boldly towards the mouth of the harbor of Rio. For a few moments the ship's prow pointed towards Raza Island, on which stands the lighthouse, but a slight turn of the wheel soon changed its relative position, and we entered the passage leading into the bay. After passing the "Sugar Loaf," a rock twelve hundred feet in height, the city lay off our port bow. All is so well defined, the water is so deep and free from obstructions of any sort, that no pilot is required and none is taken, and thus we crept slowly up towards our moorings. As the reader may well suppose, to eyes weary of the monotony of the sea, the panorama which opened before us was one of intense interest. Everything seemed matured and olden. There was no sign of newness; indeed, we recalled the fact that Rio was an established commercial port half a century before New York had a local habitation or a name. The town lies on the west side of the port, between a mountain range and the bay, running back less than two miles in depth, but extending along the shore for a distance of some eight miles, fronting one of the finest and most spacious harbors in the world, famous for its manifold scenic beauties, which, from the moment of passing within the narrow entrance, are ever changing and ever lovely. The most prominent features are the verdure-clad hills of Gloria, Theresa, and Castello, behind which extend ranges of steep, everlasting mountains, one line beyond another, until lost among the clouds. Few natural spectacles can equal the grand contour of this famous bay. People who have visited it always speak in superlative language of Rio harbor, but we hardly think it could be overpraised. It is the grand entrance to a tropical paradise, so far as nature is concerned, amid clustering mountains, abrupt headlands, inviting inlets, and beautiful islands, covered with palms, tree-ferns, bananas, acacias, and other delights of tropical vegetation, which, when seen depicted in books, impress one as an exaggeration, but seen here thrill us with vivid reality. It is only in the torrid zone that one sees these lavish developments of verdure, these labyrinths of charming arboreous effect.

Though so well known and so often written about, the harbor of Rio is less famous than beautiful. The bay is said to contain about one hundred islands, its area extending inland some seventeen or eighteen miles. The largest of these is Governor's Island, nearly fronting the city, being six miles long. Some idea of the extent of the bay may be had from the fact that there are fifty square miles of good anchorage for ships within its compass. Into the bay flows the water of two inconsiderable rivers, the Macacu and the Iguaçu, the first named coming in at the northeast and the latter at the northwest corner of the harbor.

The Organ Mountains,—Serra dos Orgãos,—capped with soft, fleecy clouds, formed the lofty background of the picture towards the north, as we entered upon the scene, the immediate surroundings being dominated by the sky-reaching Sugar Loaf Rock,—Pão d'Assucar,—which is also the navigator's guiding mark while yet far away at sea. This bold, irregular rock of red sandstone rises abruptly from the water, like a giant standing waist-high in the sea, and forms the western boundary of the entrance to the harbor, opposite to which, crowning a small but bold promontory, is the fort of Santa Cruz, the two highlands forming an appropriate portal to the grandeur which is to greet one within. The distance between these bounds is about a mile, inside of which the water widens at once to lake-like proportions. Clouds of frigate birds, gulls, and gannets fly gracefully about each incoming ship, as if to welcome them to the harbor where anchorage might be had for the combined shipping of the whole world. We have lately seen the harbor of Rio compared to that of Queenstown, on the Irish coast, twenty times magnified; but the infinite superiority of the former in every respect makes the allusion quite pointless.

The Organ Mountains, to which we have referred, and which form so conspicuous a portion of the scene in and about Rio, are so called because of their fancied resemblance in shape to the pipes of an organ; but though blessed with the usual share of imagination, we were quite unable to trace any such resemblance. However, one must not be hypercritical. The gigantic recumbent form of a human being, so often spoken of as discernible along this mountain range, is no poetical fancy, but is certainly clear enough to any eye, recalling the likeness to a crouching lion outlined by the promontory of Gibraltar as one first sees the rock, either on entering the strait or coming from Malta.

One of the most beautiful indentures of the shore, earliest to catch the eye after passing into the harbor of Rio from the sea, is called the Bay of Botafogo. The word means "thrown into the fire," and alludes to the inhuman *autos-da-fé* which occurred here when the natives, on refusing to subscribe to the Roman Catholic faith, were committed by the priests to the flames! This is the way in which the Romish creed was introduced into Mexico and South America, and the means by which it was sustained.

The principal charm of this lovely bay within a bay—Botafogo—is its flowers and exposition of soaring royal palms. The attractiveness of the handsome residences is quite secondary to that of nature, here revealed with a lavish profusion. This part of Rio is overshadowed by the tall peak of the Corcovado, "the Hunchback," one of the mass of hills which occupy a large area west of the city, and the nearest mountain to it. From its never-failing

85

springs comes a large share of the water supply of the capital. The aqueduct is some ten miles long, crossing a valley at one point seven hundred feet in width, at a height of ninety feet, upon double arches. Another large aqueduct is in contemplation, besides which some other sources are now in actual operation, as Rio has long since outgrown the capacity of the original supply derived from the Corcovado. The drainage of the town suffers seriously for want of sufficient water wherewith to flush the conduits, which at this writing, with the deadly fever claiming victims on all hands, are permitted to remain in a stagnant condition! And yet there are hundreds of hills round about, within long cannon range, which would readily yield the required element in almost limitless quantity.

We left the Vigilancia, and our good friend Captain Baker, with regret. The noble ship had borne us in safety thousands of miles during the past month, through storms and calms, amid intense tropical heat, and such floods of rain as are only encountered in southern seas. Watching from her deck, there had been revealed to us the glories of the changing latitudes, and particularly the grandeur of the radiant heavens in equatorial regions. A sense of all-absorbing curiosity prevailed as we landed at the stone steps, overlooked by the yellow ochre walls of the arsenal, in the picturesque, though pestilential city. The nauseous odors which greet one as he steps on shore are very discordant elements in connection with the intense interest created by the novel sights that engage the eye of a stranger.

With a population, including the immediate suburbs, of over half a million,— estimated at six hundred and fifty thousand,—Rio has most of the belongings of a North American city of the first class, though we cannot refrain from mentioning one remarkable exception, namely, the entire absence of good hotels. There is not a really good and comfortable public house in all Brazil. Those which do exist in Rio charge exorbitantly for the most indifferent service, and strangers are often puzzled to find a sleeping-room for a single night on first arriving here. Tijuca, situated in the hills a few miles from the city, is perhaps the most desirable place of temporary sojourn for the newly arrived traveler, who will find at least one large and comfortable public house there, favorably known to travelers as Whyte's Hotel. It is some little distance from the city, but is easily reached by tramway, which takes one to the foot of the hills of the Tijuca range, whose tallest peak is thirty-four hundred feet above tide-water. This place abounds in attractive villas, tropical vegetation, and beautiful flowers, both wild and cultivated. From here also one gets a most charming view of the distant city, the famous bay, and the broad Atlantic; indeed, the view alone will repay one for making this brief excursion. The loftiest village in these hills is called Boa Vista. There are mountains, however, on either side, which are five or six hundred feet higher than the village containing the hotel. American enterprise is engaged at this writing in constructing a narrow gauge electric tramway to the summit of Tijuca. The driving road from the base to the top is an admirable piece of engineering, and is kept in the very best condition possible.

The objectionable character of the Italian emigrants, who come hither as well as to our own States, was demonstrated by a party of them robbing and nearly murdering a resident of Tijuca who happened to be a short distance from his own house, the evening previous to the day which we spent at this resort. These Italians are mostly employed as workmen upon the railroad, though some are gardeners on the neighboring estates. In town they act as porters and day laborers on the wharves, as boatmen, and so on, but, as we were assured, are a lawless, vagabond element of the community, giving the police force a great deal of trouble.

Rio has many large and commodious public buildings and some elegant private residences, the latter generally of a half Moorish type of architecture. Some of the edifices date back a couple of centuries. The early Portuguese built of stone and cement, hence the somewhat remarkable durability of these houses. The large edifice devoted to the department of agriculture and public works is one of the most noticeable in the city. The Bank of Brazil occupies a building which is classic in its fine architecture, being elaborately constructed of hammered granite. There is no more superb example of masonry in the country. The National Mint, on the Square of the Republic, is also a fine granite building; so is that devoted to the Bourse, where enormous values change hands daily. Educational institutions are numerous, well organized, and generally availed of by the rising generation. The National College is of notable influence in the dissemination of general intelligence, and the same may be said of the Polytechnic College, an excellent and practical institution. It should be observed that any well organized educational establishment is called a college in this country.

The public library of Rio contains some two hundred thousand volumes, besides many valuable Spanish and Portuguese documents in manuscript. It is liberally conducted; black and white people alike, as well as all respectable strangers, have free access and liberal accommodations within the walls. This institution is an honor to Brazil.

Rio has a new and well organized navy yard, a large arsenal, cotton mills, and several extensive manufacturing establishments. Among the latter is the largest flour mill we have ever seen. This is an English enterprise; but so far as we could learn, it had been found impossible to compete profitably with the American flour, as now landed at Rio. A foundling hospital on the Rua Everesta de Veiga is worthy of mention. Here, as already described in relation to another Brazilian city, infants are freely received and cared for, without any inquiry being made of those who deposit them. These little ones at the outset become children of the state, and are registered and numbered as such. Oftentimes the mother pins to the little deserted one's clothes the name she desires should be given to it, and the wish is usually regarded by the officials of the institution. The authorities put each child out to nurse for a year, but receive it back again at the expiration of that time, and at a proper period send it to school, and endeavor to rear it to some useful employment or trade. While the child is thus disposed of, the payment for its board and care is very moderate in amount, and is also contingent upon its good health and physical condition. Thus the deserted one is likely to have good attention, if not for humanity's sake, then from mercenary motives. This plan is copied from that which is pursued by the great foundling hospitals of St. Petersburg and Moscow, which are certainly the best organized and largest institutions of the sort in the world. Where so large a percentage of the children born are illegitimate, such a hospital becomes a real necessity. There has been no year since this establishment was opened, in 1738, as we were told, in which less than four hundred infants were received. Sometimes parents, whose worldly conditions have greatly improved, come forward after the lapse of years and claim their children. This right on their part is duly respected by their properly proving the relationship beyond all possible doubt, and paying a sum of money equal to that which has been actually expended by the state in the child's behalf.

In the line of public amusements there is a large and well-appointed opera house besides eight other fairly good theatres, together with an excellent museum. The performances at the theatres are given in French, Spanish, and Portuguese. Italian opera is presented three times a week during the season. This year the performances were summarily stopped by the principal tenor dying of yellow fever. The theatre bearing the name of the late emperor is a sort of mammoth cave in size, and is capable of seating six thousand people, not one half of whom can hear what is said or sung upon the stage by the performers. Street bands of German musicians perform here as they do in Boston and New York; the mass of the people, being music loving, patronize these itinerants liberally. One band posted themselves daily before the popular Globe Restaurant, at the hour of the midday meal (breakfast), and performed admirably, reaping a generous response from the habitués. Most of the patrons of this excellent establishment were observed to be American, English, and French merchants, who attended to business in Rio during the day, but who went home to the elevated environs to dine and to sleep. "I have been here in business nine years," said one of these gentlemen to us, "and have been down with the fever once; but I would not sleep in Rio overnight for any amount of money, at this season of the year." This was early in June. He added: "The fever should have disappeared before this time, which is our winter, but it seems to linger later and later each succeeding year." This was a conclusion which we heard expressed by other observant individuals, but all joined in ascribing its persistency in no small degree to the imperfect drainage, and the vile personal habits of the mass of the common people, who make no effort to be cleanly, or to regard the decencies of life in this respect.

As to churches, Rio has between sixty and seventy, none of which are very remarkable, all being dim, dirty, and offensive to the olfactories. The cause of the foul air being so noticeable in all of these Romish churches is the fact that no provision whatever is made for proper ventilation, and this, too, in places of all others where it is most imperatively necessary. The offense is created by exhalations from the bodies of the least cleanly class of the population. It is such who mostly fill these churches all over the continent of Europe, Mexico, South America, and the United States. Precisely the same disgusting odor greets the senses of the visitor to these edifices, be it in one hemisphere or another, but especially in Italy and Spain.

The cathedral of Rio is a large, showy edifice, surrounded by narrow streets, and thus hidden by other buildings, so that no general and satisfactory outside effect can be had. The front and sides are of solid granite, and the whole is known to have cost a mint of money, yet the safety of the foundation is more than questionable. Like the grand church of St. Isaacs, in the Russian capital of St. Petersburg, great expense will doubtless have to be incurred to renew and strengthen it in this respect. It is believed that the site upon which Rio stands was once under the sea, and, geologically speaking, at no very remote period, which accounts for considerable trouble being experienced in obtaining secure and solid foundations for any heavy superstructure. At this writing, the cathedral is undergoing extensive repairs, inside and out, but in spite of the noise of workmen, the disagreeable lime dust, and the interference of a network of interior staging, it is still very striking in its architectural effect.

In the old part of the town, two prominent cupolas dominate the surroundings. These belong respectively to the churches of Candelaria and San Luigi. The most popular church in Rio is undoubtedly that which crowns the Gloria Hill, called the Igreja da Gloria do Onterio, which overlooks the bay. Its commanding situation is very remarkable. In shape it is octagonal, and seems to be very solidly built. In front of the church there is a broad terrace, from whence a fine view may be enjoyed. On a moonlight night the picture presented from the Gloria Hill is something worth going miles on foot to behold. This church was the favorite resort of the late royal family when they were in the city, though much of their home life and all of their summers were passed in the hills of the Organ Mountains at the emperor's favorite resort,— Petropolis.

The shops of Rio, notwithstanding they are generally small and situated upon streets so narrow that they would be called only lanes in North America,— close, confined, half-strangled thoroughfares,—will compare favorably in many respects with those of continental Europe. The larger number of the merchants here are French, together with a considerable sprinkling of German Jews. Indeed, can any one tell us where we shall not find this peculiar race represented in the trade centres of the wide world? In many of the fancy-goods stores the famous Brazilian feather flowers are exhibited for sale, but the best place to purchase these is at Bahia, where they are a specialty, and where their manufacture is said to have originated. The narrow streets, traversed by tramways, are at times almost impassable for pedestrians, and are often blocked by heavy mule teams for fifteen minutes at a time. By and by some lazy policeman makes his appearance and quietly begins to unravel the snarl, which he at length succeeds in doing, and the ordinary traffic of the thoroughfare is once more resumed. An unsightly gutter runs through the middle of some of these thoroughfares, which adds to the annoyances incident to ordinary travel. All are regularly laid out, chess-board fashion, very ill smelling, and harbor an infinite number of beggars and mangy dogs.

It is customary for local merchants who employ European clerks—and there are many English, French, and Brazilians in Rio who do so,—to give them a fixed salary, quite moderate in amount, and to furnish them with lodgings also. The latter are of a very rude and undesirable character, in the business establishment itself, either over the store, or in the back part of it. The bedding which is furnished is of a makeshift character, rarely changed, and never properly aired. Exceedingly uncleanly domestic arrangements, or the entire absence of them, are also a serious matter in this connection, from a sanitary point of view. The clerks get their food at some neighboring restaurant, and contract irregular habits, all of which is both mentally and physically demoralizing. It is among this class of foreigners that the yellow fever finds the most ready victims. To sleep in these crowded business centres, in ill-ventilated apartments, with far from cleanly surroundings, is simply to provoke fatal illness, and during an epidemic of fever these places furnish fuel for the flames. Neatness and cleanliness among domestic associations in this city are entirely lost sight of and are totally disregarded by men and women.

The Rua Direita is the State Street or Wall Street of Rio; a new name, which escapes us at this moment, has been given to it, but the old one is still the favorite and in common use. Here brokers, bankers, and commission merchants meet and bargain, and fiercely speculate in coffee. The principal shopping street is the Rua de Ouvidor, where the best stores and choicest retail goods are to be found. In the Rua dos Ourives,—"Goldsmith's Street,"—the display of fine jewelry, diamonds, and other precious stones recalls the Rue de la Paix of Paris. Diamonds are held at quite as high prices as in London or New York, and those of the best quality can be bought better at retail out of this country than in it. A poor quality of stone, off color, is imported and offered here as being of native production, and careless purchasers are not infrequently deceived by cunning dealers in these matters.

Two vehicles cannot pass each other in this avenue without driving upon the narrow sidewalk. At times a deafening uproar prevails along these circumscribed lanes. The rough grinding of wheels, noisy bootblacks, whooping orange-sellers, screaming newspaper boys, howling dogs, the rattle of the street peddler, lottery ticket venders, fighting street gamins, all join to swell the mingled chorus. And yet these crowded thoroughfares would lose half of their picturesqueness were these elements to be banished from them. They each and all add a certain crude element of interest to this every-day picture of Vanity Fair.

In their ambition to copy European and North American fashions, the gentlemen of Rio utterly disregard the eternal fitness of things, wearing broadcloth suits of black, with tall, stove-pipe hats, neither of which articles should be adopted for a moment in their torrid climate. Nothing could be more inappropriate. Linen clothing and light straw hats are the true costume for the tropics, naturally suggesting themselves in hot climates to the exclusion of woolen, heat-brewing costumes, which are necessary articles of wear in the north. Fashion, however, ignores climate and is omnipotent everywhere; comfort is subsidiary. Wear woolen clothing by all means, gentlemen of Rio, even when the thermometer hangs persistently at 95° Fahr. in the shade, and the human body perspires like a mountain stream.

The tramway system of Rio is excellent in a crude way. Statistics show that fifty million passengers are annually transported by this popular means from one part of the city to another, and into the suburbs. The street railway was first introduced here by North American enterprise, the pioneer route being that between the city proper and the botanical garden. The prices of passage vary according to distances, as is the case with the London omnibuses. The cars are all open ones, of cheap, coarse construction, and far from inviting in appearance, being entirely unupholstered, and affording only hard board seats for passengers to sit upon. They are usually drawn by one small donkey, whose strength is quite overtasked, but the ground in the city is so nearly level that the cars move very easily and rapidly.

There is one delightful excursion from Rio which nearly all strangers are sure to enjoy. We refer to the ascent of Corcovado, the mountain which looms over Botafogo Bay to the height of twenty-two hundred feet, and to the summit of which a railway has been constructed. The grades are extremely steep, and the road is what is called a centre line, worked upon the cog-wheel system, the ascent being very slow and winding. The principle is the same as that of the railway by which Mount Washington is ascended, in New Hampshire, or the Righi, in Switzerland. This road was built by the national government, but as a pecuniary speculation it does not pay, though it is of considerable indirect benefit to the city. We will not dilate upon the grand outlook to be had from the summit of the Hunchback, which takes in a bird's-eye view of the harbor and its surroundings, but will add that no one should come hither without ascending Corcovado. The top consists of two rounded masses of bare rock, and is walled in to prevent accident, there being on one side a perpendicular descent of a thousand feet. It gives one at first a dizzy sensation to look down upon the vast city spread out over the plain, from whence a hum of mingled sounds comes up with singular distinctness. Even the bells upon the mules which are attached to the tram-cars can be distinguished, and other sounds still more delicate and minute. Just so balloonists tell us that at two or three thousand feet in mid-air they can distinguish the voices of individuals upon the earth below them. The experienced traveler learns to be astonished at nothing, but there are degrees of pleasure induced by beautiful and majestic views which mount to the apex of our capacity for admiration. One can safely promise such a realizing sense to him who ascends the Corcovado.

A tramway which starts from the centre of the city will take the traveler to the base of the hill, through roads lined by palms of great age and beauty, finally leaving him near the point from whence the steam road begins the upward journey.

Nictheroy, just across the harbor of Rio, on the east side of the bay, is a sort of faubourg of the capital, with which it is connected by a line of steam ferry-boats, as Chelsea is with Boston, or Brooklyn with the city of New York. It is the capital of the province of Rio Janeiro, and has broader streets, is more reasonably laid out, and is kept more cleanly than Rio itself. Space is found for a profusion of attractive gardens, and the senses are greeted by sweet odors in the place of needlessly offensive smells, which attack one on all sides in the metropolis so near at hand. It is quite a relief to get on to one of the ferry-boats and cross over to Nictheroy occasionally, for a breath of pure air. This is the native Indian name of the place, and signifies "hidden water," particularly applicable when these land-locked bays were shrouded in dense tropical woods.

Unlike Pará, Montevideo, and Buenos Ayres, this city has no special river communication with the interior, but her commerce is large and increasing. Railroads are more reliable feeders for business than either rivers or canals. It is a fact which is not generally realized, that Brazil has over six thousand miles of well-constructed railways in operation, besides having a telegraph system covering seven thousand miles of land service. In the construction of the railroads, the cost, so far as the ground work and grading was concerned, was reduced to the minimum, owing to the level nature of the country. As was the case in New Zealand, many of these railways were constructed at great expense, in anticipation of the wants of a future population, who it was hoped would settle rapidly upon the route which they followed. That is to say, many of these roads did not open communication between populous districts already in existence. This would have been perfectly legitimate. They run to no particular objective point, and seem to stop finally nowhere. The natural sequence followed. After being built and equipped with borrowed money, they were anything but self-supporting, and pecuniary aid from the government was freely given to enable them to be kept in operation.

There must always come a day of reckoning for all such forced schemes, and the Brazilian railways were no exception to the rule. This is largely the primary cause of the present monetary troubles in this country, as well as in the Argentine Republic. The capital for the construction of these roads came mostly from England, and that country has been accordingly a heavy pecuniary sufferer. The rates charged for transportation upon most of the lines are also exorbitant, if we were rightly informed; so much so, in fact, as to prove nearly prohibitory. Scarcely any species of merchandise brought from a considerable distance inland will bear such freight charges and leave a margin for profit to the producer and shipper. Would-be planters of coffee and sugar-cane dare not enter upon raising these staples for the market, unless situated very near the shipping point, or near some available river's course, the latter means being naturally much cheaper than any form of railway transportation.

Situated on the border of two zones, Rio Janeiro has the products of both within her reach, and thus possesses peculiar advantages for extensive trade and general commerce. It is in this latter direction that her progressive and enterprising merchants are endeavoring to extend the facilities of the port. The passenger landings—not wharves—which border the water front of the city here and there are of solid granite, from which at suitable intervals broad stone steps lead down to the water's edge, as on the borders of the Neva at St. Petersburg. We have few, if any, such substantial landing-places in our North American ports. We know of no harbor on the globe which enjoys a more eligible situation as regards the commerce of foreign countries, both of the New and the Old World. The one convenience so imperatively demanded is proper wharves for the landing and shipping of cargoes, thus obviating the necessity of the expensive and tedious lighter system. It is her many natural and extraordinary advantages which has led to so steady a growth of the city, notwithstanding the very serious drawback of an unwholesome climate, aggravated by the indolence and incapacity of the local authorities in sanitary matters. Both consumption and yellow fever have proved more fatal here than at any other port in South America, so far as we could draw comparisons.

The well-equipped marine arsenal of Rio is of considerable interest and importance, as there is no other port on the Atlantic coast, between the Gulf of Mexico and Cape Horn, where a large modern vessel can go into dry dock for needed repairs. This receptacle is ample in size, and is substantially built of granite. Such an establishment as a national shipyard is a prime necessity to a commercial country like Brazil, which has eleven hundred leagues of seacoast.

In the Plaza Constitution, which is a very grand and spacious park in the heart of the city, there is an elaborate and costly statue of the father of the late emperor, of heroic size. The pedestal is surrounded by four bronze groups, representing typical scenes of early Indian life in this country. The Paseo Publico is also a garden-like spot, extending three or four hundred feet along the bay. This is a cool and favorite resort of the populace. On the corners of the principal streets and squares there are little octagonal structures called kiosks, gayly painted, where hot coffee, lottery tickets, and bonbons are sold, as well as newspapers and flowers. Here, as in Havana, the city of Mexico, Naples, and many European cities, the lottery proves to be a terrible curse to the common people, draining their pockets and diverting them from all ideas of steady-going business. It is customary also for the regularly organized business establishments to patronize the lottery with never-failing regularity, charging a certain monthly sum to expense account, but the money is nevertheless paid out for lottery tickets. The bad moral effect of this upon clerks and all concerned is very obvious. When by chance any prize, be it never so small, is awarded, a great flurry is made of the fact, and advertisements emphasize it, thus to incite fresh investments in this organized public swindle. Tickets are sold by boys and girls, men and women, and half the talk of the thoughtless multitude is about the lottery, how to hit upon lucky numbers, and so on.

It is a mistaken though popular idea that our New England consumptives have only to seek some tropical locality to alleviate their special trouble. Rio seems to be particularly fatal to persons suffering from pulmonary troubles. The same may be said of many other tropical regions. When consumption is developed in the Bahamas, Cuba, or the Sandwich Islands, for instance, it runs its fatal course with a speed never realized in the Northern States of America. Physicians do not send patients to foreign localities so indiscriminately as they used to. Almost every sort of climate is to be found within the borders of the United States, where also civilized comforts are more universally to be obtained than abroad. Besides which, an invalid does not have to brave seasickness and other ocean hardships, if sent to some eligible locality within our own borders.

Though Brazil has long been, and is still, famous for its production of diamonds, precious stones, and gold, yet these are as nothing when compared with her exports of sugar, coffee, and hides, not taking into account her product of rice, cocoa, tobacco, dyewoods, and other important staples. A large portion of the abnormal growth of her forests is valuable for its timber, resins, fibre, and fruits. It is naturally a very rich country, with a world of wealth in its soil, but miserable financial mismanagement has caused the national treasury to become utterly bankrupt, and at this writing mercantile credit is an unknown quantity, so to speak. The natural resources of the country are unlimited; therefore it must be only a question of time when a healthy reaction shall set in, and a period of sound prosperity follow.

It should be remembered in this connection that the immediate country of which we are speaking, that is, Brazil as a whole, is as large as the United States, leaving out the territory of Alaska.

CHAPTER IX.

Outdoor Scenes in Rio Janeiro.—The Little Marmoset.—The Fish Market.—Secluded Women.—The Romish Church.—Botanical Garden.—Various Species of Trees.—Grand Avenue of Royal Palms. —About Humming-Birds.—Climate of Rio.—Surrounded by Yellow Fever.—The Country Inland.—Begging on the Streets.—Flowers. —"Portuguese Joe."—Social Distinctions.

It would require many pages to properly describe Rio Janeiro with its curious phases of street life, its manners and customs, its local peculiarities, and moving panorama of events, all combining to make up a unique personality. These out-of-door scenes go far to tell the true story of any special locality. The fruit and vegetable market, near Palace Square, is a highly attractive place to visit at early morning. The negro women venders, always stout and portly creatures, with heads turbaned in many-colored bandannas, are eloquent in recommending their articles for sale, and are also very shrewd at a bargain. It is not uncommon for these middle-aged negresses to stand six feet high, without shoes or stockings, and to turn the scales at double the average weight of men of the same color and class. These women were all slaves in their girlhood. As regards prices charged for provisions, fruits, and vegetables, in the markets of Rio, they seemed to the author rather exorbitant, but doubtless permanent residents do not pay such sums as are charged to strangers for the same articles. We were heartily laughed at by a housekeeper on stating the cost of a small basket of choice fruit which we had purchased, being told that we had paid four times its market value. However, it was well worth the price to us, who had just arrived from an ocean voyage of five thousand miles and more. On shipboard fruit is necessarily a scarce article, and it was certainly worth something extra to be introduced for the first time to the luscious products of this region.

The abundance and variety of flowers, as well as their cheapness and fragrance, make them a desirable morning purchase, with all their dewy freshness upon them. Oranges, limes, pineapples, lemons, alligator-pears, cocoanuts, grapes, mangoes, with an infinite variety of other fruits, make up the stock in trade, together with squealing pigs, live turkeys, and noisy guinea-fowls. Here also are various gaudy feathered songsters, in cheap, home-made cages, besides monkeys, marmosets, and other household pets. The macaws, chained by the leg, and the screaming parrots vie with each other and with the monkeys in the amount of noise they make. Wicker baskets filled with live ducks, geese, and fowls are borne on the heads of native women, who have brought them many a long weary mile from far inland, hoping to make a few pennies by their sale. The chatter of the women, the cries of men and animals, an occasional quarrel between two noisy Italians, ending in furious vociferations and gesticulations, all add to the Babel of sound. One little marmoset put his hand into that of the author, looking so appealingly into his face that, imagining the little fellow might be hungry, some nice edibles, calculated to rejoice the monkey heart, were promptly purchased and gratefully received by the marmoset, which, in his eager haste to consume the same, stuffed the sides of either jaw to alarming proportions. The little creature was wonderfully human, and having found a kindly disposed stranger, insisted upon keeping one of his tiny hands in our own, while he rapidly filled his mouth with the other.

It is interesting to observe the artistic manner in which the native women, Indians and blacks, mingle and arrange the various fruits and vegetables, showing a natural instinct for the harmonious blending of colors and forms. A pile of yellow oranges, green limes, and mangoes had a base of buff-colored bananas picturesquely arranged with all the pointed ends of the finger-like fruit outward, while a luscious ripe pineapple formed the apex of the pile, set off jauntily by its cactus-like, prickly leaves. On the borders of the market and along the iron railing of Palace Square, black-haired, bareheaded Italian women displayed cheap jewelry, imitation shell, gilded combs, and other fancy trinkets for sale, embracing priestly knick-knacks, ivory crosses, crucifixion scenes, coral beads, high-colored ribbons, and gaudy kerchiefs. The bronzed faces of these black-eyed, gypsy-like women were very cadaverous, as though the land of their adoption did not particularly agree with them. It seems hardly possible that these peddlers could gain a livelihood trading in these tawdry and utterly useless articles among such a humble, impecunious class of customers as frequent the market, and yet their numerous wide-open, shallow tin boxes showed a considerable stock of goods.

The fish market is a curious sight in the variety of colors and shapes afforded by the inhabitants of the neighboring bay, where most of them are caught. What an array of finny monsters!—rock-fish, large as halibut, ray, skates, craw-fish, cuttle-fish, and prawns half as large as lobsters, together with devil-fish and oysters. Funny idea, but these oysters, many of them, are grown on trees! How is this possible? Let us tell you. The mangrove trees line the water's edge; many of the branches overhang the sea, and are submerged therein. To these young oysters affix themselves, and there they live and thrive. The same phenomenon was observed by the author some years ago in Cuba. These oysters are found in small corrugated shells scarcely larger than a good-sized English walnut, which they somewhat resemble.

In the fish market one sees some very original characters among the negro women who preside over the finny tribe. They are large, good-natured creatures, quick at a trade, and quite intelligent. We recall one, who was a prominent figure among her companions. She was tall, portly, and strong as a horse. Her head was decked with a bandanna kerchief of many colors, her flat nose and protruding lips indicating close African relationship. Secured behind one of her ears was a cigarette, while a friction match protruded from the other, ready for use. Her coarse calico dress, of deep red, was covered in front by a brown linen apron extending nearly to her bare feet. Her uncovered arms were about as large as a man's legs. This negress dressed the several kinds of fish with the facility of an expert, making change for her patrons with commendable promptness, and dismissing them with a good-natured smile, adding some remark which was pretty sure to elicit hearty laughter.

As we stood viewing these things, a noisy fellow made himself very obnoxious to every person whom he met. He had evidently been too often to the neighboring spirit-shops. A police officer arrested the man by touching him lightly on the shoulder and saying a few words to him; then, pointing ahead, made the fellow precede him to the lock-up. Though this disturber of the peace was half drunk, he knew too much to resist an officer, which is considered to be a heinous offense and is severely punished in Rio. It was natural to contrast this scene with the violent resistance offered by offenders with whom the police of New York and Boston have often to deal.

The streets of Rio, at all times of the day, present a motley crowd of half-naked negroes, overladen donkeys, lazy Portuguese, Italian, and Spanish loafers, smoking cheap cigars, with here and there a Jew hawking articles of personal wear, women with various heavy articles upon their heads, water carriers, vociferous sellers of confectionery, all moving hither and thither, each one intent upon his or her individual interest and oblivious of all others. The background to this kaleidoscopic picture is the low, stucco-finished houses, painted in lively red, yellow, or blue, interspersed here and there by bas-reliefs, the whole reflecting the rays of a torrid sun. Though it is all quite different, yet somehow it recalls the narrow, crowded streets and bazaars of Cairo and Alexandria. It is very natural, in passing, to regard with interest those screened balconies, and to imagine what the lives may be of the half orientally excluded women within them, while occasionally catching luminous glances from curious eyes. The notes of a guitar, or those of the piano, often reach the ear of the passer-by, sometimes accompanied by the ringing notes of a song, for the ladies of Brazil are extremely fond of music; indeed, it seems to be almost their only distraction. Of books they know very little, and any literary reference is to them like speaking in an unknown tongue. Even the one poet of Portugal, Camoens, appears to be a stranger on this side of the Atlantic. The isolation and want of intellectual resort among the average women of this country are a sad reality, and are in a degree their excuse for some unfortunate indulgences and immoralities, domestic unfaithfulness being as common here as in Paris or Vienna.

The majority of the Brazilian women marry at or before the age of sixteen, and become old, as we use the term, at thirty. The climate and the cares of maternity together age them prematurely. In early youth, and until they have reached twenty three or four years, they are almost universally very handsome, but this beauty is not retained, as is often the case among the sex in colder climes. Of their charms, it must be honestly admitted that they are almost purely physical (animal); the beauty which high culture imparts to the features, by informing the mind and developing the intellect, is not found as a rule among Brazilian women. Of course there are some delightful and notable exceptions to this conclusion, but we speak of the women, generally, of what is termed the better class. Now and then one meets with ladies who have been educated in the United States, or in Europe, upon whom early and refined associations have left an unmistakable impress. The superiority of such is at once manifest, both in general ease of manner, and the inexplicable charm which high breeding imparts.

One searches in vain for a full-faced, well-developed, hearty looking man, among the natives in the streets of this capital. The average people, both high and low, are sallow, undersized, and cadaverous. Sunken cheeks and thin figures are the rule among the men, a passing North American or Englishman only serving to furnish a strong and suggestive contrast. These people have brilliantly expressive eyes, with handsome teeth and mouths, though half shriveled up and undeveloped in body. If one pauses to analyze the matter, he comes to the conclusion that vice and short commons, unwholesome morals and an unwholesome climate, have much to do with this prevailing appearance, which must be in part hereditary, to be so universal, commencing some way back and increasing with the generations. As in Mexico, gentlemen meeting on the streets of Rio hug each other with both arms, at the same time inflicting two or three quick, earnest slaps with the flat of the hand upon the back. This is perhaps after an absence of a few days; but if they meet ten times a day, off come their hats, and they shake hands with the most earnest demonstrations, both at meeting and at parting. Kissing on both cheeks is common enough in many parts of Europe among society people, but this hugging business between men meeting upon the public streets strikes one as a waste of the raw material.

It goes without saying that the popular religion of Rio Janeiro and the country at large is that of the Romish Church, though all denominations are tolerated by the laws of the republic. In some districts it is the same here as in Mexico and continental Spain, the Protestants being persecuted in every possible manner. Nevertheless, the power of the priesthood, we were creditably informed, is on the wane. They owe the loss of it in a great measure to the gross abuse of their positions and their shamefully immoral lives. No one conversant with the true state of the case, be he Protestant or Romanist, can deny this statement. The author thought that the Roman Catholic priests of Mexico were about as wicked a set of men as he had ever met with, taken as a whole, but further experience in South America has convinced him that the Mexican priesthood have their equals in immorality in Brazil, and elsewhere south of Panama. The popular religion of the country is one of the saddest features of its national existence, forming the great drag-weight upon its moral, and indirectly upon its physical progress.

The Botanical Garden of Rio is a justly famous resort, situated about six miles from the city, behind the Corcovada, between that mountain and the sea, but it is easily reached by tramway, or better still by a delightful drive along the shore of Botafogo Bay, over a road shaded by imperial palms, together with occasional clusters of the ever beautiful bamboo, the sight of which recalled the luxuriant specimens seen in Japan and Sumatra. The nearest approach to this admirable public garden is to be found at Kandy, in the island of Ceylon, which, as we remember it, is considerably more extensive, and presents a larger variety of tropical vegetation. The examples of the india-rubber tree, especially, are finer in the Asiatic garden than we find them at Rio. A tall, slim-stemmed sloth-tree, straight as an arrow, and bare of branches or leaves except at the top, was pointed out to us here. It is so called because it is the favorite resort of that animal. This creature is very easily captured, and the natives are fond of its meat, which may be nutritious, but it can hardly be called palatable. As it is almost entirely a vegetable-feeding animal, we know not why there should be any objection to the meat it produces. The sloth climbs up into the tall branches of the tree described, though it does so with considerable difficulty, and there remains until it has consumed every leaf and tender shoot which it bears; then the voracious creature wanders off to find and denude another.

The bread-fruit tree is interesting, with its handsome feathery leaves, and its large, melon-shaped product. It grows to fifty feet in height, and bears fruit constantly for three quarters of the year, then takes a three months' rest. It is only equaled in the profuseness of its product by the banana, forming one of the staple sources of food supply to the lazy, indolent denizens of tropical regions. The candelabra-tree, with its silver-tinted foliage, is one of the beauties of this charming Brazilian garden. Among other notable trees are fine specimens of the camphor-tree, the tamarind, the broad-spreading mango, opulent in fruitfulness, the flowering magnolia, also the soap-tree, with its saponaceous berries. The cochineal cactus was thriving after its kind, near by what is called the cow-tree, which interests one quite as much as any of its companions, rising over a hundred feet in height, with a red bark and fig-like leaves. The milk which it yields is of cream-like consistency, very similar to that from a cow, and it may be used for any ordinary purpose to which we put that article. The tree is tapped, as we treat the sugar-maple, in order to obtain its very remarkable and useful product. It is nutritious, that is freely admitted; but most probably it has some medicinal properties of a latent character, though of this we could learn nothing.

The world-famed avenue of royal palms in the Botanical Garden of Rio is unique, being undoubtedly the finest tropical arboretum in the world arranged by the hand of man. We saw here a delicate little member of the palm family, a sort of baby tree, known as the small-stemmed palm of Pará. Many trees from Asia have become domesticated side by side with the maple, the pine, and the elm from New England. Some of the large trees were decked with orchids and hanging lichens, the dainty and fantastic ornamentation of nature herself, not promoted by artificial means. The humidity of the atmosphere especially facilitates the growth of this beautiful family of plants, which are as erratic in shape as they are variegated in prismatic colors.

It would require a whole chapter to do even partial justice to this remarkable garden behind the Corcovado mountain.

One sees here myriads of delicate humming-birds, wonderful animated gems of color, remarkable in Brazil for their metallic hues. Such brilliancy of lustre, glancing in the warm sunlight, is fascinating to behold. The Spaniards call these delicate little creatures "winged flowers," and the Portuguese, "flower-kissers." A lady resident of Rio told the author of the vain attempt of a patient German scientist to domesticate a few specimens of these birds. He commenced by taking them from the nest soon after they were hatched, at various periods of their growth, and even after they had learned to fly, but although infinite care was taken to supply their usual food, and also not to confine them too closely, the naturalist was fain to acknowledge the impossibility of accomplishing his object, though the experiment extended over a period of two years. The ceaseless activity of this frail little bird renders any circumscribing of its liberty fatal to existence.

Delicate, innocent, and apparently harmless as butterflies, these diminutive creatures are often very pugnacious, and when two males engage in a contest with each other, which is not seldom the case, one or the other often loses his life. If disturbed during the period of incubation, they will attack large birds and even human beings, directing their long, needle-like bills at the offender's eyes. Our informant told us the particulars of a man who, under such circumstances, came very near losing both of these organs. Scientists have succeeded in preserving over two hundred different specimens of this little feathered beauty, representing that number of species indigenous to Brazil. Some of these are only five or six times as large as a humble-bee. The artificial flowers already referred to as being for sale in the shops of Rio depend almost entirely upon the humming-bird for their delicate beauty; no other feathered creature affords such marvelous colors and exquisitely fine material for the purpose. The best specimens of this work are necessarily expensive, requiring, besides a truly artistic taste and eye, skill of execution, infinite patience, and much time, to produce them. We saw a choice design of this sort, measuring about fifteen by twenty inches, framed under a glass, the design being a bouquet of natural flowers, for which the asking price was five hundred dollars; four hundred and fifty had been refused. The feathers were almost entirely from the throat and breast of humming-birds, arranged by a woman who had made this work the occupation of her life from girlhood. We learned that such a piece of artistic effect represented nearly a year's labor!

One also finds in the Rio shops flower-pieces ingeniously formed from the scales of high-colored fishes, as well as from the wings and bodies of native insects characterized by brilliant colors, but these of course will not compare in delicacy and beauty with the products of the feathers. The Brazilian beetle is prepared in a myriad of ornamental forms and in many combinations, sometimes mingled with feathers. In the Rua dos Ourives there are two or three shops where a great variety of such objects is offered for sale. These stores have also many choice native stones of great beauty, including the true Brazilian topaz, for which there is a growing and appreciative demand.

The idea prevails that the climate of Rio is like some parts of Africa, suffocatingly hot all the time, but this is not correct. The American consul told the author that he had suffered more from the cold than from the heat in the environs of the city, where his residence is in a rather elevated district. He declared that the temperature, even in town, was rarely so extreme as is often found in the cities of the United States. He believes that the yellow fever might be effectually banished from Rio by the adoption of strict quarantine and effective sanitary measures in the city proper. As we have already intimated, consumption prevails here to an alarming extent. This is doubtless owing to the peculiar dampness of the atmosphere. We found that statistics show one half as many deaths from consumption as from yellow fever, taking the aggregate of five years. "The one disease comes annually in the heat of summer only, as a rule," said our informant, "while the other prevails more or less all the year round, year in and year out." During the two weeks which the author stopped at Rio, forty and fifty fatal cases of yellow fever a day were recorded, and doubtless more than that number actually fell victims to its ravages, as only those who died in the several hospitals were enumerated. We were in the city in June, one of the winter months in this latitude. Heretofore the fever has nearly always disappeared, as an epidemic, by the first or middle of May, even in years when it has been most prevalent and fatal. Notwithstanding the charm of novelty which so absorbs the stranger, we are free to confess there was a lurking dread of the subtle enemy which proved so swift and fatal all about us. Fifty deaths daily by yellow fever in a population exceeding half a million only served to show that it still lingered in a sporadic form where the seeds are perhaps never entirely exterminated. It most readily attacks strangers and the unacclimated, but no class is exempt. The indigent, careless, drunken portion of the population are no more liable, we were informed, to contract the disease than others of better habits. This outrages all preconceived notions of diseases of this character, but we were assured by good authority that it was really so. The day we left Rio, the English Bishop, a most estimable man, who was universally respected and beloved, died of the fell disease.

The summer season begins in October and lasts until April, and is better known here as the wet season, the rain falling with great regularity nearly every afternoon, and at about the same time. Usually an hour of liberal downpour is experienced, then it promptly clears up and becomes bright and pleasant. The warmest month is February. The winter months are May, June, July, and August; this is the dry season, during which very little rain falls. The climate appears to be particularly injurious to persons who are troubled with a torpid liver. Elephantiasis is indigenous, but it is not very common; the few cases seen were upon the streets, and were those of negroes who exposed their diseased limbs to excite public pity, making the affliction an excuse for systematic begging. A score of such unfortunates were seen daily in and about Palace Square, and one or two regularly posted themselves before the Globe Restaurant, which is the Maison Dorée of Rio Janeiro.

The well-to-do merchants do not think of living in town, but select some pleasant spot in the environs, where they erect picturesque homes, often extremely attractive to the eye architecturally, and surrounded by lovely gardens, containing both native and exotic plants and trees. The contrast between commercial and rural Rio is something very striking. One presents all the grossness and belittling aspect of money-getting, the other the graces, liberality, and ennobling appearance of culture and refinement. Of all the trees in these attractive environs, the palm, in its great variety, challenges one's admiration most. We mention it frequently, for it was our constant delight. At every turn one comes upon it, in its several species,—the cocoa-palm, the palmetto, the cabbage, the assai-palm, the fanshaped-palm, and scores of other varieties. The hand and taste of woman are seen in these gardens of the environs. Flowers are selected and arranged as only feminine taste could suggest, while the broad piazzas are simply floral bowers and gardens of placid delights.

The province round about Rio is beautified and rendered profitable by the many large coffee plantations, particularly attractive when the well-trimmed bushes are seen in full bearing, bending under the weight of red berries. Orange orchards abound, the branches of the trees heavy with the rich golden fruit; yet as an orange-producing section, Florida, in our own country, is fully its equal. The fruit of the southern part of the United States is much better and more intelligently cultivated, and is larger and fairer, than the fruit of this region. We except Bahia, however, in this remark; that is the very paradise of oranges. Besides the abundance of fruits, Flora reigns in Brazil, and near to Rio bignonias, passifloras, variegated honeysuckles, morning-glories, magnolias, and orchids mingle with the dark green mango trees and the delicate light green mimosas which meet the eye everywhere. It appears that the several species of flowers have their special season for blooming, when they are at their best, so that a large variety is always seen in bloom at all times in the year. We must confess to having felt half lost without the "Queen of Flowers," our grand favorite; but as to roses, it was found that the ever present ants maintained a fixed hostility to them, rendering it particularly difficult to rear them in this country. In all of the many lands we have visited, the author has never seen such superbly developed roses as are produced in and about the city of Boston. There is some quality in the climate of New England, added to the genius of her famous florists, especially adapted to their perfection.

The broad leafed umbrella-tree—*chapeo do sul*—is often seen in this neighborhood cultivated as a shade tree, both in town and country, while the thick clustering bamboo, so often referred to, adds its unique beauty to the environs in all directions. The banana and plantain, both cultivated and wild, thrive hereabouts, and form an important adjunct to the food supply of all classes. The banana is cultivated by offsets, and is of rapid growth, coming to maturity and bearing fruit a few months after it is planted. Brazil seems to be well called the home of fruits and flowers.

Has the reader ever chanced to hear of "Portuguese Joe," of Rio Janeiro? He is a man as well known in the capital of Brazil as the late emperor. Ostensibly he is only a successful shipchandler, wholesale grocer, purveyor—by appointment—to the American and British naval ships which put into Rio, or which are stationed here; but over and above his extensive commercial relations, we found him to be a Good Samaritan. He is quite ready for legitimate business, and has realized a handsome fortune by fair and honorable dealing. He charges a reasonable profit upon the various supplies which he furnishes, but his goods are exactly what he represents them to be, and he has the confidence of all who deal with him. His establishment grew up from a small beginning, he having come from Portugal to engage in business when only thirteen years of age. To-day he is in the prime of life, and his store on the Paraça de Dom Pedro II. is a city institution. The highest official, the wealthiest bankers, and the most influential merchants are glad to shake him cordially by the hand. Signor J. C. V. Mendes—the other title being a trade *nom de plume* of long standing—is a gentleman by nature, and a true friend to all strangers who seek his counsels on arriving at Rio. We fortunately became acquainted with Signor Mendes on the first day of our landing, and are glad to speak of his ready courtesy and desire to make all Americans at home who arrive in the capital of Brazil. It is no particular recommendation, but it is a pleasure to say that, with his calm, self-possessed manner, his brilliant black eyes and genial smile lighting up his bronzed features, he is unquestionably the handsomest man whom we chanced to meet in Rio Janeiro. Manly beauty is not an imperative adjunct to excellence, but is still a very agreeable accessory.

One naturally anticipates but will not find any social distinction as to race in this city. Color opposes no obstacle to progress in educational or official position. Pupils of the public schools meet on the same footing and mingle promiscuously. There is nothing to prevent the intelligent negro from becoming a judge or minister of state, or from filling any high civil office, if he develops proper ability. Many bureaus in the public offices are held by colored men, observably in the custom house, and the race generally is regarded with far more respect than with us in the United States.

Providence has liberally endowed the larger portion of Brazil with a fertile soil, an unrivaled flora, and a delightful climate. For a tropical country, it is remarkably temperate and salubrious. It has mountain scenery excelling that of Switzerland, with fertile valleys surpassing those of Italy, and myriads of rivers affording ample means of transportation with natural and abundant irrigation. Unlike many of her sister states, including those on the west coast of the continent, she is exempt from earthquakes and the destruction caused by devouring tidal waves. While so much of Mexico and thousands of miles of the Pacific coast are scorched by drought, there are no districts of Brazil exempt from regular and refreshing rains, the importance of which cannot be overestimated. To crown all else, the splendid harbor of her capital by its size, safety, and beauty invites the commerce of the world. It would certainly seem, when we realize all of these special advantages, that nature had intended so large and favored a portion of the globe to ultimately be the home of a great, powerful, and prosperous nation.

That the material growth of Brazil is mainly in the right direction is manifest to the most casual observer. The many lines of railways penetrating the country in every province will by and by prove to be effective means of development. Wherever the facilities are liberally afforded, not only individuals, but ideas, are sure to travel, and social and material improvement must follow. Civilization keeps pace with the iron horse. When the street rails penetrated the cañons of Utah, polygamy was doomed. Material facts are stronger than arguments of well-meaning moralists. The establishment of so many railroads through the wilds of South America may not be a paying matter, it is not so at this writing, but a great moral purpose, and that of true progress, will be subserved by them. They will be the agents of enlightenment and civilization to many wild tribes of Indians, at the same time opening broad and favorable tracts of territory for settlement by emigrants from the crowded and overstocked states of Europe.

On the homeward passage, when we visited Rio Janeiro for the second time, it was found to be rife with politics; but like Joseph's coat, of so many colors as to be confusing to a foreigner. It may reasonably be doubted if the natives themselves clearly understood what they wanted. The revolutionary element seemed very strong, and was led by men who had nothing to lose by agitation, but everything to gain by a lawless uprising. The most intelligent citizens predicted a popular revolution of some sort in the near future, and their anticipation proved to be correct. Revolution is chronic in South America.

CHAPTER X.

Petropolis.—Summer Residence of the Citizens of Rio.—Brief Sketch

of the late Royal Family.—Dom Pedro's Palace.—A Delightful
Mountain Sanitarium.—A Successful but Bloodless Revolution.—
Floral Delights.—Mountain Scenery.—Heavy Gambling.—A German
Settlement.—Cascatinha.—Remarkable Orchids.—Local Types.—A
Brazilian Forest.—Compensation.

Petropolis,—or the city of Peter,—the fashionable summer resort of the
citizens of Rio Janeiro, is a modern town, dating only from 1844, and
contains at that season of the year a population of some eight thousand. The
intense heat of the crowded city in the summer months, not to mention its
usually unhealthy condition, makes even the acclimated inhabitants seek a
refuge in the hills. So long as the fever continues to rage, merchants leave
their families here, and come up nightly to sleep and breathe the fresh, pure
air. It is only on the coast and in crowded communities that epidemics prevail.
We were told by residents that a case of yellow fever never originated at
Petropolis; that it was too elevated for the citizens to fear anything of the sort.
It is so generally throughout the country; the yellow fever prevails only in the
ports and at sea level, a peculiarity also observable in Cuba and the several
West Indian islands. When the fever prevails, as it does annually at Havana
and Matanzas, the wealthy citizens, and all unacclimated people who are able
to do so, retire inland to elevated localities, where they are comparatively safe
from the scourge. The same rule applies to the coast cities of South America,
—Pará, Pernambuco, Bahia, etc. It is a very important matter to the merchants
of Rio that they have, within two or three hours' reach of their overheated city
offices, a resort where they can sit in a dry skin and sleep in quiet and
comfort. Had they not this resort, they would be obliged to succumb to
disease, or to leave Rio for half of the year annually.

Petropolis is situated in the Organ Mountain range, about thirty miles from
the metropolis, and is something less than three thousand feet above tide-
water. The town is built in a slight depression among the well wooded hills,
forming a vale of alpine beauty, easily reached from Rio by boat and rail. The
latter portion of the trip, comprising a sharp mountain ascent, is made by a
system of railroad like that by which the summit of Corcovado is reached.
The popular route is to cross the harbor at Rio by a large and commodious
steamboat, a distance of twelve miles, and then to take the steam-cars. There
is also another railroad route, all the way by land. The late emperor's summer
palace is the prominent feature of Petropolis, together with its elaborate
gardens, covering some fifteen or twenty acres of land. Hither come the
diplomatic representatives of foreign nations to enjoy the salubrious mountain
air and the hospitable society of the best people of Rio Janeiro, and to lay
aside many of the constraints of city life. A great contrast is apparent here to
the crowded streets and narrow lanes of the uncleanly capital, while the air is

undoubtedly remarkable for its healthful and invigorating qualities. The summer palace is surrounded by elegantly arranged grounds, planted with rare flowers and choice trees from every clime. In general effect it resembles an old English country house, except for the tropical vegetation, the fine verdant lawns of grass, the only ones of any extent in the country, being particularly noticeable. This mountain resort has been called the Versailles of Brazil.

It seems appropriate to recall, in brief, the family history of the late emperor, Dom Pedro II., of whose favorite abiding-place we are speaking. He enjoyed a distinguished reputation among modern rulers, was liberal, scholarly, and possessed of great experience of men and the world at large. Having been an observant and studious traveler in many parts of the globe, his endeavor was to adopt the best well-tried systems of other governments in educational and other matters relating to political economy. His system was mild, progressive, and designed for the general good of the people over whom he presided; in fact, it was too mild for the turbulent, unlettered masses of the provinces of Brazil. They were not intellectually prepared for such leniency.

The royal family of Portugal fled hither in 1808, at the time of Napoleon's invasion of that country, but returned to Europe in 1821. A national congress assembled at Rio Janeiro the next year, and chose Dom Pedro, eldest son of King Joâo VI. of Portugal, "Perpetual Defender of Brazil." He proclaimed the independence of the country, and was chosen "Constitutional Emperor." In 1831 he abdicated in favor of his only son, Dom Pedro II., who reigned as emperor until November 15, 1889, when he was dethroned by a bloodless revolution, and, together with his family, was exiled, Brazil declaring herself a republic under the title she now bears of the United States of Brazil. The feeling was nearly universal among the Brazilians that they desired to live under a republican form of government, but Dom Pedro II. was a man of such estimable character, so just, intelligent, and popular a ruler, that the revolution, which finally dethroned him, was deferred long after it was determined upon. The peaceful manner in which it was finally achieved is perhaps without precedent, and shows how thoroughly the mind of the active spirits of the nation was made up to this end. It was a political *coup d'état*, accomplished without the burning of an ounce of gunpowder. The emperor himself seemed to accept the position as a foregone conclusion. We learned from persons who had been quite intimate with him that he had already anticipated the whole condition of affairs, foreseeing that it was inevitable. If this is so, he was wise as well as diplomatic and humane, for he had enough devoted adherents about him to have made a serious though doubtless futile conflict for possession. There are always myriads of the unthinking rabble ready to join and even fight for authority which is already established, especially when seconded, as was the case with Dom Pedro, by a strong personal popularity.

The palace at Petropolis is, with its extensive grounds, now offered for sale, the country having no further use for palaces. It is understood that a local syndicate propose to purchase the whole and cut up the land into building lots, which are very much in demand just at this writing. It would not be surprising if Petropolis were to double its population during the next four or five years. Speculators are already at work "booming" the place, and a summer home here is just what the Rio merchant requires.

Some queer stories are told about the every-day life of Dom Pedro by his neighbors. It seems, according to these reports,—for the truth of which we cannot vouch,—that he often chose as his associates and advisers uneducated persons of very humble origin, who had accumulated wealth by shrewdness and industry, besides which he latterly exhibited many very peculiar traits of character; but, as we say, it is difficult to decide whether these stories are to be relied upon. It is more than hinted that he had grown very weak minded, or, as the Scotch say, had a bee in his bonnet. At all events, it now appears that he did not possess the necessary energy and executive ability requisite to control a naturally turbulent and restless people, and that his summary dethronement, so peaceably accomplished, must have come sooner or later.

It is very natural to speculate upon the present state of affairs in this country, since the change has taken place. To render a republic possible and successful requires a liberal degree of intelligence among the common people, that is, the masses at large. Unfortunately Brazil cannot boast of such a condition among her population. The educated, cultured portion of the community is quite limited, consequently the country is hardly fit for self-government. Ignorant masses are only amenable to the strong arm, and cannot, while untaught, be controlled through the influence of reason and argument. Past experience shows us that while a republic in the United States, France, or Switzerland means freedom and order, in these half barbaric southern states it signifies an alternation of revolution and of military despotism. Subject to the rule of Dom Pedro, Brazil was alike free from despotism and from disorder, so that it may be questioned whether his liberal reign was not, under the circumstances, the truest republic for which Brazil was fitted. Indeed, while these lines are being written, the question of a return to the former style of government is openly discussed at Rio Janeiro, where a state of political imbroglio exists very similar to the conditions which caused the late disastrous civil war in Chili, on the other side of the Andes. Such a shocking outcome, however, need never be feared in Brazil as has been developed by the sister republic on the Pacific coast, since both intelligence and civilization are far more advanced in Brazil than in Chili.

The town of Petropolis and its neighborhood possesses good roads for driving purposes, this location having been for several years the pride and pleasure of the late emperor, who made the place what it now is by his liberal expenditures and the constant improvements which he instituted, paying for them out of his own private purse. The first selection of this healthful spot was also his idea, and he felt a personal pride in doing everything possible towards making it popular. The roads referred to lead one through delightful scenery and highly cultivated neighborhoods, beautified by art, until finally they lose themselves among the hills and amidst impenetrable forests. There are several fairly good hotels here, where the charges are moderate and the domestic conveniences execrable! The great variety of trees to be found in and about the town is marvelous, the palm and pine prevailing, interspersed with the beautiful feathery Brazilian cedar. The tree-ferns which grow here to a height of twelve feet are great favorites, with their bright green fronds, six feet in length, almost reaching the ground as the stalk bends gracefully with their weight. The scarlet passion flower is trained as an ornamental creeper in nearly every garden-plot, and tall fuchsias in various colors and pearl white camellias also abound. We have rarely seen the camellia in such variety of colors, or such profusion of flowers. It is often found blooming beside tall coffee-trees, themselves full of deep green clustering berries, the tree, where grown for ornamental purposes, being permitted to reach full proportions. Here one sees also a profusion of the rich green bamboo in prolific groves by the roadside, or surrounding humble cottages, thus forming a welcome shade. In midsummer, so rapid is the growth of the bamboo that every twenty-four hours adds two feet to its height, or in other words, it grows an inch each hour throughout the day and the night. Jack's fabulous beanstalk hardly surpasses the bamboo, though the former is an amusing myth, while the latter is simply a literal fact. Some very lovely gladioli and white roses were noted as adding their beauty to these charming hill gardens in the Organ Mountains. So abundant were the flowers of various kinds in the grounds which surrounded our hotel, that any one was welcome to pluck and appropriate them to the extent of his fancy. The public tables were supplied with fresh ones every day, forming great living pyramids of beautiful colors, emitting inimitable fragrance.

Our hotel was situated on gently rising ground, commanding a considerable view of the plateau on which the town stands, with Dom Pedro's palace in the middle foreground, shaded by groups of palms. It was a delight to sit out-of-doors and watch the cloud effects as they hung over the tree-covered hills and peaks, closing their ranks now and again, and sweeping over the valley like a dashing charge of cavalry; or cautiously advancing in single scuds like infantry deployed as skirmishers; or, again, mottling the sky in white and peaceful masses. At the brief twilight hour, it was like a living poem to note the varying sunset hues creeping along the valley and gleaming through the branches of the grand old trees which broke the sky-line of the mountains, and the soft lilac blush of the sky, like a profile in silhouette, with sharp curves and infinite detail. A deep, broad gulch, opening towards the west, afforded a lingering view of the golden, crimson, and pink horizon, long after the day had closed, and until the stars gleamed forth through the transparent atmosphere and glorified the advent of night.

This is nature in her happy moods. A little later, to these exquisite delights of the moment, an ugly obverse presents itself. "Only man is vile."

From opposite the open window where we sit penning these lines,—it is a Sabbath evening,—there comes the sharp rattle of diceboxes and billiard balls, together with the loud, angry talk of persons engaged at gambling games of cards, interrupted by the repeated cries of the presiding genius of the roulette table: "Make your game, signors, make your game," as he coolly rakes in the winnings of the bank. Italian, French, English, and Spanish adventurers mingle their jargon with Portuguese in the noisy throng who crowd the gambling "hell." It was said that seventeen thousand dollars were won by a Portuguese gentleman, last evening, in this "casino" just across the street, so losers to a like amount, on the same occasion, must have been rendered half desperate. The wretchedly demoralizing effect of gambling is apparent throughout all the cities of this republic, the common lotteries tempting the mass of the people, and various games of chance others who have money to risk.

Petropolis is extremely attractive in many respects, the scenery round about it very much resembling that of Switzerland. The broad streets are lined with such pretty villas and attractive gardens that one falls to making romantic pictures of possible delightful things which might naturally happen in them, and is led to peer into nooks and corners with a prying earnestness amounting almost to impertinence. These avenues contain in their centres deep canals, thirty or forty feet wide, having granite linings and the upper portion of the banks neatly sodded with grass. Through these canals the water from the surrounding hills flows in a pure, rapid stream, carrying away the drainage of the town, which is emptied into them by underground conduits. These water-ways are crossed by numerous small but substantial bridges, painted scarlet, while the rushing river imparts a delightful coolness.

The largest portion of the permanent inhabitants of Petropolis is composed of Germans, whose native tongue is heard on all sides, while the familiar clatter of wooden shoes speaks of Berlin, Dresden, and other German continental centres. The rosy-cheeked, flaxen-haired, blue-eyed children are also prima facie evidence of the prevailing nationality, though there are a large number of Italians who reside here. The latter keep small shops and are peddlers of fruit, or marble cutters and stucco workers, while many others find employment as gardeners.

The highway to a certain mining district passes through the town, and many donkeys laden with inland products are constantly to be seen in the streets en route for Rio, giving the place a business aspect hardly warranted by the local trade. From the neighboring hills charcoal burners drive their donkeys every morning, laden with that article for domestic use in the town, forming picturesque groups on the public square, where they await purchasers. Others bring small-cut wood from the hill for fuel, packed in little, narrow, toy carts, each drawn by a single donkey. Scores of donkeys bearing tall, widespread loads of green fodder are so hidden by the mass of greenery which they struggle under, that none of the animal is seen at all, leading one to imagine that Birnam wood has literally come to Dunsinane. These animals are almost always attended by women, who sell the fodder in the market and return home at night with such domestic necessities as are required. Women are the laborers here, as at home in Germany, where they perform the hard work, while their husbands guzzle beer and smoke endless tobacco.

Petropolis is, as we have said, steadily growing, but the banishment of the emperor will retard its progress, as it takes from the town its strongest element of assured success. We counted about a score of fine, large residences in course of construction. The climate here is like that of June in New England, and the verdure of the trees is perennial.

There is a charming excursion which strangers rarely fail to enjoy, namely, to a place familiarly known as the Cascades. The village adjoining these falls is called Cascatinha, and is situated in the lap of the Organ Mountains, about five miles from Petropolis. The road thither leads along the side of a small but boisterous stream, which gladdens the ear with its merry, gurgling notes, past lowly, thatched cottages, orange orchards, bamboo and banana groves, and green breadths of well-cultivated, undulating land, finally ending in the midst of a panorama of bold mountain peaks, lovely with varied gradations of tint, and subtlest effects of light and shade. Here the abundant water furnished by the river, which is artificially adapted to the purpose, forms a series of cascades and falls, at the same time furnishing the motive power for operating extensive cotton and woolen mills, which give employment to several hundred men and women. A very humble type of life mingles hereabouts with that of a much more refined character. Naked or half-clad children are seen here and there playing with those who are comparatively well dressed. Nice cottage homes adjoin those of the poorest class. Children of both sexes are observed, only partially covered with rags, who are endowed with a loveliness of eyes and features, together with handsome figures, causing one to reflect upon the unfulfilled possibilities of such childish beauty.

Men and women often bring into Petropolis and offer for sale beautiful orchids, which they find in the woods not far away. These they pack in green leaves, retaining a piece of the original bark or wood upon which they have grown. These pretty flowerings of exuberant nature are sold for a trifling price. Some are very remarkable in form and color, such as we have never before chanced to see, and for really rare ones the finders ask and receive good prices. We saw among them a specimen of the Flor del Espiritu Santo, —"Flower of the Holy Spirit,"—to find which is thought to bring to the fortunate discoverer good luck, as well as a handsome price for the orchid. These women may have passed whole days in their search of the forest, patiently breaking their way through nearly impassable jungles, before nature reveals to them one of her most dainty gems. As a rule, the forests are so dense that it is useless to try to penetrate them, except by following some beaten route,—a charcoal burner's road or a straggling way formed by a watercourse.

We well remember, but can only partially describe, the glory and beauty of the Brazilian primeval forest. The general tone of the color is brownish rather than light green, influenced by the absence of strong light, for though the sun is glowing in the open country, here it is twilight. Not one direct beam penetrates the density of the foliage, the sombre drapery of the woods. At first one is awed by the vast extent of the forest, by the dark, mournful shadows, by the gigantic trees reaching so far heavenward, forming here and there gothic arcades of matchless grandeur, and by the bewildering variety of the undergrowth. Scarcely a tree trunk is seen without its parasite, green with foliage not its own, "beyond the power of botanists to number up their tribe." These dense jungles might be in India, or a bit out of "Darkest Africa;" one is barred by an impenetrable wall of vegetation. Where palms occur, it is almost always in groups; being a social tree, it loves the company of its species. So with the bamboo, which is found in the more swampy regions, but always in groups of its own family. These damp woods are the home of the orchids; it is here that they revel in moisture, clinging to the trunks of tall, columnar trees, fattening on decayed portions of the bark, but forming bits of lovely color, while about the stems of other forest monarchs wind creeping vines of rope-like texture, binding huge trunks in a fatal embrace. Their final strangulation is slow, but it is sure,—only a question of time. Lofty trees bear charming flowers, as lowly shrubs do in our northern clime. Arborescent ferns vie with the palms in poetic beauty, with their elastic, tufted tops. Bunches of lilac and blossoms of snowy whiteness hang in the air. Drooping mosses depend like human hair from widespread branches, and soft, velvety moss carpets the way, with here and there dwarf mimosas trailing beneath the ferns. Long vines of woody climbers, in deep olive-green, twine and intertwine among the ranks of stout, aged trees, breaking out at short distances with pink, blue, and scarlet buds, rivaling the color of the birds which flash hither and thither like rays of sunlight breaking through the leafy screen. Now and again the shrill or plaintive notes of unfamiliar songsters fall upon the ear, mingling with the cooing of the wood-doves and the low drone of the dragon-fly. The magnificent arboreal growth of these forests develops itself into thousands of strange and beautiful forms, stimulated by the constant humidity of the high temperature.

The atheist must feel himself stifled for breath in the tropical forest, and his fallacious creed challenged by every surrounding object, while a new light illumines his unwilling soul with irrefutable evidences. The Supreme Being writes his gospel not in the Bible alone, but upon the grand old trees, the lowly flowers, the fleeting clouds, and upon the eternal stars. Those who seek nature for religious inspiration never fail to obtain it, untrammeled by the vulgar tenets of sectarianism or outraged by the tinsel of church forms and ceremonies.

The observant traveler from the north is fain to seek some consolation, some evidence of the glorious law of compensation, while comparing the features of these poetical latitudes with his own well-beloved but more prosaic home. He remembers that if these gaudy birds do flout in vivid colors that dazzle and charm the eye, they have not the exquisite power of song which inspires our more soberly clad New England favorites. Brilliancy of feathers and sweetness of song rarely go together, a natural fact which suggests a whole moral essay in itself. The torrid zone clothes its feathered tribes in glowing plumage, but the colder north endows hers with heart-touching melody. If the flowers of the tropics exhaust the hues of the prism, attracting us by the oddity of their forms, while blooming in exuberant abundance, the sweet and lowly children of Flora in higher latitudes greet the senses with a fragrance unknown in equatorial regions. Joy is nowhere all of a piece. Blessings, we are forced to believe, whether in the form of beauty of color, fragrance, or melody, are very equally divided all over the world, and those portions which have not one, as a rule, are almost sure to have the other. When we become eloquent and appreciative in the lively enjoyment of scenes in a new country, it is not always because they are more desirable or more beautiful than our own; it is the newness and the contrast which for the moment so captivate us. That to which we are accustomed, however grand, becomes commonplace; we covet and require novelty to quicken the observation. Were the sun to rise but once a year, in place of three hundred and sixty-five times every twelve months, we would willingly travel thousands of miles, if it were necessary, to witness the glorious phenomenon. The most charming natural objects please us in proportion to their rarity or our unfamiliarity with them.

CHAPTER XI.

Port of Santos.—Yellow Fever Scourge.—Down the Coast to Montevideo.—The Cathedral.—Pamperos.—Domestic Architecture. —A Grand Thoroughfare.—City Institutions.—Commercial Advantages.—The Opera House.—The Bull-Fight.—Beggars on Horseback.—City Shops.—A Typical Character.—Intoxication.—The Campo Santo.—Exports.—Rivers and Railways.

Santos is the name of a commercially important harbor situated on the east coast of South America about three hundred miles southwest of Rio Janeiro, after which city it is the greatest export harbor for coffee in Brazil. Otherwise it is about as uninteresting a spot as can be found on the continent. It became a city so late as 1839, and contains some twenty thousand inhabitants. Its annual export of coffee will reach an aggregate of two hundred and twenty-five thousand sacks. The bay is surrounded by a succession of hills, and is well sheltered, except on the southwest. The town is situated on the west side of the harbor, and hugs the shore, many of the houses being built upon piles. Behind the town to the westward rises a succession of mountain ranges. The immediately surrounding country is low and malarial, causing fevers to prevail all the year round. During the present season Santos has suffered more seriously from yellow fever than any other place on the coast in proportion to the number of its inhabitants. As a commercial port it has no rival in southern Brazil. Santa Catharina, Porto Alegre, and Rio Grande, the three harbors south of Santos, are rendered inaccessible for any but small craft, owing to sandbars at their entrances.

This is the present terminus of the United States and Brazil Mail steamship route from New York, and notwithstanding its many drawbacks in point of sanitary conditions, is yet growing rapidly in commercial importance. Its wretchedly unhealthy condition causes one to hasten away to the more elevated country, where St. Paul is situated, and where the traveler runs little or no risk of contracting yellow fever or malarial affections of any sort.

Santos is the port for St. Paul, with which it is connected by rail, and from which it is separated by about forty miles.

This capital of the state of São Paulo, St. Paul, contains some ninety thousand inhabitants. The province is credited with a million and a half. The city lies just under the tropic of Capricorn, southwest of Rio, about two thousand feet above the level of the sea, upon a high ridge, covering an elevated plateau of undulating hills. It enjoys the sunshine of the tropics, modified by the freshness of the temperate zone. It is venerable in years, having been founded in 1554, but it seems to have taken a fresh start of late, as its population has doubled in the last decade. As intimated, it is entirely free from yellow fever, which is so fatal at Santos, and has excellent drinking water, together with good drainage and well paved streets. The city contains some fine public buildings, and has many handsome adornments, being largely peopled by North Americans and English; the former prevail in numbers and influence, indeed, it has been called the American city of Brazil. There is also a large Italian colony settled here. St. Paul has a good system of tramways, several Protestant churches, and a number of educational and charitable public institutions, together with many of the attractions of a much larger capital. Among the popular amusements, the theatre of San José is justly esteemed, and is a well-appointed establishment in all of its belongings. There are two spacious public gardens, embellished with grottoes, fountains, choice trees, and flowers, while the private gardens attached to the dwellings are numerous and tasteful.

In the district round about the city venomous serpents are frequently met with, whose bite is as dangerous as that of the rattlesnakes of our northern climate. As the land is cleared and cultivated, they naturally and rapidly disappear. These reptiles fear man, and avoid his vicinity quite as earnestly as human beings avoid them. It is only when they are molested, trodden upon, or cornered, as it were, that they attack any one.

The city is connected with Rio Janeiro by a railway, and two other railroads run from it far inland. The Rio and St. Paul railway is fairly equipped, but the roadbed is not properly ballasted, and consequently one rides over the route in a cloud of dust, while suffering from the oscillations and jolting of the cars. This railway, however, is one of the most successful and profitable in the republic. It is some three hundred miles in length, and passes through a dozen or more tunnels, one of which is a mile and a half in length. This tunnel required seven years' labor before it was passable. There is just now a great "boom" of land values in and about St. Paul. It is towards this state that the tide of Italian emigration is largely directed, for some reason which we do not comprehend, but it is probably stimulated by a combined effort to this effect.

The passage southward from Rio Janeiro or Santos to Montevideo occupies about five days, but a large amount of rough ocean experience is generally crowded into that brief period, added to which the coasting steamers are far from affording the ordinary comforts so desirable at sea. Of the food supplied to passengers one does not feel inclined to complain, because a person embarking upon these lines does so knowing what to expect; but as regards the domestic conveniences and cleanliness generally, there is no excuse for their defective character. We are sorry to say that the class of Portuguese and Spaniards one encounters on these coasting vessels is far from decently cleanly in daily habits, carelessly adding to the unsanitary conditions.

The wind in these latitudes is not only inclined to be fierce, but it usually goes entirely round the compass at least once or twice during the voyage, and is more than liable to wind up, off the mouth of the river Plate, with a regular and furious pampero. This is a hurricane wind, which is born in the gorges of the Andes, and thence pursuing its course over nearly a thousand miles of level pampas, gains speed and power with every league of progress. The season in which these hurricanes—for in their fury they deserve to be thus designated—prevail, is from March to September, but they are liable to come at any time. The wind is considered by the people of Montevideo to be wholesome and invigorating, as far as the land is concerned, but seamen dread it on shipboard, and call it a Plate River hurricane. We know of no more disagreeable roadstead than that of Montevideo, when a pampero is blowing. We have seen ships under these circumstances, with two anchors down, obliged to resort to the use of oil on the sea, to prevent themselves from being swamped. Though the inhabitants represent a pampero to be comparatively harmless on the land, yet it does sometimes commit fearful havoc there also, especially among the unprotected herds of wild cattle on the plains, and upon all trees or plantations which lie in its devastating course. It is true that it brings with it a bracing and life-giving atmosphere from the snow-capped Andes far away, and if it could only do so with less forceful demonstration, it would be a welcome visitor in the heated days of these regions.

The most direct way to illustrate what these South American pampas are is to compare them to the vast prairies of our Western and Southwestern States. Any one familiar with those far-reaching, horizon-bounded plains knows what the pampas of the Argentine Republic are like. Beginning near the foothills of the Cordilleras, in their very shadow, as it were, these smoothed out, level lands extend hundreds of miles eastward to the great estuary of the Plate River, on the borders of the Atlantic Ocean. Though apparently sterile, the soil of the pampas, like the dry, baked land of Australia, only requires irrigation and cultivation to rival the most attractive valleys of Southern Europe. It is believed by scientists that these plains were once covered by a broad inland sea, connected directly with the Atlantic. In their present condition these pampas can hardly be called barren, since they give excellent grazing for extensive herds of wild cattle, which thrive and fatten upon the abundance of coarse, natural grass, similar to what is known as bunch grass in Texas and New Mexico. This product ripens and makes itself into standing hay, retaining its natural vitality and nutritious qualities throughout months of atmospheric exposure. After being close-cropped by the roving herds of cattle, the bunch grass renews itself, reproducing in great abundance.

Montevideo, the capital of Uruguay, is situated on the remarkable estuary of the Plate River,—Rio de la Plata, or "Silver River,"—whose spacious mouth is marked by two capes, Santa Maria and San Antonio, more than one hundred miles apart. Only a nautical observation will show just where the line of ocean ceases and that of the estuary begins. The unobservant passenger believes himself still sailing upon the broad ocean until he finally sights the land on which the city stands. The flag of Uruguay flying from various crafts —blue and white, in alternate stripes, with a glowing sun in the upper corner near the staff—indicates the near approach to the land it represents.

On the island of Flores, fifteen miles from Montevideo, there are a lighthouse and quarantine station. The island is formed by a rocky upheaval, not over twenty feet above sea level, measuring about a mile in length and two or three hundred yards in width. The fierce pamperos render the navigation of this estuary oftentimes precarious. When approaching the broad river's mouth from the north, sailors know that it is near at hand, long before land is seen, by the color of the water, which comes forth in such immense volume as to impart a distinct yellow hue to the ocean for a long distance from the coast. This effect is said to be discernible one hundred miles off the shore, but thirty or forty miles will perhaps be nearer the truth, and is at the same time a statement answering all legitimate purposes. The tide about the estuary is mostly governed by the wind, and so up the river, showing no regularity in its rise and fall. The current of the Plate opposite Montevideo runs at the rate of about three miles an hour. In extent, this ranks as the third great river of the world, draining, with its affluents, eight hundred thousand square miles of territory; a mammoth basin, which is only exceeded by those of the Amazon and the Mississippi.

The commercial activity of the port is shown by the arrival and departure daily of many large steamships, foreign and coastwise. Sixty European steamers are recorded as arriving here monthly, besides a number from the United States. The maritime business of the port is mostly in the hands of Englishmen, Americans, and Frenchmen. The native-born citizen evinces no genius in commercial matters. The department of the capital is the smallest in the republic, having an area of only twenty-five square miles, but it is fertile, well wooded and watered, its agricultural interests predominating, which is a most important fact in estimating the stability and pecuniary responsibility of any state.

The city is exceptionably well situated on a small rocky promontory, or rather we should designate it as a peninsula, jutting out into the estuary, three of its sides fronting the sea, and as its streets are nearly always swept by ocean breezes, it is cool and pleasant even in midsummer. The land rises gradually as it recedes from the shore, and then declines to the bed of a small stream which empties into the bay, thus affording a natural surface drainage. Uruguay is a little more than twelve times as large territorially as the State of Massachusetts, and is divided into thirteen departments. There are over half a million acres of land under good cultivation in the republic, the principal staples being wheat and corn. Extreme heat and extreme cold are alike unknown, the country being within the temperate zone. The mean summer temperature is 71° Fahr., that of autumn 62°, and of spring 60°. There are, therefore, but few things which the climate is too hot or too cold to produce, while for the raising of cattle on a large scale it is said to be the best section of South America, and this forms, we believe, its largest industry.

In approaching Montevideo from the sea, it is observed that the surrounding country is quite level, with scarcely a single object to break the distant view. Immediately upon landing one realizes that the city is clean and well built, though it is mostly made up of low structures one story in height. There are plenty of dwellings of two and three stories, however, in the more modern part of the town. Dominating the whole stand the lofty dome and towers of the cathedral, which faces the Plaza Constitution. The turrets are of striking proportions, each rising to the height of one hundred and thirty-three feet. The widespread dome would be grand in effect, were it not covered with glazed tiles of various colors, blue, green, yellow, and so on, the combined effect of which is anything but pleasing to a critical eye. Still, it is no more tawdry than much of the inside finish and meaningless ornamentation. There is an elaborate marble fountain in the centre of the plaza, besides some ornamental shrubbery and flowers. The very fine marble façade of the building occupied by the Uruguay Club adds to the beauty of the plaza. Near the fountain is a fanciful music stand, in which a military band is occasionally stationed to perform for the public pleasure. These South Americans would as soon give up the bull-fights as the popular outdoor evening concerts, the excellent moral effect of which no one can possibly doubt.

An abrupt hill at the head of the harbor, four or five hundred feet in height, known as the "Monte," gives the city its name, Montevideo. This hill is crowned by a small fort and lighthouse, the latter containing a revolving light which can be seen a long distance at sea. A couple of miles inland rises another hill called the Cerrito, or "little hill." Several times during revolutionary struggles, these two hills have been fortified by opposing parties, who have desired to control the city, but restless revolutionists are now at a discount, fortunately, in this republic of Uruguay, a class of uneasy spirits who have reigned quite long enough on the southern continent.

The town is built in the form of an amphitheatre, and has comparatively few edifices of importance. Its regular, straight streets and open squares are intensely Spanish. The Paseo del Molino is the fashionable part of the town, where the wealthy merchants reside in curious chalets, or *quintas* as they are called here. There is rather an extraordinary taste displayed in the matter of buildings on this Paseo. Swiss cottages, Italian villas, Chinese dwellings, and Gothic structures are mingled with Spanish and Moorish styles. This architectural incongruity is not picturesque, but, on the contrary, strikes one as very crude and ill-chosen. The charm of domestic residences in any part of the globe is a certain adaptability to the natural surroundings, and is, when well conceived, a graceful part of the whole. Inappropriate structures are to the eye like false notes in music to the ear, an outrage upon harmony. A Swiss chalet in Hindostan, or a Japanese bamboo house in England, is simply discordancy in scenic consistency. Nature should always be a silent partner in the creation and adaptation of architectural designs. In olden times the Jesuits built a large mill near this spot, and hence the name of the place.

The climate must be very equable and fine to admit of such fruit culture as exists here. The strawberries grown in the neighborhood are famous for their size and sweetness, the vines producing this favorite fruit all the year round. They are perhaps a little over-developed, and would doubtless be of finer flavor if they were smaller.

The Plaza de la Independencia is highly attractive, and so is the broad, tree-lined avenue known as the Calle del Dieziochavo de Julio, named after the anniversary of the Uruguayan declaration of independence. This, indeed, is thought to be the most effective boulevard in all South America. On festal occasions it is decorated in an original and brilliant manner, having colored draperies hanging from the windows and balconies, bright colored cambrics stretched from point to point, with the gay flag of the republic festooned here and there. Chinese lanterns are hung from the trees, and arches spanning the roadway and bearing national designs are all ablaze with ingeniously arranged gas jets. Down one side of this long avenue and up the other, it being over a hundred feet broad, a civic and military procession marches on the annual recurrence of the date which its name indicates, the several divisions headed by bands of music, with flags flying and drums beating. On such occasions the windows and balconies are filled with groups of handsome women, in gala dresses, together with pretty children in holiday costumes, who add charm and completeness to the scene. This avenue is the Champs Elysées of the southern continent, a thoroughfare of which the residents are justly very proud.

The streets and sidewalks generally are of better width in Montevideo than in most of the South American cities. Some few of the private residences display fine architectural taste, the dwellings being well adapted to the climate and the surroundings. Many of the city houses have little towers erected on their roofs, called *miradores*, from whence one gets an excellent view of the entire city and of the sea. The town is spread over a large territory, and stretches away into thinly populated suburbs, but all parts are rendered accessible by the well-perfected system of tramways which extend over fifty miles within the city and the immediate environs. In the absence of official figures, we should judge that Montevideo had a population of at least two hundred thousand. Every other nationality seems to be represented in its streets and warehouses, except that of Uruguay herself. Those "native and to the manner born" are conspicuous by their absence. Speaking of this rather curious characteristic to a friend who lives here, he replied: "There are probably fifty thousand European and North American residents doing business in this city, forming by far the most active element of the place. They are seen everywhere, to the apparent exclusion of the natives. Indigenous blood and energy could not have made this capital what it is at the present time. It is reaping the advantage of North American enterprise, English and American capital, and German shrewdness. These, combined with the natural advantages of the location and climate, will eventually make Montevideo the Liverpool of South America." Though all this goes without saying, our friend put it so aptly that his words were deemed worthy of recording. We do not hesitate to predict that the next decade will nearly double the number of the population here, as well as the aggregate of its imports and exports. No other city on the southern continent has greater advantages in its geographical position, or as regards salubrity of climate and adaptability to commerce. Were it not for the occasional visits of the howling pamperos, the climate would be nearly perfect, and even these exhibitions of a local nature are, as we have said, accepted with great equanimity by the people on land. There are few stoves, and no fireplaces or chimneys, in Montevideo. Cooking is done with charcoal on braziers out-of-doors, as is the custom in most tropical countries.

The capital of Uruguay contains the usual educational and religious, charitable and scientific, public organizations, with appropriate edifices for the same. It should certainly be considered a reading community, having more daily newspapers than London, and double as many as the city of New York; also supporting a large number of weekly newspapers and monthly magazines. As to books, so far as a casual observer may speak, they are few and far between in family circles. The men read the newspapers, and the women fill up their leisure time with music and gossip. There is a national university in Montevideo, where over six hundred pupils are regularly taught at the present time, and there are forty-eight professors attached to this admirably organized institution. We heard it highly spoken of by those who should be good judges in educational matters. The custom house, with which the stranger always makes an early acquaintance after arriving in port, is a large and costly structure, three stories in height. The opera house is worthy of particular mention, being a spacious building of the Doric order, capable of seating three thousand persons, and when it is filled at night, the interior presents a grand array of elegant costumes and female beauty, the ladies of this city being noted for their personal charms. This is a circumstance not mentioned casually as a mere compliment, but simply as a fact. The opera house covers an entire square, and has two large wings attached to the main building, one of which is devoted to business purposes, and the other contains the National Museum. There is here the nucleus of a most valuable collection, to which constant additions are being made, both by the state and through personal liberality and interest. We are sorry to say in this connection that the bull-fight, as a public exhibition, above all other styles of amusement, is the favorite one with the rank and file of the populace, which is quite sufficiently Spanish to control the matter and insure its permanency. The bull-ring, wherein these brutal and terribly demoralizing exhibitions take place on each Sabbath afternoon during the season, is situated about a league from the city proper.

It must be a country or district under Roman Catholic influence, and with more or less of a Spanish element permeating it, to admit of this style of desecrating the Sabbath, or, indeed, of indulging on any day of the week in an exhibition which is so thoroughly brutal, cowardly, and repulsive. It is a sad reflection upon the community, high and low, to state that the bull-fight is one of its popular entertainments. We have said that this is a cowardly game. The fact is, the bull is doomed from the moment he enters the arena. He has only his horns and his courage to help him in the unequal contest. The professional fighters opposed to him are all fully armed, and protected by sheltering guards, behind which they can retire at will. It is twelve experts pitted against one poor beast. Ingenious, heathenish modes of torture are devised and adopted to wound, to weaken, and to craze the victim. If it was one armed man against the bull, whether mounted or otherwise, it would be a more equal and gallant struggle,—but twelve to one! bah, it is only a cowardly game in which gallant horses and brave bulls are sacrificed by a dozen armed men. Even the matadore, who gives the final and fatal thrust with his sword, and who is looked upon as a sort of hero by the spectators, does not enter the ring to attempt the act until the bull is comparatively harmless, having been worried and wounded until he is exhausted by the struggle and the copious loss of blood, so that he is scarcely able to stand. Though reeling like a drunken man, he staggers bravely towards his fresh and well-armed enemy, showing fight to the last gasp.

Realize the moral effect of such cut-throat exhibitions upon youth! The older, cruel and hardened spectators are only rendered more so, but the young and impressionable are then and there inoculated with a love of brutality and bloodshed, fostered by every fresh exhibition which they witness.

The Exchange is a grand and spacious structure, admirably adapted to its purpose, being one of the finest business edifices in South America, to our mind infinitely superior in all respects to that of Rio, upon which so much money has been expended in meretricious designs. The author counted the names of some forty charitable institutions and associations in a Montevideo directory, eight or ten of which are maintained mostly by public endowment, such as hospitals, asylums for the poor, orphanages, industrial schools, lunatic asylums, and so on. Near the Plaza Ramirez there is a school of arts and trades, which at this writing accommodates a large body of pupils, taught by competent professors and experts. We were told that this institution was of great practical service in the cause of education, its general aim being similar to that of the Massachusetts Institute of Technology. One was hardly prepared to credit Montevideo with so many and well-sustained educational purposes as she was found to be justly entitled to. The reader will observe that we speak qualifiedly of these matters; it is only the outward and most obvious characteristics of a city, so briefly visited, of which one can speak correctly. It would have been gratifying to have remained longer in this capital, to understand more clearly the educational advantages which are offered here. In this department of progress, Montevideo seems in advance of many larger cities.

Squads of soldiers are seen lounging about the town, dressed in a uniform of the Zouave pattern, not very jaunty looking fellows, it must be confessed, but perhaps "as good food for powder as a better." The entire army of Uruguay consists of only five thousand men, of all branches. The president has also a battalion of body-guards, consisting of three or four hundred men, forming a very efficient as well as ornamental organization. This organization consists of men loyal to the administration, and beyond a doubt personally devoted to the president. The rank and file of the army embraces all shades of color, both as to mind and body, and is liable to become disaffected at the outbreak of any popular upheaval, or through the influence of designing men. This body-guard, however, being always on duty, is ready and able to turn the scale by prompt and consistent action, in favor of the established authorities, and thus nip rebellion in the bud. It is only after getting thoroughly under way that revolutionary attempts become formidable. At the inception, the strong arm promptly applied stamps out the life and courage of the mob, and renders sedition futile. "No parleying; fire promptly, and fire to kill; that ends the matter," said Napoleon. Blank cartridges and vacillation stimulate a half-formed purpose into action.

One is forced to admit that beggars are rather numerous in Montevideo,—beggars on horseback and wearing spurs. They coolly stop their small, wiry, half-fed ponies, and with magnificent effrontery beg of any stranger they chance to meet for a centavo, a copper coin worth about two cents of our American money. The incongruity of beggars mounted, while the stranger of whom they solicit alms is a pedestrian, is somewhat obvious. It must be remembered, however, that horses are very cheap in this country, and that nearly every one rides or drives. A good serviceable animal can be bought in any of the South American cities at what we should consider a mere trifle to pay for one. A well-broken young saddle-horse will bring from twenty to twenty-five dollars, but the owner, if one of the dudes about town, will expend five hundred dollars upon a silver-decked saddle, bridle, and trimmings, a Spanish peculiarity which is also observed in the city of Mexico. A pair of well-matched carriage-horses, in good condition, can be had for seventy-five or eighty dollars. Mares are not worked in this country, being solely used for breeding purposes, and have no fixed price; indeed, they are not met with in the cities. It will be seen that for a beggar to set up business here requires some capital, but not much. De Quincey would describe Spanish beggary as having become elevated to one of the fine arts.

There is a class of men in Uruguay called gauchos who devote themselves to breaking the wild horses of the pampas for domestic use. They are more Indian than Spanish, and pass their lives mostly as herdsmen of the vast numbers of animals which live in a semi-wild state upon the plains of South America. These men can hardly be said to train their horses. They only conquer them by a process of cruel discipline which thoroughly subdues the animal. After this the poor creatures are ever on the alert to obey their rider's will, prompted by a pressure of the powerful bit, and a merciless thrust of the long, sharp rowels. The gaucho reminds one of the cowboys of our Western States. He forms a very picturesque figure when seen upon his wiry little mustang, galloping along with his yellow poncho streaming behind him, his head covered by a broad-brimmed soft felt hat, his long, dark hair floating upon the breeze, and his broad, loose trousers fluttering in the wind. A lasso of braided or twisted leather sometimes swings from one hand, while the rider skillfully manages his horse with the other. Altogether the gaucho forms a picture of strong vitality and vivid color. He spends a small fortune upon his equipments, and his heavy spurs are of solid silver. He is not a hard drinker, an occasional glass of country wine satisfies him; but he will gamble all night long until he has lost his last penny to professional sportsmen, who somehow know the way to win by fair means or foul.

Few strangers who visit Montevideo for the first time will be at all prepared to see such a quantity and variety of rich jewelry in the shops. Imported dress goods of the finest quality are also offered for sale in these shops. The Parisian boulevards have no display windows which contain larger or finer diamonds, sapphires, and emeralds; indeed, this country seems to be the home of precious stones and real gems. The silversmiths exhibit goods equally artistic and elegant. The best products of Vienna, Paris, and London, in the fancy-goods line, are fully represented here. Readers who have visited Genoa will recall the fine silver filigree-work which is a specialty of that city, but some of the manufactures of this character made here are quite equal, if they do not excel, that of the Italian capital.

It seemed to be rather a singular and significant fact, that when a couple of pennies will purchase a tumblerful of the national tipple called caña, a raw liquor made from sugar-cane, and quite as strong as brandy, still comparatively few persons are seen under its influence upon the public streets. It is true that on all church festal occasions the common people have a regular carousal, and get very much intoxicated, whereupon they lose one day in repenting and two in recuperation. It is the same all over the world. The lower, uneducated classes, having no intellectual resort, seem imbued with the idea that to get thoroughly tipsy is the acme of pleasure. The inevitable punishment does not enter into the calculation at all, nor does it deter the victim from repeated excesses. It is curious to observe the peculiar effect which intoxicants produce upon people of different nationalities: the Russian gets boozy on vodka, and only becomes more loving to his species; the Mexican drinks pulque by the pint measure, and craves only to be permitted to sleep; the French guzzle brandy and wine until they become equally full of song and gayety; the American Indian is made utterly crazy and reckless by drink; the Irishman finds a fight in every glass of whiskey; and the Englishman who indulges overmuch becomes eloquent on politics and patriotism. In South America the common people who drink to excess are rendered pugnacious and revolutionary. The police arrangements of Montevideo are excellent, and the streets are safe for man or woman at any hour of the day or night, which one is forced to admit is more than can be truthfully said of the majority of large cities in either Europe or North America. There is no sickly sentimentality about crime and criminals here. If a man outrages the law, he has to suffer for it, and there is no pardoning him until he has worked out his entire penalty. It is the certainty of punishment which intimidates professional rascals. Official leniency and pardoning of criminals are a premium on crime.

Between two and three miles from the city there is a public park, which is laid out with excellent taste and skill, forming a popular pleasure resort. There are here many fine native and exotic trees, as well as flowering shrubs and blooming flowers. This spacious park, intersected by a willow-lined stream, is called the Paseo, and is ornamented with statues, fountains, and rockeries. The grounds are also occupied by several small places devoted to amusements, shooting-galleries, billiard saloons, and gambling tables, very similar to the Deer Garden in the environs of Copenhagen. Citizens of Montevideo of the humbler class come hither with their families, bringing food and drink to be disposed of in picnic fashion. Bordering the sweep of the bay, which forms the harbor, are many cottages, the homes of the rich merchants. These villas are surrounded by flower gardens and graceful shrubbery, the endless spring climate making the bloom perennial. The flat roofs of many of the town houses are partially inclosed, so as to form a pleasant resort in the closing hours of the day, where family parties are often seen gathered together. Social life among the residents of the environs is very gay, and so indeed is that of the town residents, whose hospitality is also proverbial. The Hotel Oriental is the favorite hostelry of Montevideo, built of marble and well furnished, though it is hardly equal to the Hotel Victoria, its rival, architecturally speaking.

The drinking water, and all that is used for domestic purposes in the city, is brought by a well-engineered system from the river Santa Lucia, which is tapped for this purpose at a distance of thirty or forty miles from Montevideo.

The Campo Santo of the capital is admirably arranged and particularly well kept, being in several respects like those of Pisa, Genoa, and other Italian cities. It is the most elaborate cemetery in South America, surrounded by high walls so built as to contain five tiers of niches which form the receptacles for the dead. The grounds are nearly as crowded with elaborate tombs and stone monuments as Père la Chaise, at Paris, the funereal cypress rising here and there in stately mournfulness above the marble slabs. The abundance of metallic wreaths and artificial flowers afforded another resemblance to the famous French cemetery. The freshness of many of the floral offerings showed that the memory of the departed was kept green in the hearts of those left behind. The traveler sees many such touching evidences of tenderness all over the world. Much of the marble work seen in these grounds was imported from Milan, and some from both Florence and Rome. The monumental entrance to the grounds, and the elaborate chapel within them, are both in good taste.

Beef, hides, wool, hair, and grain seem to be the principal articles of export.

Uruguay contains over half a million of people, and has an area of seventy-one thousand square miles, intersected by several railways, bringing the interior within easy reach of the capital. It is said to be growing more rapidly in proportion to its size and the present number of inhabitants than any other part of South America. The republic is best known to the world by its Indian name, Uruguay, but on many maps it is still designated as the Banda Oriental, that is, the "Eastern Border." It will be remembered that this now independent state was originally a part of the Argentine Republic, which was formerly known by that designation. Though Uruguay is one of the smallest of the independent divisions of the continent, it is yet one of the most important, a fact owing largely to its admirable commercial location. Nearly all of its territory can be reached by navigable rivers, while its Atlantic shore has a dozen good harbors. Sixteen large rivers intersect the republic in various directions, all of which have their several tributaries. Cheap internal transportation is assured by over three hundred miles of railways; also by these rivers. As already intimated, its agricultural interests are largely on the increase, the strongest element of permanency. Originally the pastoral interest prevailed over all other, but agriculture, both here and in the Argentine Republic, has taken precedence. The model farms near Montevideo are unsurpassed for extent, completeness, and the liberal manner in which they are conducted. Some large estates might be named which will compare favorably with anything of the sort which the author has ever seen in any country, where agriculture is followed on intelligent principles. Here the cultivation of the soil is carried on not solely to obtain all which can be wrung from it, in the way of pecuniary profit, but *con amore*, and with a due regard to system. As may be supposed, the return is fully commensurate with the intelligence and liberality exercised in the business. Such farming may be and is called fancy farming, but it is a sort which pays most liberally, and which affords those engaged in it the most satisfaction.

To be an honest chronicler, one must not hesitate to look at all phases of progress, successful or otherwise, on the part of each people and country visited and written about. There are always deep-lying influences acting for good or evil, which scarcely present themselves to the thoughtless observer.

One reason for the rapid growth of this republic of Uruguay is because of its gradually casting off the slough of Roman Catholic influence, a species of dry rot quite sufficient to bring about the destruction of any government. The same incubus which was of so long standing in Mexico, where its effect kept the people in ignorance and ferment for centuries, has at last been abolished, and modern progress naturally follows. In Uruguay the Romish Church has lost its prestige, having hastened its own downfall by blindly striving to enforce fifteenth century ideas upon people of the nineteenth. Monks and nuns have been expelled, and parish schools have been closed. Free schools now prevail, and general knowledge is becoming broadcast, which simply means destruction to all popish control. Intelligence is the antidote for bigotry, which explains the bitter opposition of the Roman Catholic priesthood to free schools wherever their faith prevails.

In all of these South American provinces it has been found difficult to throw off the evil inheritance of sloth and anarchy which the Spaniards imposed upon their colonial possessions. The schoolhouse is the true temple of liberty for this people. In the department of Montevideo alone there are to-day over sixty free schools, and in the whole republic nearly four hundred, something for her authorities to point at with a spirit of just pride. This enumeration does not include the private schools, of which there are also a large number in the capital.

We find by published statistics that Uruguay exports of wool, about seven million dollars' worth per annum; of beef, over six million dollars' worth; of hides, four million dollars' worth; and of wheat about the same amount in value as that of the last article named. These staples, however, are only representative articles, to which many more might be added, to show her growing commercial importance and assured prosperity.

Our next stopping-place is the important city of Buenos Ayres, on the opposite bank of the river, about one hundred and fifty miles southwest of Montevideo.

CHAPTER XII.

The city of Buenos Ayres—"Good Air"—is well named so far as its natural situation is concerned, but this condition of a pure atmosphere has been seriously affected by unsanitary conditions, naturally arising from the large influx of a very promiscuous population. A considerable percentage are Italians, and so far as personal cleanliness and decency go, they seem to be among the lost arts with them.

This thriving city is the capital of the Argentine Republic, which, next to Brazil, is the largest independent state in South America, containing fourteen provinces, each of which has its own local government, modeled after those of the United States. The average reader will doubtless be surprised, as the author certainly was, to realize that this southern republic exceeds in extent of territory the united kingdoms of Great Britain, together with France, Germany, Austria, Hungary, Italy, Spain, Portugal, Belgium, Holland, and Greece combined, the actual area being something over twelve hundred thousand square miles. The province of Buenos Ayres is just about the size of the State of New York, and contains in round numbers a population of one million. Two hundred years ago, the city of Buenos Ayres had a population of five hundred. Having the statistics at hand, it is perhaps worth while to state that, of the aggregate population of the province, a majority, or fully six hundred thousand, are foreigners, classed as follows: three hundred thousand Italians, one hundred and fifty thousand French, one hundred thousand Spaniards, forty thousand English, and twenty thousand Germans. The number of North American residents is very small, though they control a fair percentage of the exports and imports. Authentic statistics show that they number less than six hundred. Paris is not more crowded with refugees from various countries than is this Argentine capital. Why such a spot was selected on which to establish a commercial city is an unsolved riddle, as it embraces about all the natural inconveniences that could possibly be encountered on the banks of a large river. The perversity of such a selection is the more obvious, because those who made it must have passed by a score of admirable points eminently superior in all respects to the one now occupied.

The first view of Buenos Ayres on approaching it by water is peculiar, the line of sight being only broken by the church towers and a few prominent public buildings; the horizon alone forms the background of the picture. Unlike nearly all of the South American cities, there is no forest or mountain range behind or surrounding the capital. From its environs a continuous plain stretches away for nearly eight hundred miles to the foothills of the Andes. Situated between the 34° and 35° of south latitude, it enjoys a climate similar to that of the south of France, and almost identical with that of New Orleans. The site upon which the city stands is considerably above the level of the river, and though the streets are far too narrow for business purposes in the older portions of the town, they widen to a better size in the newer parts. The roadways are poorly paved, so that it is very uncomfortable to walk or drive over them. Boulevards are laid out to cut the older parts of the city diagonally, as was done in Paris and Genoa, and is now being done in Florence, so as to relieve the present insufficient capacity for the transportation of merchandise. One is apt, however, when remarking upon these particularly narrow and irregular streets in a foreign country, to forget that there are, in the older portions of the capital of Massachusetts, some quite as circumscribed and corkscrew fashioned. If we do not find all the excellences of civilization predominating, and admirable people in the majority here, we should do well to remember that we have also left them in the minority at home.

The huge custom house of Buenos Ayres, with its circular form and high walls facing the river, recalls in general appearance Castle Garden in New York harbor, or the fort on Governor's Island. In its importance as a commercial emporium, this city disputes the first place with only three others in the southern hemisphere, namely, Rio Janeiro, Sydney, and Melbourne, the latter of which has lately added greatly to its harbor facilities by deepening and widening the Yarra-Yarra River.

The dwelling-houses of Buenos Ayres are mostly built of brick, and are of a far more substantial character than those upon the west coast of the continent. They have much more the appearance of North American dwellings than Spanish, except that the windows are strongly guarded with iron bars, and the cool, shady patios present domestic scenes, mingled with flowers and fragrance, strongly local in color. The city is regularly laid out in squares of a hundred and fifty yards each, so when one is told that such or such a place is so many squares away, he knows exactly the distance which is indicated. The Plaza de la Victoria is surrounded by handsome edifices, including the opera house and the cathedral, the façade of the latter very much resembling that of the Madeleine at Paris. This square has a fine equestrian statue of some patriot, and a small column commemorating a national event. The city has a population equaling that of Boston in number, and we do not hesitate to say that it is more noted for its enterprise and general progress than any other of the South American cities. It has been appropriately called the Chicago of the southern continent. The republic, of which it is the principal city, has seven thousand miles of telegraphic wire within its area, a tangible evidence of enterprise which requires no comment. One remarkable line connects this city with that of Valparaiso, on the Pacific side of the continent, and is constructed with iron poles nearly the whole distance, crossing the Andes by means of forty miles of cable laid beneath the perpetual snows!

It may well be supposed that the inhabitants of Buenos Ayres are of a cosmopolitan character, when it is known that the daily newspapers are issued in five different languages. As shown by the statistics already given, a considerable share of the people are Italians, who form much the larger portion of the emigrants now coming hither from Europe, or who have arrived here during the last decade. As additions to the population, they form a more desirable class, in many respects, than those who seek homes further north. After the Italians, the Basques are among the most numerous of the new-comers. There are over fifty thousand of this people settled in the province of

Buenos Ayres alone, readily adapting themselves to the country. They are a strongly individualized race, whom no one is liable to mistake for any other. They maintain in a great measure the picturesque style of dress which prevails in their native land, no matter what their vocation may be here. As a rule, the Basques come with their families, bringing some moderate amount of pecuniary means with them, and at once devote themselves to agricultural pursuits. They take especially to the department of the dairy, making butter and cheese of excellent quality, for which they find a ready city market. They have a natural inclination towards cattle tending, and are looked upon by the authorities as among the very best of European emigrants. To promote this immigration to Argentina, a per capita premium has been paid heretofore by the government, who, indeed, are still ready to furnish a free passage for responsible emigrants, both of this and other nationalities. This generous offer has been so shamefully abused by the beggars, lazzaroni, and criminal classes of Naples and Sicily, that a check has necessarily been put upon it, particularly as regards the generally objectionable people of Sicily.

As a shipping port, Montevideo has a decided advantage over this Argentine metropolis. Large steamers are obliged to anchor eight or ten miles, or even more, below the city, on account of the shallowness of the river at this point. A channel has been opened to facilitate the approach of vessels of moderate tonnage, but much yet remains to be done before the experiment will be of any practical advantage. Tugboats land passengers on the quay, who arrive by the large mail steamers. Vessels of not over twenty-five hundred tons can lie at the shore and land their cargoes by means of the limited conveniences of the new dock. One would think that this want of harbor facilities was an insuperable objection and impediment in the growth of a great commercial capital, but Buenos Ayres goes straight onward, progressing in wealth and business, apparently regardless of such disadvantages. The present aggregate of its imports, in round numbers, is one hundred million dollars per annum.

Even to-day, while resting under so serious a financial cloud, with her credit at the lowest ebb, and so many of her lately wealthy merchants in bankruptcy, the city has a certain steady, normal growth, which it would appear that nothing can seriously impair. As we have intimated, the tide of immigration has been checked, though not entirely stopped, by the depressed financial and business condition of the country; still, in one closing month of the last year, October, 1891, over two thousand passengers arrived by steamship in Argentina, seeking new and permanent homes.

When a pampero is blowing, it sometimes forces nearly all of the water out of the harbor, leaving it high and dry, so to speak, though the river is thirty miles in width opposite Buenos Ayres. Passengers, baggage, and freight have in the past often been landed by means of horse carts, hung on high wheels, and driven out into the water to such a depth as would float small boats and lighters. Indeed, this was for many years the common mode of landing freight and passengers at Buenos Ayres. Two long and narrow piers which have been built partially obviate the necessity of employing carts, unless the water becomes very low. It has been said in all seriousness, and we believe it to be true, that the cost of landing a cargo of merchandise at Buenos Ayres has often been as great as the freight by vessel from New York, Liverpool, or Boston.

To construct a suitable harbor here for commercial purposes is a project attended by almost insurmountable difficulties, but the attempt is gradually being made. The water in front of the city is not only shallow, but the bottom is extremely hard, while the increase of depth down the river is so little that it would involve the dredging of soil for a distance of ten miles, together with an indefinite width. It is very doubtful if a channel in such a situation, liable to constant changes, could be effectually established and maintained at any cost. The city does not depend upon its foreign commerce alone for business, having a boundless and productive territory in its rear, of which it will always be the commercial capital. It is already a great railway centre, the republic having over seven thousand miles of iron and steel rails within its borders. Five railways radiate from Buenos Ayres at this writing, and a sixth is projected. One route has been surveyed with the idea of connecting this city direct with Valparaiso, the distance between the two capitals being about nine hundred miles. It is designed to take advantage of the road already completed to Mendoza, from whence the addition would cross the Cordilleras at a height of ten thousand feet, and pass through several tunnels, one of which would be two miles long.

It should also be remembered, while on this subject of transportation facilities, that the Paraná River is navigable for light draught steamers two thousand miles inland from Buenos Ayres, into and through one of the most productive valleys in the world. From Montevideo to Point Piedras, the river is uniformly sixty miles wide, and at Buenos Ayres it has only narrowed to about half this distance. The two main rivers which form the Plate are the Uruguay and the Paraná, which in turn unite to form the grand estuary called Rio de la Plata.

The city of Buenos Ayres has about as many miles of tramway as there are in Boston. The various routes are well managed, and afford an infinite amount of popular accommodation. This service is carried on by six different companies. It is not in the hands of one big monopoly, as with us in Boston. Competition in undoubtedly best for the public good, but the business can be more advantageously conducted by a single company. Experience has shown, however, that such a franchise is liable to great abuse in the hands of a corporation having no rivalry to fear.

The citizens suffered long and patiently for want of good water for drinking and domestic purposes. This trouble has been partially obviated for a considerable time by the establishment of extensive water-works, but they are not adequate to the demand. The means for obtaining a new and additional supply are now under consideration. A system of drainage has also been constructed, which was fully as much of a necessity as the supply of water, but which, as usual, proves to be insufficient in capacity to perform the necessary work,—at least it but partially meets the requirements for which it was designed. People grow hardened by association with danger, but the importance of good and sufficient drainage for a capital in which malarial fevers prevail hardly requires argument.

Unlike nearly all of the South American cities, Buenos Ayres has no Plaza Mayor, or public square, as a grand business and pleasure resort, a central point, par excellence, designed also for the recreation of the general public. There are, however, several spacious squares, quite large enough to represent such an idea,—nine or ten of them in fact, all of which are surrounded by fine buildings. The Plaza Victoria, for instance, already referred to, is some eight acres in extent, made brilliant at night by electric lights, which supplement the old style of gas-burners. The government house, the Palace of Justice, the cathedral, and other effective buildings front upon the Plaza Victoria. Eight or ten of the principal streets converge here, and this point is also the place of departure for several lines of tram-cars. The cathedral is in the Grecian style, the portico supported by twelve Corinthian columns, composed of brick, mortar, and stucco, but the general effect is the same as though each pillar was a monolith. The edifice is capable of containing eight or ten thousand people at a time, being equal in size and architectural effect to any ecclesiastical establishment on the continent. As this cathedral is a very remarkable one in many respects, we devote more than usual space to its description. It was rebuilt by the Jesuits in the seventeenth century, but was originally founded in 1580, and is not much inferior to St. Paul's, London, as the following dimensions will show. It is two hundred and seventy feet long by one hundred and fifty in width, having an area of forty-five hundred square rods, and stands next in size to Notre Dame, Paris. The interior of this immense building, with its twelve side chapels, is dark, dingy, and dirty, while the want of ventilation renders the air within foul and offensive. It is only on some rare festal occasions that an audience at all adequate to occupy its great capacity is seen within its walls. A hundred persons do not seem like more than a dozen in such a place. Less than a thousand only serve to emphasize its loneliness. One sees a few women, but scarcely any men, present on ordinary occasions. The latter are content to stand about the outer doors and watch the former when they come from morning mass, or the ordinary Sabbath services. Here, as in Havana, Seville, and Madrid, the Spanish ladies, who lead a secluded home life, under a half oriental restraint imposed by custom inherited from the ancient Moorish rule in continental Spain, do not resent being stared at when in the streets. Probably this is the main attraction which draws most of the señors and señoritas to the church services, though undoubtedly many of them are devout and sincere in the outward services which they perform. At least, let us give them the benefit of such a conclusion.

The national religion of Argentina is that of the Roman Catholic Church, but the power of the priesthood is strictly confined to ecclesiastical affairs, as in Uruguay. Absolute religious freedom may be said to exist here. No religious processions or church parades are permitted in the public streets. This used to be very different in times past, almost every other day in the Romish calendar being some saint's day, and it was the custom to make the most of these occasions by elaborate parades and gorgeous display. Besides some twenty-four Roman Catholic churches and chapels, there are a score presided over by Protestants of various denominations,—Episcopal, Presbyterian, Lutheran, Methodist, and so on. There is, as we were informed, a large and growing Protestant constituency in the city.

It should be mentioned very much to her credit that Buenos Ayres has supported, since 1872, a series of normal schools, in which regular courses of three years' training are given to persons desiring to fit themselves to become school-teachers. To assist those wishing to avail themselves of these advantages, the government appropriates a certain sum of money, and those persons who receive this public aid bind themselves, in consideration of the same, to teach on specific terms in the free schools for a period of three years. There are quite a number of North American ladies employed in these schools, throughout the several districts of Argentina, receiving a liberal compensation therefor, and commanding a high degree of respect. The University of Buenos Ayres, with about fifty professors and some eight hundred students, stands at the head of the national system of education. It was founded in 1821, having classical, law, medical, and physical departments. There are also four military schools, two for the army and two for the navy.

Buenos Ayres has more daily papers published within its precincts than either Boston or New York. It has several elegant marble structures devoted to the banking business, generally holding large capitals, though the financial condition of several of them at this writing is simply that of bankruptcy. This applies mainly to the state banks. There are here an orphanage, a deaf and dumb asylum, four public hospitals, and two libraries: the National Library containing some seventy thousand volumes, the Popular Library having fifty thousand. There is also a free art school, together with public and private schools of all grades. Last to be named, but by no means least in importance, the city has a number of fairly good hotels and restaurants, the latter much superior to the former. Hotels are not only a strong indication of the social refinement of a people, or of the want of it, but they are of great importance as regards the commercial prosperity of a large community. Travelers who are made comfortable in these temporary homes remain longer in a city than they would otherwise, spend more money there, and are apt to come again. If, on the contrary, the hotel accommodations are poor, travelers complain of them, and strangers avoid a city where they are liable to be rendered needlessly uncomfortable in this respect. Rio Janeiro is a notable instance in hand, a city whose hotels we conscientiously advise the traveler to avoid.

We well remember, at the great caravansary in Calcutta, the only hotel there of any size or pretension, that a party of five Englishmen and five Americans, who had come from Madras with the purpose of passing a fortnight in the former city, shortened their stay one half, simply because the hotel was so wretchedly kept, the accommodations were so abominably poor, and the discomforts so numerous. Let us put this idea in mercenary form. Ten guests, expending at least eight dollars each per day, curtailed their visit seven days. It is safe to say that they would have left six hundred dollars more in Calcutta had they been comfortably lodged, than they did under the circumstances.

We should not omit to mention the Commercial Exchange, in speaking of the public buildings of Buenos Ayres. It is a fine, large, modern structure, admirably adapted to the purpose for which it is designed. Until within a year, the edifice in Boston applied to the same purpose would not compare with that of this South American capital.

There is no dullness or torpor in this city. All is stir and bustle. Life and business are rampant, and yet, strange to say, no one seems to be in any special hurry. Everything is done in a leisurely manner. The number of handsome stores and the elegance of the goods displayed in them are remarkable, while the annual amount of sales in these establishments rivals that of some of our most popular New York and Boston concerns in similar lines of business. One may count forty first-class jewelry establishments in a short walk about town. There is hardly a more attractive display in this line either in Paris or London. Diamonds and precious stones of all descriptions dazzle the eye and captivate the fancy. The Calle Florida is one of the most fashionable thoroughfares, and presents in the afterpart of the day a very gay and striking picture of local life, a large element being composed of handsome women, attended by gayly dressed nurses, in charge of lovely children wearing fancy costumes. The young boys affect naval styles, and their little sisters wear marvelously broad Roman scarfs, and have their feet encased in dainty buff slippers. What pleasing domestic pictures they suggest to the eye of a restless wanderer!

On account of the narrowness of the streets, there is but one line of rails laid for the tramway service, so that a person goes out of town, say to Palermo, by one system of streets and returns by another. These cars move rapidly. A considerable distance is covered in a brief time, the motive power being small horses. An almost continuous line of cars, with scarcely a break, is passing any given point from early morning until night, and the citizens are liberal patrons of them. We saw some statistics relating to the number of persons carried by the tramways of this city annually, which were simply amazing, and which would make the management of the West End Railway of Boston "grow green with jealousy, or pallid with despair." Of course all this has been temporarily affected by the present financial crisis. As we have tried to show, Buenos Ayres is a wonderfully busy city, in which respect it resembles our own country much more than it does the average capitals of the south. There is none of the visible languor and spirit of delay which usually strikes one in tropical centres. People get up in the morning wide awake, and go promptly to business. There is no closing of the shops at midday here, as there is in Havana, Santiago, the capital of Chili, or some of the Mexican cities, so that clerks may absent themselves for dinner or to enjoy a siesta. A much more convenient course for both clerks and patrons is adopted, which does not block the wheels of trade. The idea of closing stores at midday to steal a couple of hours for eating and sleeping is a bit of Rip Van Winkleism entirely unworthy of the go-ahead spirit of the nineteenth century.

The Plaza Retiro is as large as the Plaza Victoria, and occupies the spot where in old Spanish days the hateful exhibitions of the bull-fights were given. Indeed, this square was formerly known as the Plaza de Toros. Many historical interests hang about the locality, around which the rich merchants of the city have erected some palatial residences, faced to a certain height with marble on the outside. These domestic retreats have courtyards constructed one beyond another, covering a considerable depth, and forming a series of patios, each appropriated to some special domestic use,—the dining court, the reception court, and the nursery. In this square, and also in the Plaza Victoria, there are always plenty of hackney coaches to be found awaiting hire, and it should be remarked that charges are very reasonable for this service in Buenos Ayres.

There are thirteen theatres in the city, and an admirable museum. The latter, rich in antiquities, is noted for its prehistoric remains of animals which once lived in the southern part of this continent, but whose species have long been extinct. This particular museum is advantageously known to scientists all over the world. The Colon Theatre is a large, well-equipped, and imposing place of entertainment, as much so as the Théâtre Française, Paris, and takes a high position in representations of the legitimate drama and the production of the better spectacular plays. This house adopts what is called here the *cazuela* in the division of its auditorium, an excellent system, very general in South American theatres, and we believe, nowhere else. It consists in giving up the entire second tier of boxes or seats to the exclusive use of unattended ladies, an arrangement which seemed to us strongly to recommend itself. To this division of the auditorium there is a separate entrance from the street, and no gentlemen are admitted under any pretext whatever. So those who desire to come to the entertainments quite unattended can do so with perfect propriety, and are safe from all intrusion in this isolated position. The ladies of this city, when they appear in public, dress very elegantly, following closely North American and European styles, while displaying the choicest imported materials well made up. Perhaps comparisons are invidious, but we feel inclined to accord precedence in the matter of personal beauty to those of Montevideo. In dress, however, the ladies of Buenos Ayres certainly excel them. Each city has its local "Worth," but many dresses are made in Paris and imported, regardless of expense.

There may be somewhere a noisier city than Buenos Ayres, as regards street life in the business section, but London or New York cannot rival it in this respect. Undoubtedly this is owing in a measure to the fact that the traffic of so large and busy a metropolis is crowded into such narrow thoroughfares, barely thirty feet in width, and often less than that, a portion of which space is taken up by the tramway tracks. The noisy vehicles which run on these rails make their full share of the racket and hubbub. Here, as in the cities of Mexico and Puebla, the drivers of the cars are supplied each with a tin horn, hung about his neck, or suspended from the car front, upon which he exercises his lungs, producing ear-piercing and discordant notes. Wheels and hoofs upon the uneven pavements increase the din, supplemented by shouts and language more forcible than proper, uttered by enraged teamsters because of the frequent blocking of the roadway. Add to these dulcet sounds the cries of itinerant fruit venders, fancy-goods sellers, and the shouts of persistent newsboys, and one has some idea of the irritating uproar which rages all day long in the older streets of Buenos Ayres.

Cows and mares are driven singly or in groups through the streets of this city, and milked at the customers' doors, so that one is nearly certain of getting the genuine article in this line, though we were assured that some roguish dealers carry an india-rubber tube and flat bag under their clothing from which they slyly extract a portion of water to "extend" the lacteal fluid. "Is there no honesty extant?" Adulteration seems to have become an instinct of trade. Asses are still driven through the streets of Paris, in the early mornings, and the milk obtained from them is distributed in the same manner, whether with a slight adulteration of water or not, we are unable to say. It is not uncommon at Buenos Ayres to see a person served on the street with fresh milk just drawn from the animal, which he drinks on the spot. A very refreshing, modest, and nutritious morning tipple. Mares, as before mentioned, are not used for working or riding in this country, but are kept solely for breeding purposes and to furnish milk. This article is considered to be more nourishing for invalids and children than cow's milk, and is often prescribed as a regular diet by the physicians.

The grand driving park of the capital, known by the name of Third of

February, is situated at Palermo, some distance from the city proper, and covers between eight and nine hundred acres. On certain days, especially on Sundays, a military band gives a public outdoor concert here, when all the beauty and fashion of the city turn out in gay equipages to see and to be seen, forming also a grand and spirited cavalcade of fine horses and carriages. The races take place at Palermo, and, as in all Roman Catholic countries, on Sundays.

The neighborhood of Buenos Ayres is generally under good cultivation, the soil and climate uniting to produce splendid agricultural results. The suburbs of Flores and Belgrano each present a very pretty group of quintas and gardens, wherein great skill and refinement of taste is evinced. The alfalfa, a species of clover used here in a green condition as fodder for cattle, and which is as rich as the red clover of New England, to which family of grasses it belongs, grows so rapidly and ripens so promptly that three crops are often realized from the same field in a single season. The immediate environs of the city are occupied by private residences, many of which are very elaborate and imposing, surrounded by charming gardens and pleasure grounds. Grottoes, statuary, and fountains abound, while orchards of various fruits are common, interspersed here and there with picturesque graperies. Some of the highways are guarded by hedges of cactus,—*agave*,—much more impenetrable than any artificial fencing. Trees of the eucalyptus family have heretofore been favorites here, originally imported from Australia, but they have ceased to be desirable, since it appears that nothing will grow in their shadow. They seem to exercise a blighting power on other species of vegetation. Figs, peaches, and oranges grow side by side, surrounded by other fruits, while the low-lying fields and open meadows nearest to the river are divided into large squares of three or four acres each, enameled with the deep green of the thick growing alfalfa, and other crops varying in color after their kind. Richest of all are the intensely yellow fields of ripening wheat still farther inland, whose softly undulating surface, gently yielding to the passing breeze, produces long, widespread floating ripples of golden light.

The love of flowers is a passion among all classes of the people, and their cultivation as a business by experienced individuals gives profitable employment to many florists, whose grounds are pictures of accumulated beauty, fragrance, and variety of hues. There is as true harmony to the eye in such blendings as there is to the ear in perfect music. The reader may be sure that where the children of Flora so much abound, bright tinted humming-birds do much more abound, dainty little living feathered gems, rivaling rubies, sapphires, and emeralds.

To insure the good health of her large and increasing population, the system of drainage in Buenos Ayres requires prompt and effectual treatment. The natural fall of the ground towards the river is hardly sufficient to second any engineering effort to this end. That typhoid fever should prevail here to the extent which it does, at nearly all seasons of the year, is a terrible reflection upon those in authority. This is a fatal disease which is quite preventable, and in this instance clearly traceable to obvious causes. Rio Janeiro, with its yellow fever scourge, is hardly more seriously afflicted than Buenos Ayres with its typhoid malaria. Indeed, it is contended by some persons living on the coast that the number of deaths per annum in the two cities arising from these causes is very nearly equal, taking into account the results of year after year. Sometimes, unaccountably, Rio escapes the fever for a twelvemonth, that is to say, some seasons it does not rage as an epidemic; but we fear, if the truth were fairly expressed, it would be found that the seeds are there all the while, and that the city of Rio Janeiro, like that of Vera Cruz on the Gulf of Mexico, is never absolutely exempt from occasional cases.

The Argentine Republic contains more than a million square miles, as already stated; indeed, immensity may be said to be one of its most manifest characteristics. The plains, the woods, the rivers, are colossal. To be sure, all of her territory is not, strictly speaking, available land, suitable for agricultural purposes, any more than is the case in our own wide-spread country. No other nation equals this republic in the value of cattle, compared with the number of the population, not forgetting Australia with its immense sheep and cattle ranches. It is believed, nevertheless, that the agricultural interest here, as in Uruguay, is gradually increasing in such ratio that it will erelong rival the pastoral. The average soil is very similar to that of our Mississippi valley, yielding a satisfactory succession of crops without the aid of any artificial enrichment. The pampas have a mellow, dry soil, the common grass growing in tussocks to the height of three or four feet, and possessing a perennial vigor which mostly crowds out other vegetation. A few wild flowers are occasionally seen, and in the marshy places lilies of several species are to be met with; but taken all together the flora of the pampas is the poorest of any fertile district with which we are acquainted. A few half-developed herbs and trefoils occasionally meet the eye, together with small patches of wild verbenas of various colors. At long distances from each other one comes upon areas of tall pampas grass as it is called, so stocky as to be almost like the bamboo, eight or ten feet high, decked with fleecy, white plumes. Birds are scarce on the pampas. There is a peculiar species of hare, besides some animals of the rodent family, resembling prairie-dogs—*biscachos*—or overgrown rats, together with an occasional jaguar and puma, found on these plains, as well as that meanest of all animals, the pestiferous skunk. Animal life, other than the herds of wild cattle, can hardly be said to abound on the pampas.

Until a few years since, Buenos Ayres enjoyed the distinction of being the capital of the province of the same name, as also of the Argentine Republic; but the present capital of the province of Buenos Ayres, called La Plata, is situated about forty miles south-east of Buenos Ayres, with which it is connected by railway. The site of the new capital was an uninhabited wilderness ten years ago, the foundation stone of this city having been laid in 1882. To-day La Plata has a population of about fifty thousand, although over seventy are claimed for it, a comprehensive system of tramways, broad, well paved streets, two theatres, thirty public schools, a national college, and six large hotels. There are many monuments and fountains ornamenting the thoroughfares, and what is now wanting is a population commensurate with the grand scale on which the capital is designed. An immense cathedral is being built, but has only reached a little way above its foundation, as work upon it has for a while been suspended. If the original plan is fully carried out, it may be half a century or more in course of construction. La Plata is suffering from the pecuniary crisis perhaps more seriously than any other part of the country. The city is lighted by both electricity and gas, issues five daily newspapers, has a very complete astronomical observatory, a public library, five railroad stations, and some very elegant public buildings. Its large possibilities are by no means improved, however. Of the buildings, the edifice of the provincial legislature, that of the minister of finance, and the legislative palace are all worthy of mention. The government house is a long, low structure, the front view of which is rendered effective by an added story in the centre, which projects from the line of the building, and is supported by high columns. The "Palace," as it is called, forming the residence of the governor of the province, is an elaborate and pretentious building, three stories in height, with two flanking domes and a dominating one in the centre. Of course La Plata has gained its start and rapid growth from the prestige of being the provincial capital, but it is now slowly developing a legitimate growth on a sound business basis, and though it can hardly be expected to ever equal Buenos Ayres in population and commercial importance, it nevertheless promises to be a prosperous city in the distant future; its citizens already call it the "Washington" of South America. A close observer could not but notice that many houses were unoccupied, and the streets seemed half deserted.

While the most of our maps and geographies remain pretty much as they were a score of years ago, and a majority of the kingdoms of the Old World have changed scarcely at all, the Argentine Republic has been steadily growing in population, progressing rapidly in intelligence, constantly extending its commercial relations, and marching all the while towards the front rank of modern civilization. A detailed statement of its extraordinary development during the last twenty years, in commerce, railway connections, schools, agriculture, and general wealth, would surprise the most intelligent reader. It is believed by experienced and conservative people, particularly those conversant with the South American republics, that Buenos Ayres will be the first city south of the equator in commercial rank and population, within a quarter of a century. The increase of this republic in population during the last two decades has been over one hundred and fifty per cent., a rapidity of growth almost without precedent. The increase of population in our own country, during the same period, was less than eighty per cent. Twenty-four lines of magnificent steamships connect the Argentine Republic with Europe, and twice that number of vessels sail back and forth each month of the year, while its railway system embraces over six thousand miles of road in operation, besides one or two yet incomplete routes, though the opening of its first line was so late as thirty-four years ago. Add to this her system of inland river navigation, covering thousands of miles, which has been so systematized as to fully supplement the remarkable railway facilities.

That Argentina rests at the present moment, as we have constantly intimated, under a financial cloud is only too well known to every one. It is a crisis brought about by an overhaste in the development of the country, especially in railroad enterprises. *Festina lente* is a good sound maxim, which the people of this republic have quite disregarded, and for which they and their creditors are suffering accordingly. It is seldom that any newly developed country escapes the maladies attendant upon too rapid growth, but this is a sort of illness pretty sure to remedy itself in due time, and rarely impedes the proper development of maturer years. If this republic has been unduly extravagant, and borrowed too much money in advancing her material interests, she has at least something to show for it. The funds have not been foolishly expended in sustaining worse than useless hordes of armed men, nor in the profitless support of royal puppets.

Nations no less than individuals are liable to financial failure, but with her grand and inexhaustible native resources, backed by the energy of her adopted citizens, this republic is as sure as anything mortal can be to soon recover from her present business depression, and to astonish the world at large by the rapidity of her financial recuperation. Her present annual crop of wool exceeds all former record in amount, and is authoritatively estimated at over thirty million dollars in value. To this large industrial product is to be added her prolific harvest of maize and wheat, together with an almost fabulous amount of valuable hides.

CHAPTER XIII.

City of Rosario.—Its Population.—A Pretentious Church.—Ocean
Experiences.—Morbid Fancies.—Strait of Magellan.—A Great
Discoverer.—Local Characteristics.—Patagonians and Fuegians.—
Giant Kelp.—Unique Mail Box.—Punta Arenas.—An Ex-Penal
Colony.—The Albatross.—Natives.—A Naked People.—Whales.—
Sea-Birds.—Glaciers.—Mount Sarmiento.—A Singular Story.

The route to Rosario is rather monotonous by railway, taking the traveler
through a very flat but fertile region, over prairies which are virtually treeless,
not unlike long reaches of country through which the Canadian Pacific
Railroad passes between Banff, in the Rocky Mountains, and Port Arthur, on
Lake Superior. The monotonous scenery is varied only by a sight of
occasional herds of cattle, feeding upon the rich grass, with here and there a
mounted herdsman, and the numberless telegraph poles which line the track.
It is at least a seven hours' journey from Buenos Ayres to Rosario.
Occasionally a marshy reach of soil is encountered where large aquatic birds
are seen, such as flamingoes, storks, cranes, herons, and the like.

Rosario, in the province of Santa Fé, is the second city in point of population
and importance in the Argentine Republic. It is a young and promising
capital, hardly yet fairly launched upon its voyage of prosperity, but so far it
has been singularly favored by various circumstances. The place is arranged
in the usual crisscross manner as regards the streets of this country, which,
unfortunately, are too narrow for even its present limited business. In place of
twenty-four feet they should have been laid out at least double that width, in
the light of all experience has developed in these South American cities. This
new town is situated a little less than three hundred miles by water from
Buenos Ayres, and about two hundred by land, railroad and steamboat
connection being regularly maintained between them. The site is admirably
chosen on the banks of the Paraná River, fifty or sixty feet above its level, and
it is destined to become, eventually, a great commercial centre. In 1854 it was
only a large village, containing some four thousand people. It is the natural
seaport, not only of the rich province of Cordova, but also of the more inland
districts, Mendoza, San Luis, Tucuman, Salta, and Jujuy, the first named
having a population of half a million. Owing to the height of the river's
banks, merchandise is loaded by "shutes," being thus conducted at once from
the warehouses to the hatches of the vessels. Already a number of foreign
steamships may be seen almost any day lying at anchor opposite the town,
while the railway communications in various directions have all of their
transportation capacity fully employed. One of these lines reaches almost
across the continent to Mendoza, at the eastern slope of the Andes, west from
Rosario. Other roads run both north and south from here. The foreign and
domestic trade of the place is second only to that of Buenos Ayres. Vessels

drawing fifteen feet of water ascend the river to this point. As a shipping port, Rosario has to a certain extent special advantages even over the larger city, being two or three hundred miles nearer the merchandise producing points.

There is already a population of some seventy-five thousand here, and, as we have intimated, the city is growing rapidly. Wharves, docks, and warehouses are in course of construction, and can hardly be finished fast enough to meet the demand for their use. There are a few substantial and handsome dwellings being erected, and many of a more ordinary class, in the finishing of which many a cargo of New England lumber is consumed. Some of the public buildings are imposing in size and architectural design, wisely constructed in anticipation of the future size of the city, whose rapid growth is only equaled by St. Paul in Brazil. The tramway, gas, and telephone have been successfully introduced. There is certainly no lack of enterprise evinced in all legitimate business directions, while attention is being very properly and promptly turned towards perfecting a carefully devised educational system of free schools, primary and progressive. When the founders of a new city begin in this intelligent fashion, we may be very sure that they are moving in the right direction, and that permanency, together with abundant present success, is sure to be the sequence.

On one side of the Plaza Mayor of Rosario stands a very pretentious church, not yet quite completed, but as the towers and dome are finished it makes a prominent feature from a long way off, as one approaches the town. In the centre of this square is a marble shaft surmounted by a figure representing Victory, and at the base are four statues of Argentine historic characters. This square is adorned with a double row of handsome acacias. As regards amusements, so far as is visible, theatricals seem to take the lead, the place having two theatres, both of which appear to be enjoying a thriving business.

When a new city is started in South America upon a site so well selected, and after so thoroughly substantial a plan, the result is no problem. The influx of European immigrants promptly supplies the necessary laborers and artisans, quite as fast, indeed, as they are required, while the ordinary growth and development of inland resources tax the local business capacity, enterprise, and capital to their utmost. Rosario needs to perfect a careful and thorough system of drainage. Fevers are at present alarmingly prevalent, arising from causes which judicious attention and sanitary means would easily obviate.

We will not weary the reader by protracted delay at this point, having still a long voyage before us.

Embarking at Montevideo, our way is southward over a broad and lonely track of ocean. If we can summon a degree of philosophy to our aid, it is fortunate. Without genial companions, surrounded by strangers, and thrown entirely upon ourselves, mental resort often fails us, life appears sombre, the wide, wide ocean almost appalling. One of the inevitable trials of a long sea voyage is the wakeful hours which will occasionally visit the most experienced traveler,—midnight hours, when the weary brain becomes preternaturally active, the imagination oversensitive and weird in its erratic conceptions, while forebodings of evil which never happens are apt to fill the mind with morbid anxieties. The very silence of the surroundings is impressive, interrupted only by the regular throbbing of the great, tireless engine, and the dashing waters chafing along the iron hull close beside the wakeful dreamer. Separated by thousands of miles from home, all communication cut off with friends and the world at large, while watching the dreary ocean, day after day, week after week, we imagine endless misfortunes that may have come to dear ones on shore. However limited may be the world of reality, that of the imagination is boundless, and sometimes one realizes years of wretched anxiety in the space of a few overwrought hours. It is such moments of passive misery which beget wrinkles and white hairs. Action is the only relief, and one hastens to the deck for a change of scene and thoughts. After experiencing such a night, how glad and glorious seems the sun rising out of the wide waste of waters, how bright and glowing the smile he casts upon the long lazy swell of the South Atlantic, as if pointedly to rebuke the overwrought fancy, and reassure the aching heart!

Be we never so dreary, the great ship speeds on its course, heeding us not; its busy motor, like heart-beats, throbs with undisturbed uniformity, forcing the vessel onward despite the joy or sorrow of those it carries within its capacious hull.

The Strait of Magellan, which divides South America from the mysterious island group which is known as Terra del Fuego, and connects the Atlantic with the Pacific Ocean by a most intricate water-way, is considerably less than four hundred miles in length, and of various widths. De Lesseps, with his successful Suez Canal and his deplorable Panama failure, is quite distanced by the hand of Nature in this line of business. It would require about ten thousand Suez Canals to make a Magellan Strait, and then it would be but a very sorry imitation. It will be remembered that the Portuguese navigator who discovered this remarkable passage, and for whom it is justly named, first passed through it in November, 1520, finally emerging into the waters of the new sea, upon which he was the first to sail, and which he named Mar Pacifico. Doubtless it seemed "pacific" to him after his rude experience in the South Atlantic, but the author has known as rough weather in this misnamed ocean as he has ever encountered in any part of the globe.

One can well conceive of the elation and surprise of Magellan, upon emerging from the intricate passage through which he had been struggling to make his way for so many weary days. What a sensation of satisfaction and triumph must the courageous and persevering navigator have experienced at the discovery he had made! What mattered all his weary hours of watching, of self-abnegation, of cold and hunger, of incessant battling with the raging sea? Henceforth to him royal censure or royal largess mattered little. His name would descend to all future generations as the great discoverer of this almost limitless ocean.

The passage leading to the strait on the Atlantic or eastern end is about twenty miles across, Cape Vergens being on the starboard side, and Cape Espiritu Santo—or Cape Holy Ghost—on the port. The entrance on the western or Pacific end is marked by Cape Pillar, Desolation Land, where the scenery is far more rugged and mountainous, the cape terminating in two cliffs, shaped so much like artificial towers as to be quite deceptive at a short distance. The narrowest part of the strait is about one mile in width, known to mariners as Crooked Reach. A passage through this great natural canal is an experience similar, in some respects, to that of sailing in the inland sea of Alaska, between Victoria and Glacier Bay, bringing into view dense forests, immense glaciers, abrupt mountain peaks, and snow-covered summits, the whole shrouded in the same solitude and silence, varied by the occasional flight of sea-birds or the appearance of seals and porpoises from below the deep waters. So irregular in its course is this passage between the two great oceans, so changeable are its currents, so impeded by dangerous rocks and hidden shoals, so beset with squalls and sudden storms, that sailing vessels are forced to double the ever-dreaded Cape Horn rather than take the Magellan route. A United States man-of-war, a sailing ship, was once over two months in making the passage through the strait, and Magellan tells us that he was thirty-seven days in passing from ocean to ocean, though using all ordinary dispatch. Within a fortnight of the writing of these notes, a European mail steamship was lost here by striking upon a sunken rock. Fortunately, owing to the proximity of the shore and moderate weather prevailing, the crew and passengers were all saved.

Winter lingers, and the days are short in this latitude. A sailing ship would be compelled to find anchorage nightly, and some days would perhaps be driven back in a few hours a distance which it had required a week to make in her proper direction. Steamships usually accomplish the run in from thirty to forty hours, there being many reaches where it is necessary to run only at half speed. If heavy fogs and bad weather prevail, they often lay by during the night, and also in snow-storms, which occur not infrequently. The sky is seldom clear for many hours together, and the sun's warmth is rarely felt, the rain falling almost daily. Even in the summer of this high southern latitude the nights are cold and gloomy, ice nearly always forming. It must be admitted that this region, of itself, is not calculated to attract the most inveterate wanderer. One is not surprised when reading the rather startling narrations of the old navigators who made the passage of the strait, encountering the constantly varying winds, and having canvas only to depend upon. The marvel is that, with their primitive means, they should have accomplished so much. There are no lighthouses in this passage from ocean to ocean, though it has been pretty well surveyed and buoyed in late years, thanks to the liberality of the English naval service, by whom this was done. There is, in fact, a dearth of lighthouses on the entire coast of South America, especially on the west side of the continent. We can recall but three between Montevideo and Valparaiso, a distance, by way of the strait, of fully two thousand miles. The lighthouses we refer to are at Punta Arenas, Punta Galesa, near Valdivia, and that which marks the port of Concepcion, at Talcahuano. The Strait of Magellan is only fit as an abiding-place for seals, waterfowl, and otters; humanity can hardly find congenial foothold here.

The natives of Patagonia, who live on the northern side of the strait, are called horse Indians, because they make such constant use of the wild horses; they do not move in any direction without them. Those on the Fuegian side are called canoe Indians, as the canoe forms their universal and indeed only mode of transportation. The former are a rather large, tall race of people, the men averaging about six feet in height; the latter are smaller in physical development, and are less civilized than the Indians of Patagonia, which, to be sure, is saying very little for the latter, who are really a low type of nomads. The Fuegians are believed to still practice cannibalism. One writer tells us that criminals and prisoners of war are thus disposed of, and that the last crew of shipwrecked seamen who fell into their hands were roasted and eaten by them. Their hostile purposes are well understood, for whenever they dare to exercise such a spirit they are sure to do so. They cautiously send out a boat or two to passing vessels, with whom a little trading is attempted, the main body of natives keeping well out of sight; but in case of any mishap to a ship, or if a small party land and are unable to defend themselves, they will appear in swarms from various hiding-places, swooping down upon their victims like vultures in the desert. The officers of the yacht Sunbeam, as recounted by Lady Brassey, found it necessary to turn her steam-pipes full force upon the swarming natives, who were doubtless preparing to make an effort to capture the yacht and her crew, hoping to overcome them by mere force of numbers. They were, however, so frightened and utterly astonished by the means of defense adopted by Lord Brassey that they threw themselves, one and all, into the sea, and sought the shore pell-mell. Humboldt, in his day, ranked these Fuegians among the lowest specimens of humanity he had ever met, and they certainly do not seem to have improved much in the mean time. One is at a loss to understand why the Patagonians should have impressed the early navigators with the idea that they were a people of gigantic size. There is no evidence to-day of their being, or ever having been, taller or larger than the average New Englander. Half-naked savages, standing six feet high, naturally impress one as being taller than Europeans clad in the conventional style of civilized people.

The waters of Magellan are very dark, deep, and sullen in aspect, with insufficient room in many places to manage a ship properly under canvas alone. In their depth and darkness these waters also resemble those of Alaska's inland sea. The shores are quite bold, and the rocks below the surface are mostly indicated by giant kelp—*Fucus giganteus*—growing over them, a kind provision of nature in behalf of safe navigation. It will not answer, however, to depend solely upon this indication; the many rocks in the strait are by no means all so designated, nor are they all buoyed. Sea-kelp is very plentiful in this region, and serves many useful purposes. It forms a nourishing food for the Fuegians under certain circumstances, when their usual supply is scarce. They dry it and prepare it in a rude way suited to their unsophisticated palates. It also forms a portion of the support of the seals and sea-otters; these creatures feed freely upon its more delicate and tender shoots. It is wonderful how it can exist and thrive among such breakers as it constantly encounters in these restless waters, which are churned into mounds of foam in squally weather; but it does grow in great luxuriance, rising oftentimes two hundred feet and more from the bottom of the sea. It is curious to watch its abundant growth and its peculiar habits. If the wind and tide are in the same direction, the plant lies smooth upon the water; but if the wind is against the tide, the leaves curl up, causing a ripple on the surface, like a school of small fish. A specimen of giant kelp was secured from alongside of the ship, broken off at arm's length below the surface of the water. It was heavy and full of parasites. Upon shaking it, myriads of marine insects, shells, tiny crabs, sea-eggs, and star-fish fell upon the deck. All of these were of the smallest species, some almost invisible to the naked eye, but how wonderful they appeared under the microscope, which developed hundreds of forms of life infinitesimal in size!

At a prominent point of the main channel is a strong box made fast by a chain, which always used to be opened by the masters of passing ships, either to deposit or to take away letters, as the case might be, each shipmaster undertaking the free delivery of all letters whose address was within the line of his subsequent course. In the whaleship service, especially during times now long past, this arrangement has been of great service, and there is no instance on record where the purpose of this self-sustaining post-office was disregarded. In these days of fast and regular post-office service, the "Magellan mail," as it was called, is of no practical account.

There are several fairly good harbors in the strait, but the only white settlement was originally a penal colony founded by the Chilian government, though it no longer serves for that purpose, the convicts having risen some years since, and overpowered the garrison. A large portion of the Patagonian shore is well wooded, besides which an available coal deposit has been found and worked to fair advantage. Steamships, which were formerly obliged to go to the Falkland Islands, in the Atlantic, five hundred miles from the mouth of the strait, when running short of fuel, can now get their supply in an exigency at Punta Arenas—"Sandy Point." It is situated in the eastern section of the strait, about a hundred and twenty-five miles from the entrance. We do not mean to convey the idea that this is a regular coaling station, though it may some time become so. The town consists of straggling, low-built log-houses, and a few framed ones, reminding one of Port Said at the Mediterranean end of the Suez Canal, with its heterogeneous population. That of Sandy Point is made up of all nationalities, strongly tinctured with ex-convicts, and deserters from the Chilian army and navy. English is the language most commonly spoken, though the place is Chilian territory. It contains some twelve or fifteen hundred inhabitants, and is the most southerly town on the globe, as well as the most undesirable one in which to live, if one may express an opinion upon such brief acquaintance.

We made no attempt to go on shore at Punta Arenas. A rain-storm was at its height while the ship lay off the town, and when it rains in these latitudes, it attends exclusively to the business in hand. The water comes down like Niagara, until finally, when the clouds have entirely emptied themselves, it stops. Jupiter Pluvius is master of the situation, when he asserts himself, and there is no one who can dispute his authority. Umbrellas and waterproofs are of no more use as a protection during the downpour, than they would be to a person who had fallen overboard in water forty fathoms deep. One of our passengers came on deck with a life preserver about his body, solemnly declaring that if this sort of thing continued much longer, the article would be absolutely necessary in order to keep afloat.

During the season the Patagonians bring into Punta Arenas the result of their hunting in the shape of seal and otter skins, together with guanaco, and silver-fox skins, which are gathered by local traders and shipped to Europe. Occasionally a few sea-otter skins of rare value are obtained from here, fully equal, we were told, to anything taken in Alaskan waters. We have said that Punta Arenas is the most southerly town on the globe. The next nearest town to the Antarctic circle is the Bluff, so called,—also known as Campbelltown,

—in the extreme south of New Zealand, where the author has eaten of the famous oysters indigenous there.

Two sorts of supplies are to be obtained by navigators of the strait, namely, fuel and good drinking water. Sometimes a valuable skin robe may be purchased of the Patagonian Indians. It is called a guanaco-skin cloak, and made from the skin of the young deer. To obtain these skins of a uniform fineness of texture, the fawns are killed when but eight or ten days old; the available product got from each one is so small as hardly to exceed twice the size of one's hand. These are sewn together with infinite care and neatness by the Indian women, who use the fine sinews taken from ostriches' legs for thread. One of these guanaco-skin cloaks represents a vast amount of labor, and a hundred fawns must die to supply the raw material. Only chiefs of tribes can afford to wear them. Strangers who are willing to pay a price commensurate with their real cost and value may occasionally buy such an article as we describe, but these cloaks are rare. One was brought on board ship and shown to us, the price of which was twelve hundred dollars, nor do we think it was an excessive valuation. It was worth the amount as a rare curiosity for some art museum.

That monarch bird of Antarctic regions, the albatross, frequents both ends of the strait, and sometimes accompanies steamships during the passage, together with cape-pigeons, gulls, and other marine birds, though as a rule the albatross is little seen except on the broad expanse of the ocean. A bird called the steamer-duck, also nicknamed by sailors the paddle-wheel duck, was pointed out to us by our captain. It is so called from its mode of propelling itself through the water, scooting over the surface of the strait while using both wings and legs, and creating considerable disturbance of the water, like a side-wheeler. The wings are too small to give it power of flight through the air. The steamer-duck is a large bird, nearly the size of the domestic goose; after its fashion, it moves with astonishing velocity, considerably faster than the average speed of a steamship. But we were speaking a moment since of the albatross, which is a feathered cannibal, and shows some truly wolfish traits. When one of its own species, a member of the same flock even, is wounded and drops helpless to the surface of the sea, its comrades swoop down upon it, and tearing the body to pieces with their powerful bills, devour the flesh ravenously. This was witnessed near the Arctic circle, between Hobart, in Tasmania, and the Bluff, in New Zealand, a few years ago, when some English sportsmen succeeded in wounding one of these mammoth birds from the deck of the steamship Zealandia. The only other known bird of our day which measures from eleven to twelve feet between the tips of the extended wings is the South American condor.

The sea hereabouts abounds in fish, which constitute the largest portion of the food supply of the few Indians who live near the coast of either shore. The Fuegians dwell in the rudest shelters possible, nothing approaching the form of a house. The frailest shelter, covered with sea-lion's skins, suffices to keep them from the inclemencies of the weather. With the exception of an animal skin of some sort, having the fur on, secured over one shoulder on the side exposed to the wind, the canoe Indians wear no clothing. We were told that several of these natives, while quite young, were taken to England by advice of the missionaries and taught to read and write, being also kindly instructed in civilized manners and customs, which they gladly adopted for the time being; but upon returning to their native land, in every instance they rapidly lapsed into a condition of semi-savagery. It had been hoped they would act as a civilizing medium with their former friends, after returning among them, but this proved fallacious, and was a great disappointment to the well-meaning philanthropists. This same experience, as is well known, has been the result of similar experiments with natives of Africa and the South Sea Islands. The author is conversant with a striking illustration of this character in connection with an Australian Indian youth, which occurred in Queensland, and which was both interesting and very romantic in its development. It simply went to prove that hereditary instincts cannot be easily eradicated, and that not one, but many generations are necessary to banish savage proclivities which are inherited from a long line of ancestors.

Gold is found to some extent in the beds of the streams in Patagonia,—free gold, washed from the disintegrated rocks. Natives sometimes bring small quantities of the gold dust into Punta Arenas, with which to purchase tobacco and other articles. Many heedless and unprincipled individuals sell them intoxicants, to obtain which these Indians will part with anything they possess, after they have once become familiar with the taste and effect of the captivating poison.

Not far from Cape Forward, near the middle of the strait, which is the most southerly portion of the American continent, three native boats were seen during our passage. The steamer was slowed for a few moments to give us a brief opportunity to see the savage occupants. These three frail, ill-built canoes were tossed high and low by the swell of the Pacific, which set to the eastward through the strait. Each boat contained a man, a couple of women, and one or two children, the latter entirely naked, the others nearly so. They were Fuegians, raising their hands and voices to attract our attention, asking for food and tobacco, to which appeal a generous response was made. Their broad faces, high cheek-bones, low foreheads, and flat noses, their faces and necks screened by coarse black hair, did not challenge our admiration, however much we were exercised by pity for human beings in so desolate a condition. They certainly possessed two redeeming features,—brilliant eyes and teeth of dazzling whiteness. The fruit thrown to them seemed best to suit the ideas and palates of the children, who devoured oranges, skin and all; but the gift of clothing which was made to the parents was laid aside for future consideration, though there are probably no "ole clo'" merchants in Terra del Fuego. The men ate hard sea biscuit and slices of cold corned beef ravenously. The plump, well-rounded shoulders and limbs of the women showed them to be in far better physical condition than the men, whose bodies consisted of little besides skin and bones. They were copper colored, and the skin of the women shone in the bright sunlight which prevailed for the moment, as though they had been varnished. If their faces had been as well formed as their bodies, they would have been models of natural beauty. How these people could remain so nearly naked with apparent comfort, while we found overcoats quite necessary, was a problem difficult to solve satisfactorily.

"They were born so," said our first officer. "As you go through life with your face and hands exposed, so they go with their entire bodies. It is a mere matter of habit,—habit from babyhood to maturity."

All of which is perfectly reasonable. It was observed that on the bottom of their boats was a layer of flat stones, and on these, just amidship, was spread a low, smouldering fire of dried vines and small twigs, designed to temper the atmosphere about them. So frail were the boats that one of the occupants was kept constantly baling out water.

It is impossible to form any intelligent estimate as to how many of these aborigines there are in and about the strait. They find food, like the canvas-back ducks, in the wild celery, adding shell-fish and dried berberries, and are a strictly nomadic people. After exhausting the products of one vicinity, for the time being, they move on, but return to the locality at a proper time, when nature has recuperated herself and furnished a fresh supply of vegetable growth and edible shell-fish. A stranded whale is a godsend to these savages, upon the putrid flesh of which they live and fatten until all has disappeared. In their primitive way they hunt this leviathan, but want of proper facilities renders them rarely successful. Occasionally they manage to plant a spear in some vital spot, deep enough to be effectual, so that the whale, after diving to the depths of the sea, finally comes to the surface, near the place where he was wounded, to thrash about and to die. Even then, unless it is at a favorable point, the large body is liable to be swept away by the strong tide setting through the strait, so that the natives seldom secure a carcass by these means.

Not long since one of the European mail steamers, on approaching the Atlantic end of the strait, sighted an object which was at first thought to be a sunken rock. If this was its character, it was all important to obtain the exact location. A boat was lowered and pulled to the object, when it was found to be the carcass of a dead whale, in which was a stout wooden spear which had fatally wounded the creature. Securely attached to the spear, by means of a rope made of animal sinews, there were a couple of inflated bladders. The spear was evidently a Fuegian weapon, and though it had finally cost the whale his life, the dead body had been carried by the current far beyond the reach of those who had caused the fatal wound. The discovery showed the crude manner in which these savages seek to possess themselves of a whale occasionally and thus to appease their barbaric appetites. They could not pursue one in their frail boats, but the creature is sometimes found sleeping on the surface of the sea, which is the Fuegian opportunity for approaching it noiselessly, and for planting a spear in some vital part of the huge body. Whales, when thus attacked, do not show fight, but their instinct leads them to dive at once.

A few whales were observed within the strait during our passage, some so near as to show that they had no fear of the ship. It was curious to watch them. There was a baby whale among the rest, five or six feet in length, which kept very close to its dam; it suddenly disappeared once while we were watching the school, though only to rise again to the surface of the sea and emit a tiny fountain of spray from its diminutive blow-hole. In passing a small inlet which formed a calm, sheltered piece of water, still as an inland lake, there were seen upon its tranquil bosom a few white geese, quietly floating, while close at hand upon some rocks, a half score of awkward penguins were also observed, with their ludicrous dummy wings, and their bodies supported in a half standing, half sitting position.

Ducks seem to be very abundant in the strait, but geese are scarce. An occasional cormorant is caught sight of, with its distended pouch bearing witness to its proverbial voracity. All the birds one sees in these far away regions have each some peculiar adaptability to the climate, the locality, or to both. The penguin never makes the mistake of seeking our northern shores, nor is the albatross often seen north of the fortieth degree of south latitude. True, were the former to emigrate, he would have to swim the whole distance, but the latter is so marvelously strong of wing that it has been said of him, he might breakfast, if he chose, at the Cape of Good Hope, and dine on the coast of Newfoundland.

Terra del Fuego,—"Land of Fire,"—which makes the southern side of the strait, opposite Patagonia, is composed of a very large group of islands washed by the Atlantic on the east side and the Pacific on the west, trending towards the southeast for about two hundred miles from the strait, and terminating at Cape Horn. The largest of these islands is East Terra del Fuego, which measures from east to west between three and four hundred miles. One can only speak vaguely of detail, as this is still a *terra incognita*. These islands do indeed form "a land of desolation," as Captain Cook appropriately named them, sparsely inhabited to be sure, but hardly fit for human beings. They are deeply indented and cut up by arms of the sea, and composed mostly of sterile mountains, whose tops are covered with perpetual snow. When the mountains are not too much exposed to the ocean storms on the west coast, they are scantily covered with a species of hardy, wind-distorted trees from the water's edge upward to the snow line, which is here about two thousand feet above the sea. In sheltered areas this growth is dense and forest-like, especially nearest to the sea; in others it is interspersed by bald and blanched patches of barren rocks. In some open places, where they have worn themselves a broad path, the glaciers come down to the water, discharging sections of ice constantly into the deep sea, crowded forward and downward by the immense but slow-moving mass behind,—a frozen river,—thus illustrating the habit of the iceberg-producing glaciers of the far north.

One never approaches this subject without recalling the lamented Agassiz and his absorbing theories relating to it.

The author has seen huge glaciers in Scandinavia and in Switzerland, forming natural exhibitions of great interest; each country has peculiarities in this respect. In the last-named country, for instance, there is no example where a glacier descends lower than thirty-five hundred feet above the sea level, while in Norway the only one of which he can speak from personal observation has before it a large terminal moraine, thus losing the capacity for that most striking performance, the discharge of icebergs. The best example of this interesting operation of nature which we have ever witnessed, and probably the most effective in the world, is that of the Muir glacier in Alaska, where an immense frozen river comes boldly down from the Arctic regions to the sea level, with a sheer height at its terminus of over two hundred feet. From this unique façade, nearly two miles in width, the constant tumbling of icebergs into the sea is accompanied by a noise like a salvo of cannon. This glacier, it should be remembered, also extends to the bottom of the bay, where it enters it two hundred feet below the surface of the water, thus giving it a height, or perhaps we should say a depth and height combined, of fully four hundred feet. Icebergs are discharged from the submerged portion continually, and float to the surface, thus repeating the process below the water which is all the while going on above it, and visible upon the perpendicular surface. Nothing which we have seen in the Canadian Selkirks, in Switzerland, Norway, or elsewhere, equals in size, grandeur, or clearly defined glacial action, the famous Muir glacier of Alaska.

The most remarkable peak to be seen in passing through the Strait of Magellan is Mount Sarmiento, which is inexpressibly grand in its proportions, dominating the borders of Cockburn's Channel near the Pacific end of the great water-way. It is about seven thousand feet in height, a spotless cone of snow, being in form extremely abrupt and pointed. This frosty monarch sends down from its upper regions a score or more of narrow, sky-blue glaciers to the sea through openings in the dusky forest. Darwin was especially impressed by the sight of these when he explored this region, and speaks of them as looking like so many Niagaras, but they are only miniature glaciers after all. One sees in the Pyrenees and the St. Gothard Pass similar cascades flowing down from the mountains towards the valleys, except that in the one instance the crystal waters are liquid, in the other they are quite congealed. The group or range of which Sarmiento is the apex is very generally shrouded in mist, and is visited by frequent rain, snow, and hail storms. We were fortunate to see it under a momentary glow of warm sunshine, when the sky was deepest blue, and the ermine cloak of the mountain was spangled with frost gems.

It would seem that such exposure to the elements in a frigid climate, and such deprivations as must be constantly endured by the barbarous natives who inhabit these bleak regions, must surely shorten their lives, and perhaps it does so, though "the survival of the fittest," who grow up to maturity, is in such numbers that one is a little puzzled in considering the matter. A singular instance touching upon this point came indirectly to the writer's knowledge.

It appears that four Fuegian women, one of whom was about forty years of age, and the others respectively about twenty, twenty-five, and thirty, were picked up adrift in the strait a few years ago. It was believed that they had escaped from some threatened tribal cruelty, but upon this subject they would reveal nothing. These fugitives were kindly taken in hand by philanthropic people at Sandy Point, and entertained with true Christian hospitality. When first discovered they were, as usual, quite naked, but were promptly clothed and properly housed. No more work was required of them than they chose voluntarily to perform; in short, they were most kindly treated, and though the best of care was taken of them in a hygienic sense, they all gradually faded, and died of consumption in less than two years. They seemed to be contented, were grateful and cheerful, but clothing and a warm house to live in, odd as it may seem, killed them! They were born to a free, open air and exposed daily life, and their apparently sturdy constitutions required such a mode of living. Civilized habits, strange to say, proved fatal to these wild children of the rough Fuegian coast.

CHAPTER XIV.

The Land of Fire.—Cape Horn.—In the Open Pacific.—Fellow
Passengers.—Large Sea-Bird.—An Interesting Invalid.—A Weary
Captive.—A Broken-Hearted Mother.—Study of the Heavens.—The
Moon.—Chilian Civil War.—Concepcion.—A Growing City.—
Commercial Importance.—Cultivating City Gardens on a New Plan.
—Important Coal Mines.—Delicious Fruits.

Magellan named this extreme southern land, of which we have been speaking, "the Land of Fire," because of the numerous fires which he, from his ships, saw on the shore at night, and which were then supposed by the discoverers to be of a volcanic character. The fact probably was that the Indians did not fail to recognize the need of artificial heat, especially at night, though they had not sufficient genius to teach them to construct garments suitable to protect them from the inclemency of the weather. These fires were kindled in the open air, but the natives camped close about them, sleeping within their influence.

Cape Horn, the extreme point of South America, on the outermost island of the Fuegian group, is a lofty, steep black rock, with a pointed summit, which has stood there for ages, like a watchful sentinel at his post. Two thirds of Patagonia and Terra del Fuego—the western part—belong to Chili, and the balance of both—the eastern part—belongs to the Argentine Republic. A recently consummated treaty between these two nationalities has fixed upon this final division of territory, and thus settled a question which has long been a source of dispute and ill feeling between them. This division makes Cape Horn belong to Chili, not a specially desirable possession, to be sure, but it is an indelible landmark.

The sail along the coast northward after leaving the Pacific mouth of the strait affords very little variety of scenery; the dull hue of the barren shore is without change of color for hundreds of miles, until the eye becomes weary of watching it, as we speed onward through the long, indolent ocean swell. Arid hills and small indentures form the coast line, but as we get further northward, this dreary sameness is varied by the appearance of an occasional small settlement, forming a group of dwellings of a rude character, possibly a mining region or a fishing hamlet, connected with some business locality further inland. Sometimes a green valley is descried, which makes a verdant gulch opening quite down to the sea.

This dense monotony becomes more and more tedious, until one longs to get somewhere, anywhere, away from it.

In the dearth of scenic interest, we fall to studying the various passengers traveling between the Pacific ports, a great variety of nationalities being represented. Among those of the second-class was a handsome Italian boy, with marvelous eyes of jet and a profusion of long black hair. He had a small organ hung about his neck, and carried an intelligent monkey with him. The boy and his monkey joined in the performance of certain simple, amusing tricks to elicit money from the lookers-on. Both boy and monkey were happy in the result achieved, the former in liberal cash receipts, the latter in being fed liberally with cakes and bonbons. The capacity of monkeys for the rapid consumption of palatable dainties is one of the unsolved mysteries of nature.

Schools of porpoises played about the hull of the ship, and clouds of sea-birds at times wheeled about the topmasts, or followed in the ship's wake watching for refuse from the cook's department. Occasionally the head of a large, deep-water turtle would appear for a moment above the surface, twisting its awkward neck to watch the course of the steamer, while shoreward the mottled surface of the gently undulating waves betrayed the presence of myriads of small fish, over which hovered predatory birds of the gull tribe. Now and again one would swoop swiftly downward to secure a victim to its appetite. Few albatrosses were seen after leaving the Pacific mouth of the strait. They are lovers of the stormy Antarctic region, with the tempestuous atmosphere of which their great power of wing enables them to cope successfully. The author has seen one of these birds off the southern coast of New Zealand which spread eleven feet from tip to tip of its extended wings. It was caught with a floating bait by one of the seamen and drawn on board ship, where it was measured, but not until a long contest of strength had taken place between men and bird. The albatross was slightly wounded in the mouth and throat by the process of catching him with a baited hook. But they are hardy creatures, and unless injured in some vital part pay little heed to a small wound. After this bird had been examined, it was liberated, and resumed its graceful flight about the ship as though nothing unusual had happened.

An invalid girl of Spanish birth, who was perhaps sixteen years of age, very tenderly cared for by her mother, was propped up daily in a reclining seat upon deck, where she might find amusement in watching the sea and distant shore, while inhaling the saline tonic of the atmosphere. Poor child, how her large, dark eyes, pallid lips, and painful respiration appealed to one's sympathy! It required no professional knowledge to divine her approaching fate. She was really in the last stages of consumption, and was on her way to a popular sanitarium near the coast, hoping against reason that the change might prove restorative and of radical benefit. It was pleasant to observe how promptly every one on board strove to add to her comfort by simple attentions and services, and how the choicest bits from the table were secured to tempt her capricious appetite. The grateful mother's eyes were often suffused with tears, carefully hidden from the gentle invalid. Her maternal heart was too full for the utterance even of thanks.

"Ah," said she to us in a low tone of voice, "she is the last of my three children, two boys and this girl. The two boys faded away just like this. Do you think there is any hope for her, señor?" "Why not, señora? We should never cease to hope. The land breeze and the springs where you are going may do wonders."

Heaven forgive us. The child's fate was only too plainly to be read in her attenuated form, and the dull action of her almost congested lungs.

One day a small, weary sea-bird, newly out of its nest, flew on board our ship quite exhausted, and being easily secured, was given to the young girl to pet. It soon became quite at home in her lap, eating small bread crumbs and little bits of meat from her fingers. Confidence being thus established between them, the little half-fledged creature would not willingly leave its new-found benefactress. It seemed to be a providential occurrence, affording considerable diversion to the sick one. For a while, at least, she was aroused from the listlessness which is so very significant in consumption, and her whole heart went out to the confiding little waif. It was a pretty sight to see the bird nestle contentedly close to her bosom, the pale-faced girl scarcely less fragile than the little feathered stranger she had adopted. No one thought that Death was hovering so very near, yet the third night after the bird flew on board the young girl lay in her shroud, with an ivory crucifix, typical of the Romish faith, in one hand, and the other resting upon the inanimate bird she had befriended, which had also breathed its last.

Attempted consolation to a freshly bleeding heart is almost always premature, and there are few, very few, human beings competent to offer it effectually under the best circumstances. The sad-eyed mother listened to a few well-meant words of this character, but slowly shook her head and made no reply. Time only could assuage the keenness of her sorrow. By and by she spoke, with her eyes still resting upon that pale, dead face, where nothing but a wonderful peace and serenity were now expressed.

"Have birds souls, do you think?" she asked, in a low, trembling voice.

"Possibly," was the reply; "but why do you ask?" "Because," she continued, speaking very slowly, "that tiny creature and my darling died almost at the same moment, and if so, her spirit would have company on its way to the good God."

The unconscious poetry of the thought, so quietly expressed by the sorrowing mother, as she sat beside the corpse with folded hands and burning eyes, which could not find the relief of tears, was very touching.

The motor of the big ship throbbed on, the routine of duty continued unchanged, passengers ate, drank, and were merry, the sea-birds wheeled about us uttering their sharp contentious cries, and we pressed forward through the opposing wind and tide, as though nothing had happened. Only a mother's loving heart was broken. Only a soul gone to its God. Surely such sweet innocence must be welcome in heaven. But ah! the great mystery of it all!

Most intelligent people will agree with us that no study known to science can compare with astronomy for absorbing interest. At sea one finds ample time, convenience, and incentive to study the sky, populous with countless hosts of constellations. Especially is it interesting to watch the numerous phases of the moon, beginning with her advent as a delicate crescent of pale light in the eastern sky, after the sun has set, and continuing to the period when she becomes full. Each succeeding night it is found that she has moved farther and farther westward, until, arriving at the full, she rises nearly at the same time that the sun sets. From the period of full moon, the disc of light diminishes nightly until the last quarter is reached, and the moon is then seen high over the ship's topmast head, before day breaks in the east. Thus she goes on waning, all the while drawing closer to the sun, until finally she becomes absorbed in his light. The interesting process completed, she again comes into view at twilight in the west, in her exquisite crescent form, once more to pass through a similar series of changes.

The superstition of sailors touching the moonlight is curious. No foremast hand will sleep where it shines directly upon him. They are voluble in relating many instances of comrades rendered melancholy-mad by so doing. "They talk about the moon making the ebb and flow of the tide," said an able seaman to the author. "There's lots of queer things about the moon, but *that's* d—d nonsense, saving your honor's presence." Thus Jack eagerly absorbs superstitious ideas, and ignores natural phenomena. No humble class of men are so intelligent in a general way, and yet at the same time so universally superstitious, as those who go down to the sea in ships.

In coming on to the west coast it is natural, perhaps, for the reader to expect us to refer briefly to the late civil war in Chili, but we have not attempted in these notes to depict the local political condition of any of the states of South America. In the past they have most of them shown themselves as changeable as the wind, and remarks which would depict the status of to-day might be quite unsuited to that of to-morrow. The average reader is sufficiently familiar with the struggle so lately ended in Chili. One party was led by the late President Balmaceda, in opposition to the other, known as the Congressional party. That which brought about this open warfare was the refusal of Congress any longer to recognize the president on account of his high-handed, illegal, and venal official conduct. A line will illustrate the cause of the outbreak. It was the Constitution of the country as against a Dictatorship. The President of the Chilian Republic, like the President of the United States, has a personal authority such as nowadays is wielded by few constitutional monarchs. Balmaceda proved to be a tyrant of the first water, abusing the power of his position to condemn to death those who opposed him, without even the semblance of a trial. He succeeded in attaching most of the regular army to his cause by profuse promises and the free use of money, while the navy went almost bodily over to the side of Congress. The contest assumed revolutionary proportions, and many battles were fought. As a casual observer, the author heartily coincided with the Congressional party, and rejoices at their wholesale triumph.

The suicidal act which ended Balmaceda's life was no heroic resort, but the deed of a coward fearing to face the consequences of his murderous career. It is not the man who has been actuated by high and noble sentiments who cuts his throat or blows out his brains. Such is the act of the cunning fraud who realizes that he has not only totally failed in his object, but that his true character is known to the world. Suicide has been declared to be the final display of egoism, and it certainly leaves the world with one less thoroughly selfish character. The disappearance of such an individual may produce a momentary ripple on the surface of time, but it fails to leave any permanent mark.

Nearly three hundred miles south of Santiago, capital of Chili, on the Pacific coast, is situated the city of Concepcion. It stands on the right bank of the river Biobio, six or seven miles from its mouth, and contains about twenty-five thousand inhabitants. The people seem to be exceptionally active and enterprising, though at this writing suffering from the effects of the late civil war. It is the third city in point of size and importance in the republic, and dates from over three hundred years ago. It will be remembered also that it once held the place now occupied by Santiago as capital of the country. The city is built in the valley of Mocha, under the coast range of hills, and is justly famed, like Puebla in Mexico, for its pretty women and beautiful flowers. It is a clean and thrifty town, with handsome shops, a charming plaza, and an attractive alameda. This latter deserves special mention. It is a mile long, and beautified with several rows of tall Lombardy poplars, the sight of which carried us to another hemisphere, where those lovely Italian plains stretch away from the environs of Milan towards the foothills of the neighboring Alps and the more distant Apennines. Great things are prognosticated for Concepcion in the near future by its friends, and it is already the principal town of southern Chili. The streets are well paved, and lined by handsome business blocks, together with pleasant dwelling-houses, built low, to avoid the effect of earthquakes, the universal material being sun-dried bricks, finished externally in stucco. The façades are painted in harlequin variety of colors, yellow, blue, and peach-blossom prevailing. The town has really more the appearance of a northern than a southern city, and has long been connected with Valparaiso by railway.

Some of the most extensive coal mines on this part of the continent have been discovered in this vicinity, and are being worked on a large scale. In fact, Coronal, not far away, is the great coaling station on the Chilian coast for steamships bound to Europe or Panama. One would suppose that this coal mining must be quite profitable, as we were told that twenty-five and even thirty dollars per ton was realized for it delivered at the nearest tide-water. The port of Concepcion is some seven miles from the city, where the river Biobio flows into the ocean at Talcahuano,—pronounced Tal-ca-wha'no,—a small town on Concepcion Bay possessing an excellent harbor. There are here a large marine dock, an arsenal, and a seaman's hospital. Close by the shore is a spacious and convenient railway station. The bay is some six miles wide by seven in length. There is a resident population of nearly four thousand, who form an extremely active community. The majority of the houses are of a very humble character and, like those of Concepcion, are built of adobe.

Spanish capitals in the West Indies and South America were originally placed, like Concepcion, some distance from the coast, to render them more secure against the attack of pirates and lawless sea-rovers, who might land from their vessels, burn a town on the seashore, after robbing it of all valuables, and easily make good their escape; whereas to march inland and attack a town far from their base, or to proceed up a shallow river in boats for such a purpose, was a far more difficult, if not indeed an impossible thing to do. Thus Callao is the harbor of Lima; Valparaiso, of Santiago; and Talcahuano, of Concepcion. The situation of the last named capital is admirable, at the head of the bay, which affords one of the best harbors on the west coast of the continent. When the transcontinental railway from Buenos Ayres, on the Atlantic side, is finished, surmounting the passes of the Andes,—already "a foregone conclusion,"—it will have its termination here at Talcahuano, which must then become a great shipping point for New Zealand and Australia. Half a dozen lines of European mail steamers already touch here regularly. The river is too shallow to admit of vessels drawing more than a few feet of water ascending it so far as Concepcion, but Talcahuano is all sufficient as a port.

Few places have been so frequently devastated by fire, flood, and earthquakes, or so often ravaged by war, as has this interesting city. In the early days the Araucanian Indians put the settlers to the sword again and again. This was the bravest of all the native Indian tribes of South America, and is still an unconquered people. The city was laid in ruins so late as 1835 by an earthquake, though no special signs of this destructive visitor are to be seen here to-day. Still, one cannot but feel that with such possibilities hanging over the locality, there must be few people willing to expend freely of their means for substantial building purposes, or to make Concepcion a permanent place of abode. Human nature adapts itself to all exigencies, however, and the place grows rapidly, notwithstanding the discouraging circumstances which we have named. It is not the native but the foreign element of the population which is doing so much for this region. Were the mingled native race to be left to themselves, there would be few signs of progress evinced; they would rapidly lapse into a condition of semi-barbarism. The Chilian proper is a very poor creature as regards morals, intelligence, or true manhood; his instincts are brutal and his aims predaceous.

Like all South American cities, Concepcion is laid out by rule and compass, the fairly broad streets crossing each other at right angles. There is a large and costly cathedral, but a wholesome fear of earthquakes has caused it to be left without the usual twin towers, which gives it an unfinished appearance. The place also contains other churches, a well-appointed theatre, two hospitals, and several edifices devoted to charitable purposes. Opposite the cathedral stands the Intendencia, a large and handsome government house. Telephones and electric lights have long been adopted, and the telegraph poles do much abound. In these foreign places, so far away from home, to see the streets lined, as they are with us, by big, tall poles, holding aloft a maze of wires, is very suggestive; but where can one go that they are not? It is curious to realize that we can step into an office close at hand and promptly communicate with any part of the world. We may have sailed over the ocean many thousands of miles, and have consumed months to reach the spot where we stand, but electricity, like thought, annihilates space, and will take our message instantly to its destination, though it be at the farthest end of the globe. These marvelous facilities are no longer confined to populous centres. Electricity not only bears our messages to the uttermost parts of the world, but it propels the tramway cars in Rome, Boston, and Munich, while it also lights the streets of New York, Auckland in New Zealand, as well as of London and Honolulu.

The importance of Concepcion is manifest from the fact that several new railway connections terminating here have lately been accomplished; but the important event already referred to, of the transcontinental railway, will finally insure her commercial greatness. The town is surrounded by a widespread, fertile country, abounding in both mineral and agricultural wealth, equal to, if not surpassing, any other province in Chili. The city was financially strong before the late civil war, and has still some very wealthy residents. The principal bank of Concepcion, with a capital of one million dollars, paid a dividend to its stockholders in 1890 of sixteen per cent. on the previous year's business. The cathedral and government house, already spoken of, front on the plaza, a large open square ornamented with statuary, trees, and flowers, the latter kept in most exquisite order and constant bloom by means of a singular and original device. It seems that each separate plot of these grounds is owned or cared for by a different family of the citizens, and that a spirit of emulation is thus excited by the effort of the several parties to make their special plot excel in its beauty and fragrance. This keeps the whole plaza in a lovely condition, and makes it the pride of the city.

Society and business circles are mostly composed of foreigners, the German element largely predominating. The native, or humbler classes, as we have already intimated, are a wretchedly low people. They "wake" their dead before burial, much after the style which prevails in Ireland, except that the process is more exaggerated in manner. Drinking and debauchery characterize these occasions, which are continued often for three days at a time, or so long as the means for indulgence in excess last. In case of youthful deaths, the child's cheeks are painted red, and the head is crowned in a fantastic manner, the body being dressed and placed in a sitting position, thus forming a strange and hideous sight. Such treatment of a corpse could only be tolerated by a barbarous people. In the environs of the town, Lazarus jostles Dives. There are here many hovels, as well as a better class of residences. Some of them are wretchedly poor, built of mud and bamboo, the inhabitants half-naked and wholly starved, if one may judge by their appearance. On Saturday, which in Spanish towns and cities is called "poor day," the streets of Concepcion are full of either assumed or real mendicants. The Spanish race is one of chronic beggars,—they seem born so. Scarcely less of a nuisance than the beggars are the army of half-starved, mongrel, neglected dogs, that throng in the streets of the city, rivaling Constantinople.

It should be mentioned that Concepcion has a good system of tramway service, and that the cars have attached to them a class of neat, pretty, and modest girls for conductors, who wear natty straw hats, snow white aprons, and are supplied with a leather cash bag hung by a strap about the neck. It seems rather incongruous that while so many evidences of real progress abound in this city, water, the prime necessity of life, should be peddled about the streets by the bucketful. Now is the time to perfect a system of drainage, and to introduce an adequate supply of good water, from easily available sources.

The inexhaustible coal fields already mentioned, which are situated but a few miles away, must prove to be a lasting source of prosperity to Concepcion. They are far more important and valuable, all things considered, than a gold or silver mine near at hand would be. Indeed, it is found in the long run that the latter kind of mineral discoveries do not always tend to the material benefit of the community in which they are found. The earth produces far more profitable crops than gold and precious stones, even when considered in the most mercenary light. The business prospects of Concepcion, as we have pointed out in detail, are exceedingly promising. That the city is destined eventually to rival Valparaiso seems more than probable, and yet there is another side to this favorable aspect thus presented, which it is not wise to ignore. True, the climate is equable and healthy, but that great drawback, the liability to earthquakes and tidal waves, still remains, like a dark, portending shadow. In spite of this startling possibility there is something of a "boom" already instituted, at this writing, as to the prices of land in and about both the port and city of Concepcion. It is a fact that people will soon become calloused and heedless of almost any familiar danger. Jack turns in and quickly falls to sleep, when the watch below is called and relieves him from the deck, though the ship is in the midst of cyclone latitudes, and while a half-gale is blowing. The people of Torre del Grecco, at the base of the volcano, do not sleep any less soundly to-day because Pompeii was utterly destroyed by Vesuvius eighteen or nineteen centuries ago. The earthquake of 1835 first shook Talcahuano nearly to pieces, and then completed its destruction by a tidal wave which swept what remained of it into the sea.

It goes without saying that most of the fruits and staple products of the tropics are to be found both at Concepcion and at the port of Talcahuano. Each place we visit seems to have some specialty in this line. Here, it is the watermelon. Favored by the soil and the climate, this fruit is developed to its maximum in weight, richness of flavor, and general perfection. They are sold cheap enough everywhere. A centavo will buy a large ripe one. Street carts and donkeys are laden with them, and so are the decks of all outgoing vessels. It is both food and drink to the poor peons, who consume the fruit in quantities strongly suggestive of cholera, dropsy, or some other dreadful illness. Any one accustomed to travel in our Southern States, in the right season of the year, will have observed how voraciously the negro population, young and old, eat of the cheap, ripe crop of watermelons; but these South American peons have a capacity for storage and digestion of this really wholesome article, beyond all comparison. A child not more than ten years of age will devour the ripe portion of a large melon in a few minutes, and no ill effects seem to follow. An adult eats two at a meal which would weigh, we are afraid to say how much, but they are considerably larger than the average melons which are brought to New England from the South. After all, the watermelon is healthful food, though it is more filling than nourishing. It will be remembered that the famous fasting individual, Dr. Tanner, after eating nothing for forty days and forty nights, took for his first article of nourishment, at the close of this time of fasting, half a watermelon, and that he retained and digested it successfully.

CHAPTER XV.

Valparaiso.—Principal South American Port of the Pacific.—A Good
Harbor.—Tallest Mountain on this Continent.—The Newspaper Press.
—Warlike Aspect.—Girls as Car Conductors.—Chilian Exports.—
Foreign Merchants.—Effects of Civil War.—Gambling in Private
Houses.—Immigration.—Culture of the Grape.—Agriculture.—
Island of Juan Fernandez.

Valparaiso—"Vale of Paradise"—was thus fancifully named because of its
assumed loveliness. True, it is beautifully situated, and is a fine city of its
class, located in an admirable semicircular bay, not upon one, but upon many
hills, backed by a crescent-shaped mountain range. But when one compares
its harbor to that of Naples, or Sydney in Australia, for picturesqueness of
scenery, as is often done, it only provokes invidious remarks. The matchless
harbor of Rio Janeiro, on the eastern coast of the continent, already fully
described in these pages, is far more charming in general effect and in all of
its surroundings, not to mention that it is more than twenty times as large.
Valparaiso is the principal seaport of Chili, and indeed, for the present, it is
the main port of the entire west coast of South America. By consulting the
map it will be readily seen that Chili must ever be a maritime nation,
depending more upon an effective navy than an army. The possession of the
national ships of war by the Congressional party in the revolution so lately
terminated gave them virtual control of the cities along the coast, at the
outbreak of the émeute, and this means they employed against the Presidential
party with the most ruthless effect. They did not hesitate to savagely
cannonade and shell a city, though two thirds of the occupants were their own
friends and supporters, provided it was held ostensibly, and for the time being
only, by the supporters of Balmaceda. The outrageous bombardment of
Iquique is an instance in illustration of this charge. The Chilian delights to be
cruel; it is his instinct to destroy and to plunder. He is by nature boastful,
passionate, and headstrong. This disposition seems to be born in the race, is in
fact a matter of heredity, fostered by bull-fights and kindred entertainments.
But the country must now pay for the enormous destruction of property of
which the directors of the civil war have been guilty. The European powers
have already begun to send in their demands for damages done to their non-
combatant merchants. England comes first with a bill calling for payment of
sixty million dollars. Spain, Italy, and Germany will follow. It is estimated
that a hundred million dollars will be required to settle these foreign demands.
Chili must pay. There is no avoiding it. Reckless destruction will be found to
be rather an expensive amusement in future for these South Americans. Their
outrageous and murderous treatment of citizens of the United States who land
upon their shore is also like to cost them a heavy sum in way of penalty. The
present is a good opportunity to teach them a salutary lesson. The Chilians

will not be in a hurry to repeat crimes which they find entail sure and swift punishment.

A majority of the population of Chili lives, as a rule, within a few miles of the sea, and her coast line extends from Cape Horn northward over two thousand miles to the borders of Bolivia and Peru. With this extraordinary length, she has an average width of hardly more than a hundred miles, bordered on the east by the western slope of the Andes, whose eastern side belongs to the Argentine Republic, and on the west by the Pacific Ocean. The present estimated area of the republic is about two hundred and twenty thousand square miles, containing a population of considerably less than three millions, though its capacious territory could be so divided as to make twenty-five states as large as Massachusetts. Sixteen hundred miles of steam railroads render the principal sections of Chili accessible to one another. The coast line has from time to time been undergoing decided changes through volcanic action. In 1822, after a visible commotion, the shore was permanently raised three feet at Valparaiso, and four feet at Quintere. This change extended over an area of a hundred thousand miles. Another but lesser elevation took place in the same region in 1835.

There seems to be no accounting for the vagaries of a land subject to volcanic influences.

The harbor of Valparaiso is well protected on the east, south, and west, but it is open to the north, from which direction come very heavy winds and seas during a couple of months in the winter season, often causing serious casualties among the shipping which may chance to be anchored in the harbor. A "norther" is as much dreaded here as it is at Vera Cruz and along the Gulf of Mexico generally.

The entrance to the harbor is on its north side, and is a mile in width, more or less. The flags of nearly all nations are seen here, though the Stars and Stripes are less frequently to be met with than others. The city lies at the base of the closely surrounding hills, up whose sides and in the ravines the dwelling-houses have been constructed, tier above tier. Over all, further inland, looms the frosted head of grand old Aconcagua, twenty-two thousand feet and more in height, believed to be the tallest mountain in the western hemisphere. This mighty member of the Andean Cordillera is said to be ninety miles away, but it is so lofty and dominant, as seen through the clear atmosphere, that it appears almost within cannon range. At this writing the harbor presents quite a warlike aspect. English, American, French, German, and Chilian men-of-war are anchored here, looking after their several national interests, as affected by the civil war. The bugle calls of the several ships, the morning and evening guns, the display of naval bunting, together with the flitting hither and thither of well-manned boats, all unite to form a gay and suggestive scene. The Chilian cruisers in the hands of the revolutionists would not hesitate to batter down any government buildings on the coast, destroying incidentally the domestic residences and merchandise of non-combatants, were they not restrained by the presence of foreign flags and guns. When Balmaceda undertook by a proclamation to shut up the ports of Chili, and declared them blockaded, he was told by the several naval commanders on the coast that he could not establish a paper blockade, and that if the merchant ships of their several countries were in any way interfered with, he would have to fight somebody else besides the revolutionists. The ports were therefore kept as open to legitimate commerce as they ever were.

The author was disappointed at not being able to reach Santiago, the capital of Chili, which is situated at the foot of the western slope of the Andes, nearly two thousand feet above tide-water. It is connected with Valparaiso by railway, and under ordinary circumstances can be reached in eight hours. The difficulties caused by the civil war, and the suspicion with which all foreigners were regarded, proved impossible to surmount without a protracted effort, and submitting to any amount of red tape. Santiago was founded by one of Pizarro's captains, in 1541, and now contains about two hundred thousand inhabitants. There are some Americans and many English resident in Santiago, together with Germans and Frenchmen, the foreigners being mostly merchants. We were told of two familiar statues which are to be seen in a public square of the city, in front of the post-office. One represents George Washington, the other Abraham Lincoln, both of which were stolen from Lima during the late conflict between Chili and Peru.

But this is a digression. Let us once more return to the commercial port of Valparaiso.

A considerable portion of this city has been reclaimed from the sea, and still more land suitable for the erection of business warehouses near the shore is being added to this part of the town. Local enterprise, however, is pretty much suspended for the time being, owing to the disturbed condition of political affairs. The mountains near at hand supply ample stone and soil for the purpose of extending the area of this business portion of the town. Sixty or seventy years ago, the city contained only a single street, on the edge of the harbor; to-day it has all the appearance and belongings of a great commercial capital, and a population of a hundred and thirty thousand. Except Rio Janeiro and Buenos Ayres, we saw nowhere thoroughfares more full of energetic life and business activity. The main avenue is the Calle Victoria, which runs round the entire water front, occupied by the banks, hotels, insurance offices, and the best shops in the town.

There are four large daily newspapers published in Valparaiso, whose united circulation exceeds thirty thousand copies. "El Mercurio" has the eminent respectability of age, having been published regularly for a period of half a century. The facility for news-gathering is very good, as this city is connected with the world at large by submarine cable, but no such detailed and complete summary of intelligence is attempted as our North American journals exhibit daily. While on this subject, we may add that there are no newspapers in Europe, or elsewhere, which will compare with those of the United States in the average ability and journalistic merit which characterizes them. We do not say this in a boastful spirit, but simply make the statement as an incontrovertible fact.

Some of the business structures along the harbor front of Valparaiso are fine edifices architecturally, and many of the retail stores will compare favorably with the average of ours in Washington Street, Boston. The elegant class of goods displayed in some of these establishments shows that the population is an habitually extravagant and free-living one. We were told, by way of illustration, that millionaires were as plenty as blackberries before the late civil war, while many wealthy men, foreseeing the catastrophe which was about to occur, shrewdly prepared for it, and by careful management saved their property intact. Many of the private houses on Victoria Street are spacious, elegant, and costly, the occupants living in regal style, to support which must cost a very heavy annual outlay. It appears that President Balmaceda discovered, during the late struggle, where and how to lay his hands upon the resources of a few of these citizens, and that such he completely impoverished, under one pretext and another, using their property to support his armed minions, and to swell the aggregate of funds which he sent for deposit in his own name to Europe. One or two cases of this sort were related to us in which the citizens were not only made to give up the whole of their private property, but were finally imprisoned and sentenced to death upon a charge of treason, without even the semblance of a trial!

It is no marvel, to those who know the facts of his career, that a man who was guilty of such crimes, when at last brought to bay, finding himself betrayed and deserted by his pretended friends, should have blown out his own brains. The posthumous papers which he left, and wherein he tries to pose as a martyr, are simply a ludicrous failure. José Manuel Balmaceda was in the fifty-second year of his age when he committed suicide, and was at the time hiding for fear of the infuriated citizens of Santiago, who would certainly have hanged the would-be dictator without the least hesitation or formality, if they could have got possession of his person.

The tramway-cars of Valparaiso are of the two-story pattern, like those of

Copenhagen and New Orleans, also found in many of the European cities. They have as conductors, like Concepcion, very pretty half-breed girls, who appear to thoroughly understand their business, and to fulfill its requirements to universal satisfaction. If an intoxicated or unruly person appears on the cars, the conductress does not attempt personally to eject him. She has only to hold up her hand, and the nearest policeman, of whom there are always a goodly number about, jumps on to the car and settles the matter in short order. Girls were thus first employed in order that the men who ordinarily fill these places might be drafted into the army, during the late war between Chili and Peru, and as the system proved to be a complete success, it has been continued ever since. The fare charged on these tram-cars is five cents for each inside passenger, and half that sum for the outside; and, as in Paris, when the seats are all full, a little sign is shown upon the car, signifying that no more persons will be admitted, none being allowed to stand. The same rule is enforced in London, and the thought suggested itself as to whether our West End Railway Company of Boston might not take an important hint therefrom.

The ladies and gentlemen of the city are a well dressed class, the former adopting Parisian costumes, and the gentlemen wearing a full dress of dark broadcloth, with tall stove-pipe hats. The women of the more common class wear the national "manta," and the men the "poncha." The former is a dark, soft shawl which covers in part the head and face of the wearer. The latter is a long, striped shawl, with a slit cut in the centre, through which the head of the wearer is thrust. Nothing could be more simple in construction than both of these garments, and yet they are somehow very picturesque.

As we have already intimated, it is soon learned, upon landing at any port of the commercial world, what the staple products of the neighborhood are, by simply noting the visible merchandise made ready for shipment. Here we have sugar, wool, and cotton prevailing over all other articles. Guano and nitrate, which also form specialties here, are represented, though the supply of the former is pretty much exhausted. The nitrate trade is controlled by an Englishman of large fortune, Colonel North, known here as the "Nitrate King." This valuable fertilizer is the deposit of the nitrate of soda in the beds of lakes long since dried up, the waters of which originally contained in solution large quantities of this material. These lakes in olden times received the flow of a great water-shed, and having no outlet, save by evaporation, accumulated and precipitated at the bottom the chemical elements flowing into them from the surrounding country. The article is now dug up and put through a certain process, then shipped to foreign countries as a fertilizer, believed to put new heart into exhausted soil. England consumes an immense quantity of it annually, and many ships are regularly employed in its transportation.

The custom house, situated near the landing at Valparaiso, is a somewhat remarkable structure, having a long, low façade surmounted by tall, handsome towers. This is eminently the business part of the town, and is called "El Puerto." The larger share of the residences of the merchants and well-to-do citizens is situated on the hillsides, to reach which it is necessary to ascend long flights of steps. At certain points elevators are also supplied by which access is gained to the upper portions of the town, after the fashion already described at Bahia, on the east coast.

The majority of people doing business in Valparaiso are English, and English is the almost universal language. Even the names upon the city signs are suggestive in this direction. Among the public houses are the "Queen's Arms," the "Royal Oak," the "Red Lion," and so on. Besides an English school, there are three churches belonging to that nationality. There are numerous free schools, both of a primary and advanced character, an elaborately organized college, two or three theatres, and the usual charitable establishments, including a public library. The principal part of the city is lighted by electricity, and the telephone is in general use. A special effort has lately been made to promote the education of the rising generation in Chili, and we know of no field where the endeavor would be more opportune. Such an effort is never out of place, but here it is imperatively called for. The almost universal ignorance of the common people of Chili is deplorable, and little improvement can be hoped for as regards their moral or physical condition, except through the means of educating the youth of the country. A commissioner-general of education was appointed some time ago, who has already visited Europe and North America to study the best modern methods adopted in the public schools. This is a tangible evidence of improvement which speaks for itself, and is a great stride of this people in the right direction. Of course the late political crisis will greatly retard the hoped-for results, just as it will put Chili back some years in her national progress, whatever may be the final outcome in other respects.

Gambling is a prevailing national trait in this country, by no means confined to any one class of the community. The street gamin plays for copper centavos, while the pretentious caballero does the same for gold coins. It is quite common in family circles, held to be very aristocratic, to see the gaming table laid out every evening, as regularly as the table upon which the meals are served. Money in large sums is lost and won with assumed indifference in these private circles, whole fortunes being sometimes sacrificed at a single sitting. Gambling seems to be held exempt from the censure of either church or state, since both officials and priests indulge in all sorts of games of chance. There are the usual public lotteries always going on to tempt the poorer classes of the people, and to capture their hard-earned wages.

One virtue must be freely accorded to the business centre of this city, namely, that of cleanliness, in which respect it is far in advance of most of the capitals on the east coast of South America. Being the first seaport of any importance in the South Pacific, it is naturally a place of call for European bound steamers coming from New Zealand and Australia, as well as those sailing from Panama and San Francisco. In view of the fact that six hundred and fifty thousand people emigrate from Europe annually, seeking new homes in foreign lands, the Chilian government, in common with some others of the South American states, has for several years past held forth the liberal inducement of substantial aid to all bona fide settlers from foreign countries. Each newcomer who is the head of a family is given two hundred acres of available land, together with lumber and other materials for building a comfortable dwelling-house, also a cart, a plough, and a reasonable amount of seed for planting. Besides these favors which we have enumerated, some other important considerations are offered. Only a small number, comparatively speaking, of emigrants have availed themselves of such liberal terms, and these have been mostly Germans. If such an offer were properly promulgated and laid before the poor peasantry of Ireland and Spain and Italy, it would seem as though many of those people would hasten to accept it in the hope of bettering their condition in life. Whether such a result would follow emigration would of course depend upon many other things besides the liberality of the offer of the Chilian government. The Germans form a good class of emigrants, perhaps the best, often bringing with them considerable pecuniary means, together with habits of industry. The late civil war has put a stop to emigration for a period at least, and will interfere with its success for some time to come, if indeed Chili ever assumes quite so favorable a condition as she has sacrificed.

There are some districts, including Limache and Pauquehue, where grape culture has been brought to great perfection, and where it is conducted on a very large scale. Wine-making is thus taking its place as one of the prosperous industries of the country. The amount of the native product consumed at home is very large, and a regular system of exports to other South American ports has been established. All of the most important modes of culture, such as have been proven most successful in France and California, have been carefully adopted here. Tramways are laid to intersect the various parts of these extensive vineyards, to aid in the gathering and transportation of the ripe fruit, while the appliances for expressing the juice of the grape are equally well systematized. One vineyard, belonging to the Consiño family, near Santiago, covers some two hundred acres, closely planted with selected vines from France, Switzerland, and California, the purpose being to retain permanently such grades as are found best adapted to the soil and the climate of Chili. The white wines are the most popular here, but red Burgundy brands are produced with good success. The vines are trained on triple lines of wires, stretched between iron posts, presenting an appearance of great uniformity, the long rows being planted about three or four feet apart. Every arrangement for artificial irrigation is provided, it being an absolute necessity in this district of Chili. Trenches are cut along the rows of vines, through which the water, from ample reservoirs, is permitted to flow at certain intervals; particularly when the grape begins to swell and ripen. The fruit is not trodden here, as it is in Italy, but is thoroughly expressed by means of proper machinery.

Geographically, Chili is, as we have intimated, a long, narrow country, lying south of Peru and Bolivia, ribbon-like in form, and divided into nineteen provinces. It has been considerably enlarged by conquest from both of the nationalities just named; including the important territory of Terapaca. The name "Chili" signifies snow, with which the tops of most of the mountain ranges upon the eastern border are always covered. Still, extending as she does, from latitude 24° south to Cape Horn, she embraces every sort of climate, from burning heat to glacial frosts, while nearly everything that grows can be produced upon her soil. Though she has less than three million inhabitants, still her territory exceeds that of any European nationality except Russia. The manifest difference between the aggregate of her population and that of her square miles does not speak very favorably for the healthful character of the climate. There is no use in attempting to disguise the fact that Chili has rather a hard time of it, with sweeping epidemics, frequent earthquakes, and devouring tidal waves. The country contains thirty volcanoes, none of which are permanently active, but all of which have their periods of eruption, and most of which exhibit their dangerous nature by emitting sulphurous smoke and ashes. The unhygienic condition of life among her native races accounts for the large death-rate prevailing at all times, and especially among the peon children, thus preventing a natural increase in the population. Unless a liberal immigration can be induced, Chili must annually decrease in population. As regards the foreign whites and the educated natives who indulge in no extravagant excesses, living with a reasonable regard for hygiene, doubtless Chili is as healthy as most countries, but there is still to be remembered the erratic exhibitions of nature, a possibility always hanging like the sword of Damocles over this region. A whole town may, without the least warning, vanish from the face of the earth in the space of five minutes, or be left a mass of ruins.

It is in the districts of the north that the rich mines and the nitrate fields are found, but the central portion of the country, and particularly towards the south, is the section where the greatest agricultural results are realized, and which will continue to yield in abundance after the mineral wealth shall have become quite exhausted. The southern portion of the country embraces Patagonia, which has lately been divided between Chili and the Argentine Republic. In short, Chili is no exception to the rule that agriculture, and not mining products, is the true and permanent reliance of any country.

A little less than four hundred miles off the shore of Valparaiso, on the same line of latitude, is the memorable island of Juan Fernandez. It is politically an unimportant dependence of Chili, though of late years it has indirectly been made the means of producing some income for the national treasury. There was a period in which Chili maintained a penal colony here, but the convicts mutinied, and massacred the officers who had charge of them. These convicts succeeded in getting away from the island on passing ships. No attempt has been made since that time to reëstablish a penal colony on this island. To-day the place is occupied by thriving vegetable gardeners, and raisers of stock. Every intelligent youth will remember the island as the spot where De Foe laid the scene of his popular and fascinating story of "Robinson Crusoe." The island is about twenty miles long by ten broad, and is covered with dense tropical verdure, gentle hills, sheltered valleys, and thrifty woods. Juan Fernandez resembles the Azores in the North Atlantic. Though generally spoken of in the singular, there are actually three islands here, forming a small, compact group, known as Inward Island, Outward Island, and Great Island. Many intelligent people think that the story of Robinson Crusoe is a pure fabrication, but this is not so. De Foe availed himself of an actual occurrence, and put it into readable form, adding a few romantic episodes to season the story for the taste of the million. It was in a measure truth, which he stamped with the image of his own genius. Occasionally some enthusiastic admirer of De Foe comes thousands of miles out of the beaten track of travel to visit this group of islands, by the way of Valparaiso. Grapes, figs, and other tropical fruits abound at Juan Fernandez. It is said that several thousand people might be easily supported by the natural resources of these islands, and the abundance of fish which fill the neighboring waters. An English naval commander stopped here in 1741, to recruit his ships' crews, and to repair some damages. While here he caused various seeds to be planted for the advantage of any mariners who might follow. The benefit of this Christian act has been realized by many seamen since that date. Fruits, grain, and vegetables are now produced by spontaneous fertility annually, which were not before to be found here. The English commander also left goats and swine to run wild, and to multiply, and these animals are numerous there to-day.

Juan Fernandez has one tall peak, nearly three thousand feet high, which the pilots point out long before the rest of the island is seen. It was from this lofty lookout that Alexander Selkirk was wont to watch daily in the hope of sighting some passing ship, by which he might be released from his imprisonment. There are about one hundred residents upon the group to-day, it having been leased by the Chilian government as a stock ranch for the breeding of goats and cattle, as well as for the raising of vegetables for the market of Valparaiso. There are said to be thirty thousand horned cattle, and many sheep, upon these islands. Occasional excursion parties are made up at Valparaiso to visit the group by steamboat, for the purpose of shooting seals and mountain goats. Stories are told of Juan Fernandez having been formerly made the headquarters of pirates who came from thence to ravage the towns on the coast of the continent, and it is believed by the credulous that much of the ill-gotten wealth of the buccaneers still remains hidden there. In search of this supposititious treasure, expeditions have been fitted out in past years at Valparaiso, and many an acre of ground has been vainly dug over in seeking for piratical gold, supposed to be buried there. Some of the shrewd stock raisers of Juan Fernandez are ready, for a consideration, to point out to seekers the most probable places where such treasures might have been buried.

CHAPTER XVI.

The Port of Callao.—A Submerged City.—Peruvian Exports.—A Dirty and Unwholesome Town.—Cinchona Bark.—The Andes.—The Llama.—A National Dance.—City of Lima.—An Old and Interesting Capital.—Want of Rain.—Pizarro and His Crimes.—A Grand Cathedral.—Chilian Soldiers.—Costly Churches of Peru.—Roman Catholic Influence.—Desecration of the Sabbath.

The passage northward from Valparaiso to Callao occupies about four days by the steamers which do not stop at intermediate ports. We entered the harbor in the early morning while a soft veil of mist enshrouded the bay, but as the sun fairly shone upon the view, this aerial screen rapidly disappeared, revealing Callao just in front of us, making the foreground of a pleasing and vivid picture, the middle distance filled by the ancient city of Lima, and the far background by alpine ranges. Callao is an ill-built though important town, with a population of about thirty thousand, and serves as the port for Lima, the capital of Peru. It has a good harbor, well protected by the island of San Lorenzo, which, with the small island of El Fronton, and the Palminos reef, forms a protection against the constant swell of the ocean. There are nearly always one or two ships of war belonging to foreign nations in the harbor, and large steamships from the north or the south. The sailing distance from Panama is fifteen hundred miles. The Callao of to-day is comparatively modern. Old Callao formerly stood on a tongue of land opposite San Lorenzo, but in 1746 an earthquake submerged it and drowned some five thousand of the inhabitants, foundered a score of ships, and stranded a Spanish man-of-war. In calm weather one can row a boat over the spot where the old city stood, and see the ruins far down in the deep waters. The present city has twice been near to sharing the same fate: once in 1825, and again in 1868. It is, therefore, not assuming too much to say that Callao may at any time disappear in the most summary fashion. The sunken ruins in the harbor are a melancholy and suggestive sight, the duplicate of which we do not believe can be found elsewhere on the globe. Though seismic disturbances are of such frequent occurrence, and are so destructive on the west coast of South America, they are hardly known on the Atlantic or eastern side of the continent. That they are frequently coincident with volcanic disturbances indicates that there is an intimate connection between them, but yet earthquakes often occur in regions where volcanoes do not exist. This was the case, not long since, as most of our readers will remember, in South Carolina. It has been noticed by careful observers that animals become uneasy on the eve of such an event, which would seem to show that earthquakes sometimes owe their origin to extraordinary atmospheric conditions.

San Lorenzo is about six miles from Callao, and is four miles long by one in width. It is utterly barren, presenting a mass of brownish gray color, eleven hundred feet high, at whose base there is ever a broad, snow white ruffle, caused by the never-ceasing ocean swell breaking into foam. An English smelting company has established extensive works near the shore of the island, for the reduction of silver and copper ores. The approach to Callao from the sea affords a fine view of the undulating shore, backed by the snowy Cordilleras, the shabby buildings of the town, with the dismantled castle of San Felipe forming the foreground. In landing one must be cautious: there is always considerable swell in the harbor.

The staple products of this region are represented by packages of merchandise prepared for shipment, and which are the first to attract one's attention upon landing, such as cinchona bark from the native forests, piles of wheat in bulk, hides, quantities of crude salt, sugar packed in dried banana leaves, bales of alpaca wool, and, most suggestive of all, some heavy bags of silver ore. Little is being done in mining at present, though the field for this industry is large. The difficulty of transportation is one of the great drawbacks, yet Peru has over a thousand miles of railways in her rather limited area. Gold, platinum, silver, and copper are all found in paying quantities. Coal and petroleum also exist here, in various inland districts. The guano deposits, which have yielded so much wealth to Peru in the past, are practically exhausted, while the nitrate-producing province of Tarapaca has been stolen by Chili, to which it now belongs. It is thought that the nitrate deposits can be profitably worked for fifty years to come.

A crowd of the lazy, ragged population were loafing about the landing, watching the strangers as they came on shore at the wet and slippery stone steps.

It is very plain that the great importance of Callao has departed, though there is still an appearance of business activity. Not long ago, a hundred vessels at a time might be seen at anchor inside of San Lorenzo; now, a score of good-sized ships are all one can count. This is owing to various causes: an unreasonable high tariff is one of them, exorbitant port charges is another, and the general depression of business on the west coast is felt quite as strongly here as at any of the ports. Like Santos, on the other side of the continent, Callao is ever an unhealthy resort, where a great mortality prevails in the fever season. The absence of good drainage and inattention to hygienic rules will in part account for the bad repute that the port has among the shipping masters who frequent the coast. The streets are particularly malodorous about the water front. The dirty vultures seem to be depended upon to remove offensive garbage.

A certain remarkable occurrence sometimes takes place in this harbor, which, so far as the writer knows, is without precedent elsewhere. A ship may come in from sea and anchor at about sunset, in good order and condition, everything being white and clean on board, but when her captain comes on deck the next morning, he may find that his ship has been painted, inside and out, a dark chocolate color during the night, the atmosphere at the same time being impregnated with a peculiar odor, arising from this "paint," or whatever it may be, which clings tenaciously to every object, wood or iron. While it is damp and freshly deposited, it can be removed like fresh paint, but if it is permitted to dry, it is as difficult to remove as ordinary dried paint would be. No one can tell the origin of this nuisance, but most seamen whose business brings them to Callao have been through this experience. Of course it must be an atmospheric deposit, but from whence? It has never been known to occur upon the neighboring land, but only in the harbor. Scientists have given the matter their attention, and have concluded that it may be caused by sulphurous gases produced in the earth below the water, which rise to the surface and disseminate themselves in the surrounding atmosphere.

From any elevated point in the city one may enjoy a delightful view, the main features of which are the Andes on the land side, and seaward, the broad heaving bosom of the Pacific. The corrugated peaks of the former, clad in white, seem like restless phantoms marching through the sky. Over the latter, long lines of inky blackness trail behind northern or southern bound steamers, while here and there a tall, full-rigged ship recalls the older modes of navigation.

The smoother water inside of San Lorenzo is alive with small boats, some under sails, some propelled by oars, shooting in and out among the shipping which lie at anchor before the town. A pair of large whales assisted at this scene for our special benefit, just inside the harbor's mouth. It must have been only play on their part,—leviathans at play,—but they threw up the sea in such clouds of spray with their broad tails, as to make it appear like a battle-royal seen from a mile away.

We mentioned the fact of seeing cinchona bark in bales ready for shipping. Of all the products of South America, gold, silver, and precious stones included, the most valuable is the drug which is called quinine, made from the bark of the cinchona tree. There is no other one article known to the materia medica which has been used in such large quantities or with such unvarying success by suffering humanity. It was first introduced into Europe from Peru, and was then known as Peruvian bark. It was supposed at that time to be found only in this section of the continent; but subsequently it was discovered to abound in all the forests along the course of the Andes, and especially on their western slope. So large has been its export that it was found the source of supply was rapidly becoming exhausted, until local governments awoke to the importance of the matter, and protected by law the trees which produce it. These are no longer ruthlessly cut down to die, when yielding their valuable harvest, but only a certain quantity of the desirable bark is taken from each tree annually, so that nature replaces the portion which had been removed, by covering the trunk with a fresh growth. The cinchona tree, having been transplanted from South America, is now successfully cultivated in the islands of the Malacca Straits, Ceylon, India, and other tropical regions.

The tree which produces this valuable febrifuge belongs to the same family as the coffee plant. In appearance it is very like our native beech tree, having remarkably white wood.

The llama is found nearly all over South America, and is often seen as a beast of burden at Callao, taking the place here which the donkey or burro fills in Mexico. It has been described as having the head and neck of a camel, the body of a deer, the wool of a sheep, and the neigh of a horse. We do not agree with those who pronounce the llama an awkward creature. True, the body is a little ungainly, but the head, the graceful pose, the pointed, delicate ears, and the large, lustrous eyes are absolutely handsome. It can carry a burden weighing one hundred pounds over hard mountain roads, day after day, while living upon very scanty food. It is slow in its movements, patient when well treated, and particularly sure-footed. It is of a very gentle disposition, but when it finds the weight placed upon its back too heavy, like the Egyptian camel, it immediately lies down and will not rise until the load is lightened.

The llama, or "mountain camel," as it has been aptly called, is the only domesticated native animal. The horse, ox, hog, and sheep are all importations which were entirely unknown here four centuries ago. The llama has two notable peculiarities: when angry it will expectorate at its enemy, and when hurt will shed tears. The expectoration is of an acrid, semi-poisonous nature, and if it strikes the eyes will, it is said, blind them. The llama, guanaco, alpaca, and vicuña were the four sheep of the Incas, the wool of the first clothing the common people; the second, the nobles; the third, the royal governors; and the fourth the Incas. The first two are domesticated, guanacos and vicuñas are wild, though they all belong to the same family.

The manners and customs of any people new to the traveler are always an interesting study, but in nothing are they more strongly individualized than in the pursuit of amusements. A favorite dance, known here as the *zama cueca*, is often witnessed out-of-doors in retired corners of the plaza or the alameda, as well as elsewhere. It requires two performers, and is generally danced by a male and female, being not unlike the Parisian cancan, both in the movement and the purpose of the expression. The two dancers stand opposite each other, each having a pocket handkerchief in the right hand, while the music begins at first a dull, monotonous air, which rapidly rises and falls in cadence. The dancers approach each other, swaying their bodies gracefully, and using their limbs nimbly; now they pass each other, turning in the act to coquettishly wave the handkerchief about their heads, and also to snap it towards each other's faces. Thus they advance and retreat several times, whipping at each other's faces, while throwing their bodies into peculiar attitudes. Again they resume the first movement of advance and retreat, one assuming coyness, the other ardor, and thus continue, until, as a sort of climax, they fall into each other's arms with a peal of hearty laughter. A guitar is the usual accompanying instrument, the player uttering the while a shrill impromptu chant. When a male dancer joins in this street performance, as is sometimes the case, it is apt to be a little coarse and vulgar.

There is very little in Callao to detain us, and one is quite ready to hasten on to Lima, the capital of Peru, hoping to escape the stench and universal dirtiness of the port.

The city of Lima has at this writing about one hundred and sixty thousand inhabitants, and is situated six miles from Callao, its shipping port, with which it is connected by two rival railways. These roads are constructed upon an up-grade the whole distance, but the rise is so gradual as to be almost imperceptible, though Lima is over five hundred feet higher than Callao. The capital, which is clearly visible from the water as we enter the harbor, presents from that distance, and even from a much nearer point of view, a most pleasing picture, being favorably situated on elevated ground, with its many spires and domes standing forth in bold relief. It has, when seen from such a distance, a certain oriental appearance, charming to the eye of a stranger. But it is deceptive; it is indeed distance which lends enchantment in this case, for upon arriving within its precincts one is rudely undeceived. The apparently grand array of architecture on near inspection proves to be flimsy and poor in detail: everything is bamboo frame and plaster; no edifice is solid above the basement. Still, one can easily imagine how attractive the place must have been in those viceregal days, the period of its false glory and prosperity. The capital stands almost at the very foot of the Cordillera which forms the coast range, and is built upon both sides of the Rimac, over which stretches a substantial stone bridge of six arches, very old and very homely, but all the more interesting because it is so venerable. The width of the river at this point is over five hundred feet. In the winter season it is a very moderate stream, but when the summer sun asserts itself, the snow upon the neighboring mountains yields to its warmth, and the Rio Rimac then becomes an alpine torrent. It is like the Arno at Florence, which at certain seasons has the form of a river without the circulation. The anecdote is told here of a Yankee visitor to Lima who was being shown over the city by a patriotic citizen, and who on coming to this spot remarked to his chaperon: "You ought either to buy a river or sell this bridge."

At the entrance of this ancient structure stands a lofty and very effective archway, with two tall towers, and a clock in a central elevation. Prominent over the arched entrance to the roadway is the motto *Dios y La Patria*,—"God and Country." Nothing in Lima is of more interest than this hoary, unique, moss-grown bridge.

One pauses before the crumbling yet still substantial old structure to recall the vivid scenes which must have been enacted in the long, long past upon its roadway. Here madly contending parties have spilled each other's blood, hundreds of gaudy church processions have crossed these arches, bitter civil and foreign wars have raged about the bridge, dark conspiracies have been whispered and ripened here, solitary murders committed in the darkness of night, and lifeless bodies thrown from its parapet; but the dumb witness still remains intact, having endured more than three hundred years of use and abuse.

It is not necessary to unpack one's waterproof or umbrella in Lima. It never rains here, any more than it does in the region of Aden, at the mouth of the Red Sea. All vegetable growth is more or less dependent upon artificial irrigation, and in the environs where this is judiciously applied the orange and lemon trees are heavy with golden fruit, forming a rich contrast with the deep green of the luxuriant plantain, the thick, lance-like agave, and the prolific banana. The city and its environs would be as poorly off without the water of the Rimac as would the Egyptians if deprived of the annual overflow of the fertilizing Nile. Though the river is so inconsiderable at certain seasons, still it does supply a certain quantity of water always, which is improved to the utmost. Dews some times prevail at night, so heavy as to be of partial benefit, giving to vegetation a breath of moisture, and taking away the dead dryness of the atmosphere. This, however favorable for vegetation, is considered unwholesome for humanity. The flowers and shrubbery of the plaza droop for want of water, and are only preserved by great care on the part of those in charge of them. In some of the private gardens the pashinba palm-tree is seen, very peculiar in its growth, being mounted as it were upon stilts, formed by the exposed straight roots which radiate, like a series of props, to support the tall trunk. At its apex is a singular, spear-like stem, pointing straight skyward, without leaf or branch, just beneath which are the graceful, long, curved palm leaves, exquisite in proportions, bending like ostrich feathers. At first sight this tree looks like an artificial production, in which nature has taken no part. Lying only twelve degrees south of the equator, Lima has a tropical climate, but being also close to the foothills of the Andes, she is near to a temperate district, so that her market yields the fruits and vegetables of two zones.

Pizarro, the ambitious and intrepid conqueror of Peru, here established his capital in 1535, and here ended his days in 1541, dying at the hands of the assassin, the natural and retributive end of a life of gross bigotry, sensuality, recklessness, and almost unparalleled cruelty. In a narrow street,—the Callejon de Petateron,—leading out of the Plaza Mayor, a house is pointed out as being the one in which Pizarro was assassinated. Both Pizarro in Peru and Cortez in Mexico owed their phenomenal success to exceptional circumstances, namely, to the civil wars which prevailed among the native tribes of the countries they invaded. By shrewdly directing these intestine troubles so as to aid their own purposes, each commander in his special field achieved complete victory over races which, thus disunited and pitted against each other, fell an easy prey to the cunning invaders. Neither of these adventurers had sufficient strength to contend against a united and determined people. Such an enemy on his own ground would have swept the handful of Spaniards led by Pizarro from the face of the earth by mere force of numbers.

Soon after its foundation, Lima became the most luxurious and profligate of the viceregal courts of Spain, and so continued until its declaration of independence, and final separation from the mother country. The most worthless and restless spirits about the throne of Spain were favored in a desire to join Pizarro in the New World. The home government, while purging itself of so undesirable an element, added to the recklessness and utter immorality which reigned in the atmosphere of Lima. Forty-three successive viceroys ruled Peru during the Spanish occupancy. The nefarious Inquisition, steeped in the blood of helpless and innocent natives, was active here long after its decadence in Madrid, while the local churches, convents, and monasteries accumulated untold wealth by a system of arbitrary taxation, and iniquitous extortion exercised towards the native race. What better could have been expected from Pizarro than to inaugurate and foster such a state of affairs? Under the influence of designing priests and lascivious monks, he was as clay in the potter's hands, being originally only an illiterate swineherd, one who could neither read nor write. The state documents put forth during his viceregency, still preserved and to be seen in the archives of Lima, show that he could only affix his mark, not even attempting to write his own name. Though Charles V. finally indorsed and ennobled him with the title of Marques de la Conquista, and appointed him viceroy of the conquered country, he was still and ever the illegitimate, low-bred hind of Truxillo in continental Spain. The palace of this man, who, with the exception of Cortez, was the greatest human butcher of the age in which he lived, is still used for government offices, while the senate occupies the council chamber of the old Inquisition building, infamous for the bloody work done within its walls. H. Willis Baxley, M. D., the admirable author, writes on the spot as follows: "When the apologists of Pizarro attempt to shield his crimes, and excuse his acts of cruelty by his religious zeal and holy purpose of extending the dominion of the cross, they may well be answered that the religion was unworthy of adoption which required for its extension that the wife of the Inca Manco, then a prisoner in Pizarro's power, should be 'stripped naked, bound to a tree, and in presence of the camp be scourged with rods, and then shot to death with arrows!' This cold-blooded brutality, and to a woman, should brand his name with eternal infamy."

As we have intimated, Lima, like Constantinople, looks at its best from a distance, viewed so that the full and combined effect of its many domes and spires can be taken in as a whole; but whether near to it or far from it, few places in South America possess more poetical and historical interest. Its past story reads like an Arabian Nights' tale. Though the city is by no means what it has been, and wears an unmistakable air of decayed greatness, and though foreign invaders and civil wars have done their worst, Lima is still an extremely attractive metropolis. Even the vandalism of the late Chilian invaders, who outraged all the laws of civilized warfare (if there is any such thing as civilized warfare), regardless of the rights of non-combatants, could not obliterate her natural attractions and historical associations. The Chilian soldiers destroyed solely for the sake of destroying, mutilated statuary and works of art generally, besides burning historical treasures and libraries; and yet these Chilians claim to be the highest type of modern civilization on the southern continent. They strove to ruin whatever they could not steal and carry away with them from Peru, and, almost incredible to record, they wantonly killed the elephant in the zoölogical garden of Lima, and purloined the small animals. Noble, chivalrous Chilians! The rank and file of these people are the very embodiment of ignorance and brutality. The Chilian soldier carries, as a regular weapon, a curved knife called a *curvos*, with which he cuts the throats of his enemies. At close quarters, instead of fighting man-fashion, as nearly all other nations do, he springs like a fierce bull-dog at his opponent's throat, and with his curvos cuts it from ear to ear. After a battle, bands of these fiends in human shape go over the field, seeking out the wounded who are still alive, deliberately cutting their throats, and robbing their bodies of all valuables. It is Chilian tactics to take no prisoners, give no quarter. These brave soldiers would have burned Lima to the ground after gaining possession, had it not been for the interference of the foreign ministers, who had national men-of-war at Callao with which to back their arguments. These guerrillas—for that is just about what the Chilian soldiers are—knew full well that if even a small European battalion of disciplined men were landed and brought against them, they would simply be swept from the face of the earth.

Lima is laid out with the streets in rectangular form, the central point being the Plaza Mayor, in the shape of a quadrangle, each side of which is five hundred feet in length. On the north side of this admirably arranged square stand the buildings occupied as government offices, together with the bishop's palace, and the cathedral overshadowed by its two lofty towers. The corner-stone of this edifice was laid by Pizarro with great ceremony. The spires, although presenting such an effective appearance, are constructed of the most frail material, such as bricks, stucco, and bamboo frames, but still, as a whole, they are undeniably imposing. In this dry climate they are, perhaps, enduring also. Like the façade of the church of St. Roche, in Paris, this of the Lima cathedral is marked by bullet-holes commemorating the Chilian invasion. The church is raised six or eight feet above the level of the plaza, as is usual in South America, standing upon a marble platform, reached by broad steps, well calculated to enhance the really graceful proportions, and add to the effect of its broad, high towers. The interior is quite commonplace, with the usual tinsel, poor carvings, and wretched oil paintings, including several grotesque Virgin Marys. These were too poor even for the Chilians to steal. Beneath the grand altar rest the ashes of Pizarro, the cruel, ambitious, reckless tool of the Romish Church. The cathedral was built in 1540, but has undergone complete repairs and renovations from time to time, being still considered to be one of the most imposing ecclesiastical edifices in America.

Its original cost is said to have been nine million dollars, to obtain which Pizarro robbed the Inca temples of all their elaborate gold and silver ornaments. According to Prescott, the Spaniards took twenty-four thousand, eight hundred pounds of gold, and eighty-two thousand ounces of silver from a single Inca temple! Prescott is careful in his statements to warn us of the unreliability of the Spanish writers, nearly all of whom were Romish priests. Where figures are concerned they cannot be depended upon for a moment. They also took special care to cover up the fiendish atrocities of the Inquisition, and the extortions of the church as exercised towards the poor, down-trodden native race.

One's spirits partook of the sombre and austere atmosphere which reigns at all times in this ancient edifice. It was very lonely. Not a soul was to be seen during our brief visit to the cathedral at noonday, except a couple of decrepit old beggars at the entrance, the faint, dull glare of the burning candles about the altar only serving to deepen the shadows and emphasize the darkness.

The area of the Plaza Mayor embraces eight or nine acres of land, and has often been the theatre of most sanguinary scenes, where hand-to-hand fights have frequently taken place between insurgent citizens and soldiers of the ruling power of the day, while many unpopular officials have been hanged in the towers of the cathedral, from each of which projects a gibbet! The middle of the plaza is beautified by a bronze fountain with arboreal and floral surroundings. There was formerly some statuary here, which the brave Chilians stole and carried away with them, even purloining the iron benches, which they transported to Valparaiso and Santiago. The streets running from this square, with the exception of the Calle de los Mercaderes, have an atmosphere of antiquity, which contrasts with the people one meets in them. Even the turkey buzzards, acting as street scavengers, are of an antique species, looking quite gray and dilapidated, as though they were a hundred years old. In Vera Cruz the same species of bird, kept for a similar purpose, have a brightness of feather, and jauntiness withal, quite unlike these feathered street-cleaners of Lima. The "Street of the Merchants," just referred to, is the fashionable shopping thoroughfare of Lima, where in the afternoons the ladies and gentlemen are seen in goodly numbers promenading in full dress.

There is here the usual multiplicity of churches, convents, and nunneries, such as are to be found in all Spanish cities, though the latter establishments have been partially suppressed. Some of the churches of Lima are fabulously expensive structures; indeed, the amount of money squandered on churches and church property in this city is marvelous. During the late war many articles of gold and silver, belonging to them, were melted into coin, but some were hidden, and have once more been restored to their original position in the churches. The convent and church of San Francisco form one of the most costly groups of buildings of the sort in America. The ornamental tiles of the flooring are calculated, not by the square yard, but by the acre. There are over a hundred Roman Catholic churches in Lima, few of which have any architectural beauty, but all of which are crowded with vulgar wax figures, wooden images, and bleeding saints. These churches in several instances have very striking façades: that of La Merced, for instance; but they are mere shams, as we have already said,—stucco and plaster; they would not endure the wear of any other climate for a single decade.

With all this outside religious show in Lima, there is no corresponding observance of the sacred character of the Sabbath. It is held rather as a period of gross license and indulgence, and devoted to bull-fights, cock-fighting, and drunkenness. The lottery-ticket vender reaps the greatest harvest on this occasion, and the gambling saloons are all open. Children pursue their every-day sports with increased ardor, and the town puts on a gala day aspect. At night the streets are ablaze, the theatres are crowded, and dissipation of every conceivable sort waxes fast and furious until long past midnight. The ignorant mass generally has drifted into observing the rituals of the Romish Church, but there are many of the native Indians in Peru who cherish a belief of a millennium in the near future; a time when the true prophet of the sun will return and restore the grand old Inca dynasty. Just so the Moors of Tangier hold to the belief that the time will yet come when they will be restored to the glory of their fathers, and to their beloved Granada; that the halls of the Alhambra will once more resound to the Moorish lute, and the grand cathedral of Cordova shall again become a mosque of the true faith.

The fact that the bull-ring of Lima will accommodate sixteen thousand people, and that it is always well filled on Sundays, speaks for itself. At these sanguinary performances a certain class of women appear in large numbers and in full dress, entering heartily into the spirit of the occasion, and waving their handkerchiefs furiously to applaud the actors in the tragedy, while the exhibitions are characterized by even more cruelty than at Madrid or Havana.

CHAPTER XVII.

A Grand Plaza.—Retribution.—The University of Lima.—Significance
of Ancient Pottery.—Architecture.—Picturesque Dwelling.—
Domestic Scene.—Destructive Earthquakes.—Spanish Sway.—
Women of Lima.—Street Costumes.—Ancient Bridge of Lima.—
Newspapers.—Pawnbrokers' Shops.—Exports.—An Ancient Mecca.
—Home by Way of Europe.

The large square in Lima, known as Plazuela de la Independencia, is grand in its proportions. One prominent feature is the bronze statue of Bolivar, the famous South American patriot. It also contains the old palace of the Inquisition, which looks to-day more like a stable than a palace. This detestable institution attained to greater scope and power here than it did even in Mexico. According to its own records, during its existence in the capital of Peru, fifty-nine persons were publicly burned alive as heretics, because they would not acknowledge the Roman Catholic faith, thousands were tortured until in their agony they agreed to anything, while thousands were publicly scourged to the same end. Could the truth be fully known as regards the bigoted reign of the priesthood at the time referred to in Peru, it would form one of the most startling chapters of modern history. But they were their own chroniclers, and suppressed everything which might possibly reflect upon themselves or upon their church. Retribution was slow, but it has come finally. The former convent of Guadeloupe is now occupied for a worthy object as a high school; the main portion of the cloisters of San Francisco have made way for the college of San Marco; that of San Carlos has supplanted the Jesuits; San Juan de Dios is now occupied as a railway station; while the once famous and infamous convent of Santa Catalina serves to-day as the public market.

The University of Lima was the first seat of education established in the New World, or, to fix the period more clearly in the average reader's mind, it dates from about seventy years before the historic Mayflower reached the shore of New England. The National Library contains some forty thousand volumes, also a collection of Peruvian antiquities, besides many objects of natural history, mostly of such examples as are indigenous to this section. There is one large oil painting in this building by a native artist named Monteros, the canvas measuring thirty by twenty feet. The title is "Obsequies of Atahualpa." This was carried away by the thieving Chilians, but was finally restored to Peru. It should be mentioned, to their lasting shame, that the books which they stole at the same time have not been returned.

The ancient pottery one sees in the collection of Peruvian antiquities is wonderfully like that to be found in the Boulak Museum at Cairo, in Egypt, Etruscan and Egyptian patterns prevailing over all other forms, which strongly suggests a common origin. Besides those which we have named, there are several other educational and art institutions in the city, together with three hospitals, two lunatic asylums, a college of arts, and the National Mint. One hospital, bearing the name of the Second of May Hospital, is a very large and thoroughly equipped establishment, occupying a whole square, and having accommodations for seven hundred patients. There are four theatres, one of which is conducted by the Chinese after their own peculiar fashion. The outsides of the dwelling-houses are painted in various brilliant colors, a practice which is found to prevail all over the southern continent, and which exhibits an inherent love among the people for warm, bright hues. The roofs of most houses serve as a depository for hens and chickens, noisy gamecocks especially asserting themselves before daybreak, forbidding all ideas of morning naps, unless one is accustomed to the din. Many of the dwellings are picturesque and attractive, with overhanging balconies and bay windows, the latter oftentimes finished very elaborately with handsome wood carvings and open-work lattices. As to the prevailing style of architecture, it is Spanish and Moorish combined, each building being constructed about a central patio, which is often rendered lovely with flowers and statuary, together with small orange and lemon trees in large painted tubs.

The abundance of cracks in the walls of the dwellings, both inside and out, is a significant hint that we are in an earthquake country. A slight shake is hardly spoken of at all; they come so often as to be comparatively unheeded.

In the environs of Lima the houses are built of adobe, rarely over one story in height, with very thick walls, this style having been found the best to resist the earthquakes, which must be very serious indeed to affect a low adobe house with walls two feet and a half thick. About these residences, which, not to put too fine a point upon the matter, are really nothing but mud cabins, there is often seen an attractive and refining feature, namely, small, but exceedingly pretty plots of cultivated flowers. It is astonishing how perfectly they serve to throw a flavor of refinement over all things else. The variety and fragrance of the Lima roses are something long to be remembered, and the people here seem to have a special love for this most popular of flowers. We had missed them nearly everywhere else in South America; therefore they were thrice welcome when they greeted us at Lima.

There is a dwelling-house in this city belonging to an old and rich family, which is worth a pilgrimage to see. It is built of stone, artistically carved, with a square balcony and bay window on each side of the tall, spacious, and elaborately ornamented doorway. It is clearly Moorish in type, and must be nearly or quite three hundred years old. Photographs are found of its façade in the art stores of Lima, and most visitors bring one away with them as a memento of the place. The house stands even with the thorough-*fare, and is only two stories in height, but is a beautiful relic of the past. It would be quite in accordance with the surroundings, were it to be transported to Cairo or Bagdad.

On the way from the Plaza Mayor to this attractive bit of Morisco architecture, one gets frequent glimpses of pretty, cool, flower-decked patios, about which the low picturesque dwellings are erected, and where domestic life is seen in partial seclusion. An infant is playing on the marble paved court, watched by a dark Indian nurse. An ermine-colored cockatoo with a gorgeous yellow plume is gravely eying the child from its perch. Creeping vines twine about the slim columns which support a low arcade above the entrance floor. Farther in, a bit of statuary peeps out from among the greenery, which is growing in high-colored wooden tubs. The vine, which clings tenaciously to the small columns, is the passion plant, its flowers seeming almost artificial in their regularity, brightness, and abundance. A fair señora in diaphanous robes reclines at ease in a low, pillowed seat, and the señor, cigarette in mouth, swings leisurely in a hammock.

188

It was a pretty, characteristic family picture, of which we should be glad to possess a photograph.

Few cities have a more agreeable climate. The range of the thermometer throughout the year being for the winter season from 68° to 75°, and in the summer from 80° to 88°. The Humboldt current, as it is called, sweeps along the coast from the Antarctic circle, causing a much lower temperature here than exists in the same latitude on the other side of the continent. Lima, it will be remembered, is situated about twelve degrees from the equatorial line. The climate is of exquisite softness, beneath a sky serenely blue; every breath is a pleasure, tranquillizing to both mind and body. Rain is of very rare occurrence, as we have intimated, but earthquakes are frequent. The most destructive visit of this sort in modern times was in 1745, which at the same time destroyed the port of Callao. Though Lima is blessed with such a seemingly equable climate, for some unexplained reason it is very far from being a healthy place. The great mortality which prevails here is entirely out of proportion to the number of inhabitants. There must be some local reason for this. Even in the days of the Incas, the present site of the city was deemed to be a spot only fit for criminals; that is to say, a penal colony was located here, where the earlier Peruvians placed condemned people, and where a high rate of mortality was not regarded as being entirely objectionable. The Campo Santo of Lima, in the immediate environs of the city, is built with tall thick walls containing niches four ranges high, and recalls those of the city of Mexico. It is not customary to bury in the ground. Some of the monuments are quite elaborate, but the place generally has a neglected appearance, and no attempt seems made to give it a pleasing aspect. It has neither flowers nor trees.

The Spaniards, during a sway which lasted over three hundred years, were terrible taskmasters in Peru, enslaving, crushing, and massacring the natives, just as they did in Cuba and Mexico. The Indians were looked upon as little more than beasts of burden, and their lives or well-being were of no sort of account, except so far as they served the purposes of the invading hordes of Spaniards. The race which has been produced by intermarriage and promiscuous intercourse is a very heterogeneous one, born of aborigines, negroes, mulattoes, Spaniards, and Portuguese. In religion, as well as in daily life, the habits of the people are Castilian, whether red, yellow, or black. There is also a considerable Chinese population, which, however, as a rule, maintains isolation from other nationalities so far as intermarriage or close intimacy is concerned. Many of the Chinese keep cheap eating-houses, and always seem to be industrious and thrifty. They are the outcome of the coolie trade, by which the Peruvian plantations were for years supplied with laborers,—slave labor, for that is exactly what it was to all intents and purposes, call it what we may. But this cruel and unjust system has long been suppressed. Most of the small shops are kept by Italians, and the best hotels by Frenchmen. The banking-houses are usually conducted by Germans, while Americans and Englishmen divide the engineering work, the construction of railways, with such other progressive enterprises as require a large share of brains, energy, and capital.

The women are generally handsome and of the Spanish type, yet they differ therefrom in some important and very obvious particulars. Their gypsy complexions, jet black hair and eyes, white, regular teeth, with full red lips, form a combination very pleasing to the eye. It must be acknowledged, however, that their complexions are aided by cosmetics. The features are small and regular, the ears being set particularly close to the head, which is always a noticeable peculiarity when it prevails. They are vivacious and mirthful, yet not forward or immodest. As regards the youthful portion, conventionality prevents all exhibition of the latter trait. In dress they follow the styles of Boston, New York, and Paris. As their brothers have been mostly educated in the cities named, they very generally speak French and English. Many of the ladies have themselves enjoyed the advantages of English, French, or North American schools in their girlhood. A certain etiquette as regards the society of men is very strictly observed here. No gentleman can associate with a young lady unless she is chaperoned by her mother or a married sister. From what we know of Spanish and Italian character, we are not at all surprised at the punctiliousness adhered to in both countries in this regard. There are very good reasons why such rules are imperative, not only in South America, but in continental Europe. Like most of the Spanish women, these of Lima, after the age of twenty-five, though they are rather short, and of small frames, nearly always develop into a decided fullness of figure.

There is a semi-oriental seclusion observed at all times as regards the sex in this country. They are rarely seen upon the streets, except when driving, or going and coming from church; but one need not watch very closely to see many inquisitive eyes peeping from behind the curtained balconies which overhang the thoroughfares, and to catch occasionally stolen glances from pretty, coquettish owners, who would be very hospitable to strangers if they dared.

Human nature is much the same in Lima as elsewhere. When seen on the streets, the ladies generally wear the black "manta" drawn close about the head and shoulders and partially covering the face. The manta is a shawl and bonnet combined, or rather it takes the place of a bonnet, and suggests the lace veil so universally worn at Havana, Seville, and Madrid, also recalling the yashmak worn by the women of the East. The Lima ladies cover half the face, including one eye; those of Egypt only cover the lower part of the face, leaving both eyes exposed.

We are speaking of the better class of the metropolis. Among the more common people, instances of great personal beauty are frequent. One sees daily youthful girls on the streets who would be pronounced beautiful under nearly any circumstances, an inheritance only too often proving a fatal legacy to the owner, forming a source of temptation in a community where morals are held of such slight account, except among the more refined classes, of whom we have been speaking.

One peculiarity is especially noticeable here among the native race: it is that the Peruvians seem to be mere lookers-on as regards the business of life in their country. All of the important trade is, as we have said, in the hands of foreigners. The English control the shipping interests, almost entirely, while the skilled machinists are nearly all Americans, with a few Scotchmen. We repeat this fact as showing the do-nothing nature of the natives, and also as signifying that for true progress, indeed, for the growth of civilization in any desirable direction, emigration from Europe and North America must be depended upon.

The heavy alcoves of the old stone bridge at Lima are appropriated by the fruit women, whose tempting display forms glowing bits of color. The thorough-*fares are crowded by itinerant peddlers of all sorts of merchandise. Milk-women come from the country, mounted astride of small horses or donkeys; water carriers trot about on jackasses, sitting behind their water jars and uttering piercing cries; Chinese food venders, with articles made from mysterious sources, balance their baskets at either end of long poles placed across their shoulders; the lottery-ticket vender, loud voiced and urgent, is ever present; newspaper boys, after our own fashion, shout "El Pais," or "El Nacional;" chicken dealers, with baskets full of live birds on their head and half a dozen hanging from each hand, solicit your patronage; beggars of both sexes, but mostly lazy, worthless men, feign pitiful lameness, while importuning every stranger for a centavo; bright, careless girls and boys rush hither and thither, full of life and spirit,—black, yellow, brown, and white, all mingling together on an equal footing. The absence of wheeled vehicles is noticeable, the tramway-cars gliding rapidly past the pedestrians, while pack-horses and donkeys transport mostly such merchandise as is not carried on the heads of men and women. Of the better class of citizens who help to make up this polyglot community of the metropolis, one very easily distinguishes the American, French, German, and English; each nationality is somehow distinctively marked.

The stock of goods offered for sale in the pawn-*brokers' shops, as a rule, is very significant in foreign cities; here the shelves of these dealers are full of valuable domestic articles, which the fallen fortunes of the once rich Lima families have compelled them to part with from time to time in a struggle to keep the wolf from the door. The Chilians took all they could readily find of both public and private property, and though they ruined financially some of the best families, they did not succeed in getting everything which was portable and valuable. Heirlooms are offered in these shops for comparatively trifling sums, such as rich old lace; diamonds; superbly wrought bracelets in gold, rubies, topazes, and other precious stones, set and unset; gold and silver spoons and forks of curious designs, and of which only one set were ever manufactured, intended to fill a special order and suit the fancy of some rich family. Drinking-cups bearing royal crests, and others with the arms of noble Castilian families engraved upon them, are numerous. There are also swords with jeweled hilts, gold and silver table ornaments, together with antique china, which might rival the Satsuma of Japan. Curio hunters have secured many, nay, nearly all, of the very choicest of these domestic relics, which they have mostly taken to London, where they obtained fabulous prices for them.

We were told of an enterprising Yankee who invested one thousand dollars in these articles, took them to England, and promptly realized some eleven thousand dollars above all his expenses upon the venture. Returning to Rio Janeiro, on the east coast, he purchased precious stones with his increased capital, and, strange to say, although he was by no means an expert, among his gems he secured an old mine diamond of great value at a low figure, which, having been crudely cut, did not exhibit its real excellence. Taking the whole of his second purchase to Paris, he disposed of his gems at a large advance, and finally returned to New York with a net capital exceeding forty thousand dollars. This enterprising and successful individual bore the euphonious name of Smyth,—Smyth with a *y*,—Alfred Smyth.

The three watering-places, or country villages of Miraflores, Baranco, and Chorillos, are connected with Lima by railway, and in these resorts many city merchants have their summer homes, occupying picturesque ranches. The Chilians sacked and burned these places during the war, but they have been mostly rebuilt, and are once more in a thriving condition.

Peru was celebrated for centuries as the most prolific gold and silver producing country in the world; her very name has long been the synonym for riches. Although the product of the precious metals is still considerable, yet it is quite insignificant compared with the revenue which she has realized from the export of guano and phosphates. The former article, as we have already said, has become virtually exhausted, and the latter source of supply, still immensely prolific and valuable, has been stolen from her bodily by the Chilians, so that Peru has now to fall back upon industry and the remaining natural resources of the soil.

The most remarkable peculiarity in the physical formation of Peru is the double Cordillera of the Andes, which traverse it from southeast to northwest, separating the country into three distinct regions, which differ materially from each other in climate, soil, and vegetation. To the proximity of the range nearest to the coast is undoubtedly to be attributed the frequent earthquakes which disturb the shore, whether the volcanoes are apparently extinct or not. It may be reasonably doubted if any of the volcanoes are absolutely extinct, in the full sense of the term. They may be inoperative, so far as can be seen, for an entire century, and at its close break out in full vigor. In consulting the authorities upon this subject we find that, since 1570, there have been sixty-nine destructive earthquakes recorded as having taken place on the west coast of South America. The most terrible of them was that already referred to, which destroyed Callao in 1745. It is stated that the shocks at that time continued with more or less violence for three consecutive months, and the records of the event further state that there were two hundred and twenty distinct shocks within the twenty-four hours following the enormous tidal wave which overwhelmed Callao. At present, hardly a week passes without decided indications of volcanic disturbance occurring, but these are of so slight a nature, comparatively speaking, that but little attention is paid to them by the native population, though it is true that sensitive strangers often turn pale at such an event and tremble with fearful anticipations.

About twenty miles south of Lima, on elevated ground which overlooks the Pacific, is the prehistoric spot known as Pachacamac, in the valley of the Lurin River. The name signifies the "Creator of the World," to whom the city and its temples were originally dedicated. Here, upon the edge of the desert, once stood the sacred city of a people who preceded the Incas, and who have left in these interesting, mouldering ruins tokens of their advanced civilization, as clearly defined as are those of Thebes, in far away Egypt. Another fact should not be lost sight of in this connection, that many ancient remains to be found in this neighborhood evince a higher degree of intelligence, in their constructive belongings, than do any evidences left to us respecting the days of the Incas, with whom we are in a measure familiar. The archæologists, whose profession it is to carefully weigh even the slightest tangible evidence which time has spared, long since came to this conclusion.

Pachacamac was the Mecca of South America, or at least of the most civilized portion of it, if we may judge by present appearances, and by the testimony of history as far back as it reaches.

The ruins at Pachacamac consist of walls formed of adobe and sun-dried bricks, some of which can be traced, notwithstanding the many earthquakes which have shaken the neighborhood. The site of the ruins is a hilly spot, and the sands have drifted so as to cover them in many places, just as the Sphinx and the base of the pyramids have been covered, near Cairo. Specific ruins are designated as having once been the grand temple of the sun, and others as the house of the sacred virgins of the sun. It is very obvious that the Incas destroyed a grand and spacious temple here, which legend tells us was heavily adorned with silver and gold, to make way for one of their own dedicated to the worship of the sun. Who this race were and whence they came, with so considerable a system of civilization, is a theme which has long absorbed the speculative antiquarian. It is easy enough to construct theories which may meet the case, but it is difficult to support them when they are subjected to the cold arguments of reason and the test of known history. Actual knowledge is a great iconoclast, and smashes the poetical images of the unreliable historian with a ruthless hand. The Spanish records relating to the period of early discovery here, as also of Pizarro's career and the doing of the agents of the Romish Church, have long since been proven to be absolutely unworthy of belief.

About the ruins of Pachacamac was once a sacred burial place, where well-preserved mummies are still to be found, but the great, silent, ruined city itself does not contain one living inhabitant. The graveyard—the Campo Santo—remains, as it were, intact, but the proud city, with its grand temples dedicated to unknown gods, has crumbled to dust.

Curiously carved gold and silver vases and ornaments, exhibiting the exercise of a high degree of artistic skill, have been exhumed in the vast graveyard surrounding these ruins, whose extent, if judged by the number of interments which have taken place here, must have been ten times larger than the present site of Lima, and it must have contained a population many times larger than that of the present capital of Peru. In the mouths of the well-preserved mummies found buried here, we are told that gold coins were found, presumably placed there to pay for ferriage across the river of death. Here we have a fact also worthy of note. It thus appears that this people must have had a circulating medium in the shape of gold coin. As the placing of coin in the mouth of the deceased was a custom of the ancient Greeks, may it not be that these people came originally from Greece or from some contiguous country?

There are numerous other ancient remains in the neighborhood of Lima, of which even tradition fails to give any account. Antiquarians find many clues to special knowledge of the past in the remains which can be exhumed in places on the coast of Chili and Peru, in the ancient graves where the nitrous soil has preserved not only the bodies of a former people, but also their tools, weapons, and domestic utensils.

* * * * *

To reach the United States from Callao, the most direct course is to sail northward fifteen hundred miles to Panama, and cross the isthmus, again taking ship from the Atlantic side; but the author's family awaited him in Europe, and as the Pacific mail service exactly met his requirements, he sailed southward, touching at several of the ports already visited, crossing the Atlantic by way of the Canary and Cape de Verde Islands to Lisbon, thence to Southampton and to London. Joining his family, he crossed the Atlantic from Liverpool to Boston, after an absence of seven months, traveling in all of this equatorial journey some thirty thousand miles without any serious mishap, and having acquired a largely augmented fund of pleasurable memories.

Lightning Source UK Ltd.
Milton Keynes UK
UKHW012200220722
406263UK00002B/81